THE SECRET FRONT

Wilhelm Hoettl, an Austrian by origin, joined the German Secret Service, the political intelligence service built by Himmler and Heydrich, in 1938 and held important posts throughout the Balkans and Italy as chief liaison officer with foreign intelligence organisations. Hoettl was personally responsible for the abduction of Mussolini's son in law Count Ciano from Allied-held Rome, and at the end of the war was involved in the desperate German peace-campaigns.

ALSO BY WILHELM HOETTL

Hitler's Paper Weapon

THE SECRET FRONT

The Inside Story of Nazi Political Espionage

·Wilhelm Hoettl

With an Introduction by Ian Colvin

**PHOENIX
PRESS**

5 UPPER SAINT MARTIN'S LANE
LONDON
WC2H 9EA

A PHOENIX PRESS PAPERBACK

First published in Great Britain
by Weidenfeld & Nicolson in 1953
This paperback edition published in 2000
by Phoenix Press,
a division of The Orion Publishing Group Ltd,
Orion House, 5 Upper St Martin's Lane,
London WC2H 9EA

A CIP catalogue record for this book
is available from the British Library.

Printed and bound in Great Britain by
Clays Ltd, St Ives plc

ISBN 1 84212 218 5

Contents

INTRODUCTION
by
IAN COLVIN

THIS is an account of the German S.D. or Secret Service, its development out of the Secret Police and the Nazi Party machine; how it furthered the war effort of Hitler, absorbed its rival the Wehrmacht Military Intelligence Service, and was finally liquidated by the Allies.

The author, Wilhelm Hoettl, is an Austrian intelligence officer who joined the German Secret Service in 1938, and later served under Schellenberg in Branch VI. His duties took him in the first years of the war to the Vienna offices of the S.D. as adviser on Southern Eastern affairs.

This gave him particular insight into German subversive activities against Czechoslovakia, Yugoslavia, Rumania and Hungary. He was promoted to the Head Security Office in Berlin in 1943 and continued in political espionage, to which was added the task of starting a secret service in the weakening ally, Fascist Italy.

So Wilhelm Hoettl has much to relate that is of historical interest about the gradual undermining and sudden overthrow of European states.

His secret service work brought him into closest contact with the Horthy Government in Hungary, with Ciano and the Fascist régime, and with the agents of many powers, including Britain and America during the years 1938–45.

A most significant part of his story is that which deals with the final intrigues in Switzerland to convince the Alan Dulles group of the American Secret Services early in 1945 that there was a real danger of prolonged German resistance in the so-called Alpine 'redoubt' of Bavaria and Austria. This myth of the redoubt, as Hoettl reveals, was used to try and get better terms of occupation from the Western Allies. No historian writing the last chapters of the Second World War will be able to dispense with this evidence, which comes to us through Hoettl from Kaltenbrunner and Schellenberg direct, the chief executives of Hitler's policy in the last phases of the war, but to some extent prepared to intrigue on their own.

The Secret Front was first published in Austria, with the title *Die Geheime Front* under the pseudonym Walter Hagen. Since then the identity of the author has become so widely known that he has assumed his real name in the English edition.

As to the veracity of his account, I have the valuable supporting evidence of the translator, Colonel R. H. Stevens, late of the British Foreign Service. Colonel Stevens who was trapped and kidnapped by Schellenberg's Secret Service in November 1939, in what has since become known as the Venlo incident, was able in the years of internment 1939–45 to extend his already wide knowledge of the German Secret Services. His verdict on the evidence of Hoettl will therefore be of particular interest to the reader.

'It has been my task to translate *The Secret Front*,' he writes, 'I am left with three predominant impressions: firstly, that the author has written from personal, first-hand knowledge; secondly, that he has brought to bear on his work a keen and critical mind, which has been capable of making the best of the material at its disposal; and thirdly, that he has done his sincere utmost to present a factual, honest and objective account of the facts as he knows them, to write history unbiased by past loyalties or prejudices—and has succeeded admirably.

'Of particular interest to me are the series of character sketches of leading Nazi personalities with which the author opens his book; for with most of these men—Himmler, Heydrich, Schellenberg, Mueller and the rest—I came into sharp personal contact during my five and a half years captivity in the hands of the Gestapo. The author undoubtedly knows them more intimately than I. The fidelity with which he has sketched them gives me all the more confidence to accept as equally faithful and true his version of the events which he later describes and of which I had but little detailed knowledge.'

In editing Colonel Stevens' translation I have spent several days with Wilhelm Hoettl in Austria, examining the sources for his account of the German Secret Service, on which he has enlarged in the English edition. Plainly his description of the origins of the Service does not pretend to be exhaustive. It serves to introduce the reader to a State Department that was adapted to the needs of a totalitarian régime and on several occasions intervened to alter the course of history by such methods as planting forged documents, calumniating men who opposed dictatorship and war, and fabricating unsuccessful conspiracies in order to unmask and forestall real ones.

Then Hoettl goes on to show the working of this machine in his own special territory, Central, South-east and Southern Europe. I have prevailed upon him to abandon the impersonal style of the historian and give us his first-person corroboration of certain historic episodes.

Nevertheless the Secret Service officer will always reserve certain facts and certain sources from public scrutiny. Hoettl has given me in such instances convincing answers as to his sources. He does not wish to follow the style of the novel in which L. C. Moyzisch wrote his spy story *Cicero*, and Hoettl reveals practically nothing of his own methods and successes in the battle of wits with the Allies—though he is open enough about his part in peace talks.

But he has told me an amusing anecdote of his spytime in Budapest, which I may mention here. He managed to steal the wartime confidential waste of the American Legation. This was done by bribing the Hungarian firm which built confidential waste shredding machines, known as 'the Wolf'. A special machine was built and delivered to the American Legation which disgorged shredded waste at intervals, but without actually shredding the documents fed into it, which were stealthily removed by a maintenance mechanic. So for a short time this 'wolf' was used to obtain State Department documents before the suspicions of the American diplomats in Hungary were aroused.

I found Hoettl, a bronzed, phlegmatic Austrian aged thirty-seven, living in Bad Aussee among those very lakes and mountains of the Salzkammergut that were to have been the heart of the mythical 'redoubt' in 1945.

He lives not far from those eerie Dead Mountains, an almost lunar landscape, near which Kaltenbrunner and other war criminals wandered and hid as the Reich collapsed in dust. And although I have spoken about the German Secret Service as something liquidated by the Allies, it is obvious that it has really split up like quicksilver in all directions, East and West, leaving certain indeterminate globules like Hoettl on the scene of the catastrophe susceptible to every tremor coming from either East or West.

Life has not ceased to be exciting to him. Now and then he glimpses a colleague in the Russian service; he was recently interrogated by the Americans on his connections with the Soviet zones of occupation, and he tells me that the Russians would like to have the opportunity of interrogating him too. In his mountain fastness Hoettl keeps silent and wary, though an article in the magazine *Spiegel* of May 1953, describing his many-hued record somewhat inaccurately, stung him into demanding a published correction.

I came away from my scrutiny of his work satisfied that he has attempted an objective study of his special subject. If it is not more fully documented, that is because so many Reich documents were destroyed in the last orgy of Hitler's myth-making exit, while the Allies obligingly confiscated the bulk of the remaining documents—far too numerous for our historians ever to digest fully. This has left the field open to German propagandists and myth merchants to reconstruct history the way they would like it to be read, on the plea that without supporting documents, memory is 'best evidence'. There are plenty of signs of that to-day, but it is a charge from which I have no hesitation in absolving Hoettl.

Whatever his ethical motives, if any, he has no other purpose than to present secret history as he saw it in the making. If there are gaps in his field of vision, others will fill them out. If he has a national bias, that is understandable. If he under-rates the secret opposition to Hitler in Germany, he is not alone in that. Through the enemy eyes of Hoettl, we have nevertheless a vivid enough picture here of the helpless plight of those countries who were ignorantly called 'Hitler's jackals' at the end of the war and have since become Russia's satellites.

His particular qualification for his job under Schellenberg was a talent for the study of minor peoples and political movements that was a tradition in the Austrian Service and long kept that Empire of many races together under the Habsburgs. The man himself, if he emerges at all from his own book, does so as a sort of intelligence chameleon shyly stretching its neck out of a cranny in the grey Alpine redoubt. He has not distorted that self-portrait by any inserted professions about democracy. The author is above everything a realist, and as such we shall no doubt hear of Wilhelm Hoettl again.

IAN COLVIN

CHAPTER I

THE SHAPE OF A SECRET SERVICE

I DO not propose to start by moralizing on my reasons for entering the German Secret Service. It happened in 1938 after the invasion of Austria, and it was called the *Sicherheitsdienst* or Security Service. Every State tends to emphasize that its secret services are for the sole purpose of security, though naturally they include espionage and often sabotage in their scope. Our tasks were of that nature, and I accept the words 'German Secret Service' as being a proper description of my department.

The immediate foreign aim of the German Secret Service then was to profit by the fall of Austria, leave the Allies no breathing space and demolish the Little Entente. I was a student then without very clear ideas about the future, but interested in my historical studies.

I was recruited to the Secret Service while still at Vienna University, a post-graduate in history, specializing in Southeast European questions. The Secret Service was interested in establishing liaison with my faculty of the University and in setting up a special institute to train students for subversive work in European countries. These experts were to become organizers of intelligence cells for Germany. A Prussian intelligence officer, Polte, recruited me, asking searching questions about the mentality of the various national groups which made up what was once the Habsburg Empire. The tensions between states and their minorities interested him.

I was sent to Berlin, where I lived in a small room in a back street in Koepenick, and began my period of training. Our wartime headquarters in Berlin were in the Berkaerstrasse in Schmargendorf, a West Berlin suburb. There 500 people were working in three shifts on a twenty-four hour service. The offices were modern, built in red brick and well appointed. Formerly a home for old people, there were many small cubicle-like rooms. This building was requisitioned at the outbreak of the war, and housed only the S.D. foreign liaison section, dealing with operations abroad and evaluation of material from abroad. Before the war, a much smaller nucleus worked at the Wilhelmstrasse under the auspices of the Foreign Ministry.

My chief during the first years of the war was S.S. General Johst. Our Berlin offices were very heavily guarded by Waffen S.S. Each official had his own pass for the building, and very strict care was taken in the issuing of passes for the technical departments. These were housed in offices in the West Berlin suburb of Wannsee, and included the departments forging passports, laboratories for criminal police and the secret wireless station which trained officials for what was later known as 'Funkspiel'—radio signalling to agents in the field or misleading foreign agents. These services were peculiar to the Secret Service as distinct from the Military Intelligence and were very jealously guarded.

Promotion was more rapid after the war began and I became a Major by 1943 and a Lieutenant-Colonel in 1944 with the title of Acting Head of Branch VI, Intelligence and Counter-Espionage in Central and South-east Europe.

My headquarters for the South East were in Budapest. My offices were near the old castle at Ofen, the ancient part of Budapest, and were in a small seventeenth-century palace which had belonged to the Counts Batyany and was built during the Turkish Wars. I had only a staff of six, and my duties were to keep in touch with the Hungarian Secret Service as well as with German minorities. I lived in rooms beside my office.

My salary was paid into my banking account at the Credit Anstalt in Vienna, but whenever I served abroad I was paid in dollars—700 dollars a month living allowance and 500 dollars travelling expenses. We had limitless funds available for paying agents in Reichsmarks, but dollars and Swiss francs were very scarce. My work began in political matters, but as the war continued these activities became more military in nature. I sent many agents behind the Russian lines during the last eighteen months of the war. As much as 5,000 dollars was the average for top agents and informants working behind the lines, and 50,000 dollars was the biggest sum spent on a group of people, such as a group of Germans living in the Argentine who were involved in spying against the United States. I am not at liberty to reveal the names of these people, because they are still alive and working there.

I think this will suffice to show the reader that I was deep in secret service work. But the purpose of this book is not to unveil the technical workings of a secret service. I wish instead to show how the course of history was affected by some of the activities of the German Secret Service.

I do not imagine that the British Secret Services, certainly not in home affairs, have ever been instruments of policy in the same degree as the organization for which I worked. To some extent it even fabricated incidents or hastened impending events, so that German policy could reap an advantage from them.

After describing the personalities with whom my work brought me into contact, I want to describe some of these secret political actions which have become part of history. And then I will relate the activities of the German Secret Service in the broader field, dealing with the fate of the Central European and South-eastern states that were my immediate concern.

During all these years we worked in rivalry with our own services. The Secret Service or S.D. had its origins in and owed its allegiance to the S.S., the Secret Police or Gestapo and the Nazi Party. As such it was an executive organ of Hitler's policy, though it sought for preference to pursue a course of realism.

The main rivalry lay with the Military Intelligence Service, an older organization but more senile and half-hearted in its approach to the urgent problems of the war. As it was supported by the General Staff of the Army and subordinate to the High Command of the Wehrmacht, with a high degree of independence, being responsible only to the Commanders-in-Chief of Services, it was no easy matter for the Secret Service to limit and eventually absorb the Military Intelligence Service. Yet that is what eventually happened. The revolutionary force ate up the reactionary force, but by then the war was too far gone for any improvement to result from unification.

I must ask the reader to bear with a brief note on the structure of the Secret Service and the Military Intelligence before we proceed to the main narrative. It will make clearer the events that follow in the course of my story.

There were two main organizations—the Military Intelligence Service under the command of Admiral Wilhelm Canaris until 1944; and the S.D. or Secret Service, directed in 1944 by S.S. Major-General Walter Schellenberg, who also took over the foreign branch of the Military Intelligence Service.

The directing Headquarters of the Military Intelligence Service was the Foreign Intelligence Office at the High Command of the Armed Forces (O.K.W.). At its head until 1944 stood Admiral Canaris. Under him were two Deputies, Admiral Buerkner who in reality had nothing whatever to do with security matters, and Lieutenant-General Piekenbrock, who was the real Second-in-Command as regards intelligence.

Buerkner was also Head of the Foreign Bureau (*Amtsgruppe Ausland*). Its functions were more of a politico-military nature and included such duties as liaison with the Foreign Ministry and the various Attaché Sections of the General Staffs.

In addition Canaris, as Chief of the Intelligence Service, had under him the 'Central Section'—an administrative machine which had no intelligence functions and dealt mainly with questions of organization, finance and law.

Finally, the Chief of the Intelligence Service had under his command the 'Special Unit z b V 800', later renamed the Brandenburg Division. This unit was primarily at the disposal either of Branch II (see diagram) or was attached to front-line formations for duty as Commando Troops.

The Foreign Intelligence Office presided over three branches —Branch I, collection and circulation of military intelligence; Branch II, psychological warfare, subversive activities, sabotage; Branch III, counter-espionage and security.

Each Army Group had its own Intelligence Sections, organized on the same lines into three branches. Armies and Divisions had similar organizations, called in these cases Intelligence Troops or Intelligence Reporting Centres. After the 1944 re-organization the last-named were renamed Close Reconnaissance Units or simply Commandos.

Intelligence and Security units also existed in each Military

District, organized to serve their own Military Headquarters in the same way as their counter-parts at the front. These district offices were modelled exactly on the Berlin Central office in three branches. Similar organizations were set up in neutral and friendly countries, where they were called War Organizations (K.O.). They were not concerned directly with the countries in which they were situated but used as bases for action against neighbouring or enemy countries.

The military and other attachés constituted a further source of intelligence information. They were not subordinate to the Military Intelligence Service but to the appropriate Attaché Section of Army, Navy or Air General Staff.

The German Political Secret Service had its origins in Branch III of the *Sicherheitsdienst-Hauptamt* or Security Services Head Office. It was finally renamed Branch VI of the R.S.H.A. or Head Office of Reich Security Services. This Secret Service was under the command of S.S. Major-General Schellenberg and was divided into a number of regional sections for active intelligence work, organization, sabotage, industrial intelligence and so on (see diagram).

In Germany itself Branch VI had so-styled 'Observers' in each S.D. Secret Service Region with tasks very similar to those of the Military Intelligence Offices but on a much smaller scale to begin with. In neutral and friendly countries the organizations of the Secret Service came under the control of a 'Principal Representative, Branch VI'.

Some of the German Legations in friendly countries had also a Police Attaché, though he had little or no connection with Secret Service activities and confined himself to liaison on purely police matters.

The functions of Branch VI differed so completely from those of any of the other branches of the Reich Security Services and Schellenberg himself was so emphatic in his opinion that Secret Service and Police must be kept absolutely apart, that it gradually attained a unique position within the framework of the Security Services and had little or nothing to do with the Gestapo and other branches. This unique position was further strengthened when Branch VI absorbed the Military Secret Service and took over a large number of Military Officers.

The Foreign Ministry possessed its own Intelligence machine which had at its disposal all German diplomatic representatives abroad.

Finally, there was a host of 'Special Institutions' such as, to quote one example, the so-called Air Force Research Service which dealt among other things with secret telephone and wireless monitoring.

The diagram opposite shows the organization of the German Secret Service after Schellenberg took over the Military Intelligence Service in 1944, and the Military Intelligence Service as it existed separately until then.

THE GERMAN SECRET SERVICE
Organization after 1944

Branch VI Overseas Political Secret Service		Military Branch Military Intelligence Service	
VI.A	Organization	Mil.A	Organization
VI.B	Western Europe	Mil.B	West
VI.C	Russo-Japanese sphere of influence	Mil.C	East
VI.D	Anglo-American sphere of influence	Mil.D	Sabotage
VI.E	Central & S.E. Europe	Mil.E	Technical Section
VI.F	Technical Section	Mil.F	Front line reconnaissance
VI.G	Scientific & experimental Section		Instructional Regiment 'Kurfürst'
VI.I	Sabotage		Special Commando: 'Dora'
VI.Wi	Economic Section		

THE GERMAN MILITARY SECRET SERVICE (*up to* 1944)

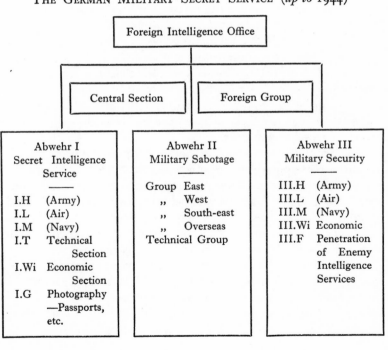

CHAPTER II

PEOPLE I KNEW

ANY mention of the German Secret Service evokes, in the same breath, the name of Heydrich. Admittedly, its creation was not the work of a single individual; a great number of men of the most varied character combined to fashion it and give it its particular character. There was Admiral Canaris, until 1944 the Head of the separate Wehrmacht Military Intelligence Service, with his two Deputies, Admiral Buerkner and Lieutenant-General Piekenbrock. Others were the notorious Himmler, the supreme Commander of the S.S., and Major-General Walter Schellenberg, Head of the Political Secret Service, who in 1944 also took over Canaris' job. But Reinhard Heydrich was the most formidable of them all, a man whom you could never forget, if he ever crossed your path.

Who was Heydrich? When, as a young man of twenty-seven, he joined the S.S. in the summer of 1931, all that was known about him was that he was a Naval Lieutenant who had been thrown out of the Navy by the 'reactionary' German Admiralty on account of his National Socialist sympathies; and Heydrich himself assiduously assisted in spreading this story, which was nearly true—but not quite.

In reality, other considerations, quite unconnected with politics, contributed largely to the reasons for his dismissal. In Kiel, where he was stationed, Heydrich had started an affair with the daughter of a naval architect, with the not unusual natural consequences. The young Lieutenant's reputation was not very savoury, and he had had any number of affairs which he had carried off with a distressingly frivolous irresponsibility. In spite of this, the naval architect was quite prepared to give his daughter in marriage to Heydrich, and he approached his prospective son-in-law with this very obvious and natural solution, confident that there would but remain to settle the details of the wedding. He met with a most cynical refusal.

Nothing, declared Heydrich, would induce him to marry a girl who had succumbed with so little ado to his advances; a young woman of that kind could not aspire to become the wife of an officer!

When intervention by more senior naval officers was of no avail, and Heydrich still bluntly refused to marry his victim, the indignant father brought the case to the notice of the Naval Commander-in-Chief, Admiral Raeder, a strict and rigid officer, who forthwith dismissed Heydrich from the Service.

The details of this little story were known to very few, and Heydrich was at great pains to see that they did not spread beyond this immediate circle. I have heard what I believe to be the correct version from S.S. General Hermann Behrens, a colleague of Heydrich in the Secret Service. On one occasion in 1940 an ex-naval officer innocently told the true story at some party. Heydrich got to hear of it, and the unfortunate man was straightway flung into a concentration camp on a charge of slander and accompanied by an explanatory memorandum which ensured that he would never emerge again.

As 'an officer persecuted on account of his National Socialist leanings' Heydrich was received with open arms by the Hamburg S.S. At that time the S.S. was still a small organization, made up for the most part of raw-boned, simple-minded yokels, and the extremely intelligent new recruit very swiftly came to the front and was soon brought to the notice of S.S. Reichsfuehrer Himmler as a young man destined for great things.

Heydrich was an ambitious man with clear-cut ideas about his own future. It was neither by chance nor at the suggestion of others that he came into contact with the Secret Service and the Secret Police; he himself took the initiative and submitted voluminous memoranda to Himmler on the necessity for, and the organization of, institutions of this nature. Himmler was immediately convinced and he gave Heydrich full authority to raise the so-called *Sicherheitsdienst* (Security Service) within the framework of the S.S., promising him at the same time that when the National Socialist Party assumed power he would be entrusted with the organization of a secret police force, coupled probably with the reform of the existing State Police Service.

In spite of this, Heydrich's name, even in Party circles, remained almost completely unknown. There was certainly an instruction issued by the Fuehrer's Deputy to the effect that the S.S. Security Service under Heydrich would henceforth be recognized as the general Intelligence Service and that other Information Sections of the Party and the S.A. would cease to exist; but who and what Heydrich was, nobody had any clear idea. It was all part of Heydrich's plan to remain for the time being in the background; he wished to be regarded as an ordinary, faithful member of the Party and subordinate of his Chief, Himmler.

In March 1933 Himmler was appointed Police President in Munich. He immediately posted Heydrich to the political section of the Police Headquarters, where, as Head of the Section, he fashioned in the space of a few short months a most efficient instrument, the new Bavarian Political Police.

Heydrich had nothing but contempt for idealists and ideologies; and it was typical of his extreme cynicism rather than of his liberality of mind that in choosing his immediate colleagues he attached far greater importance to willing subservience and absolute obedience than to any political adherence to the National Socialist Party. Many of those nearest to him were not Nazis, but simply well-disciplined, industrious, unthinking policemen.

Heinrich Mueller, later Chief of the entire Gestapo, was, for example, an admitted opponent of National Socialism right up till 1933; but he was very quickly appointed to high office in the S.S. by Heydrich, although the Party objected again and again on the grounds of the man's past record. It was only just before the war that Himmler succeeded with great difficulty in persuading the Party Chancellery to yield, and that the Gestapo Chief was at last admitted as a member of the N.S.D.A.P.

This was no isolated exception; enthusiastic and idealistic National Socialists like Heydrich's own Deputy Chief of Security Services, Dr. Werner Best, carried but little weight simply on account of their idealism, and Best, indeed, was eventually sent to Berlin as Heydrich's representative, to penetrate the Prussian police services.

Heydrich's first aim was to take over the Political Police of Prussia, the greatest of the German provinces. In name, Hermann Goering, as Prussian Prime Minister, was also supreme chief of the Prussian Political Police; in reality, it was run by Dr. Rudolf Diels, a man who had already distinguished himself as a first class organizer and administrator of Secret Police under the Prussian Reich-Commissar, Franz von Papen.

Diels, a tall dark figure with almost Mongolian features, was an eloquent and efficient schemer. For the first time Heydrich came in conflict with an opponent worthy of his steel. Thanks partly to his exceptional administrative talent and partly to the pull which membership of an extremely influential student Corps gave him, Diels had, even as a young man of barely thirty-two years of age, acquired for himself a position of exceptional strength before the Nazis came into power. He was himself no Nazi, but rather a supporter of the German National Party and the right wing 'Stahlhelm' ex-soldiers' organization. In the fight against the Prussian Social Democrat Government —and particularly against Karl Severing, the Minister for the Interior—he had supported von Papen wholeheartedly. When he saw, however, that nothing could stop the victorious progress of National Socialism, he changed camps in good time. He succeeded in getting in touch with leading members of the N.S.D.A.P., and when Goering was appointed Prime Minister, he placed his capabilities—and his secret information—at his disposal. In 1932 Diels had taken possession of the very voluminous Prussian State Police secret files on political personalities, so he told me, and in them particular attention had been paid to such National-Socialist leaders as came within the jurisdiction of the Prussian State Police. All the more important Nazi leaders who had ever lived in Berlin had detailed personal files. Nothing, not even details of the most intimate personal nature, had escaped the eyes of the watchful and zealous Police, and all this valuable material was in the exclusive hands of Diels. Goering was not slow to realize that he could turn this knowledge of Diels' to great political advantage, and immediately confirmed him in his old appointment. Goering's rise to such heights in the Reich is perhaps attributable in no small degree to the fact that, thanks to Diels, he became acquainted with so

many of the skeletons in the cupboards of the Nazi Party
hierarchy.

Having then successfully survived the change of Government,
Diels proceeded to dig himself well and truly in, with his headquarters in Berlin, exactly as Heydrich was doing from Munich.
This, obviously, was a state of affairs which could not last for
long; two men of much the same character, both imbued with
an equal ambition and both striving for the same prize could
not work peacefully together. Diels put up a great fight. More
than once Heydrich seemed to have the prize in his grasp, only
to find that by some skilful counter-move Diels had succeeded
in convincing Goering that his services were indispensable.
At last, in April 1934, Diels had to give in. Goering allowed
himself to be persuaded to hand over the command of the
Prussian Secret State Police to Heydrich in his capacity as
Himmler's Deputy, and Diels was side-tracked and sent off to
Cologne as Regional Governor. It was, however, with the
utmost reluctance that Goering had consented to this solution,
and it seemed as though he were about to change his mind at
the very last moment. Diels was attending a farewell function
with members of his late office, when Goering suddenly telephoned him and said that after all he had decided not to let him
go for the time being. But it was a decision which Goering was
not able to implement, and a few days later he had to give way
again, and this time irrevocably.

His relations with Diels did not, however, come to an end.
Very rarely did Goering ever completely abandon a man who
had once been under his wing; towards such people he felt a
species of fidelity complex and continued to regard himself as
their protector, even when, for the time being, he found himself unable to shield them from their opponents. Diels was
condemned as 'intolerable' both as Regional Governor in
Cologne and later in Hanover, and Goering seized the
opportunity of getting him back on his own staff, where
he was entrusted with the direction of the whole German
inland waterway system. Diels married a cousin of Goering's,
whose first husband had been Goering's brother, a Police
Officer.

With an eye on Goering's leanings towards nepotism, Diels

may well have regarded this marriage as a stepping-stone towards fresh fields of activity in public life; but things did not
work out quite as he hoped. As early as 1943 Diels realized
that Germany must inevitably lose the war, and he did his
utmost to persuade his new brother-in-law to draw the logical
political conclusions in good time. But he failed completely,
as many others had failed before him, to rouse Goering from his
lethargy. Even so, his relationship with the Reichs Marshal
rendered him one last, invaluable service; it saved his life, when
he was arrested after 20th July, 1944 and his execution seemed
inevitable, although apparently he had but flirted nervously on
the fringe of the conspiracy. His name was on an old list of
people with whom Heydrich (though he had been murdered
in the meantime) intended one day to settle accounts.

While in prison at Gestapo Headquarters in the Prinz
Albrecht Strasse in Berlin, Diels promised Goering, represented
by a lawyer, that he would allow himself to be divorced, and in
return Goering gave him a written guarantee that he would
procure his release. Both parties kept their word, and in this
way Diels, Heydrich's most talented and dangerous opponent,
saved his neck.

Another of Heydrich's competitors deserving of mention is
Dr. Hans Bernd Gisevius, although he was in no way in the same
class as Diels. Gisevius had originally served under Diels in
the Prussian Secret State Police. He was physically imposing
and a great talker. But Diels had found his ambition and intriguing, as he preferred to call it—somewhat irksome, and he
accordingly side-tracked him into an unimportant job in the
State Police Office. Gisevius then succeeded in getting himself
transferred into the Police Section of the Ministry of the Interior. In the National Socialist Minister for Internal Affairs,
Dr. Frick, a colourless and typically supine Civil Servant devoid
of initiative or constructive thought, he found a superior ideal
for his purpose, and he used him as a pawn in the ambitious
game of political chess he was playing.

Gisevius' ideas were not without danger for Heydrich. He
wished to have all those provincial Police Services, which had
not already been grabbed by Heydrich, placed under a centralized
control in the Police Section of the Ministry of the Interior,

and he managed to carry on his underground warfare against Heydrich for quite a considerable time; as late even as 1936, as Frick's representative in Wurtemburg, he was in the thick of a plot to organize all the provincial Police Services, with the exception of the Prussian, into one corporate anti-Heydrich entity.

All his efforts, however, failed to prevent Heydrich from becoming eventually the Chief of the entire national Security Service, and it was most probably this defeat which drove him, an old comrade of the Stahlhelm organization, first into the camp of the opponents of National Socialism and later, when he joined the Military Intelligence under Major-General Oster, into the ranks of the anti-Hitler conspiracy. But even in this circle he was not an important or influential figure. The publication of his two books—the first to reveal the secret history of the National Socialist Movement—and his subsequent appearance as one of the chief witnesses for the prosecution at the Nuremberg trial resulted in his being credited—in public opinion, at least—with an important rôle, which in reality he had never played.

On one further occasion was Heydrich's rise to the top placed in jeopardy. Just after he had been appointed Chief of the entire German Security Service, vague rumours started to circulate that his antecedents were not, from the view-point of the Third Reich, all that they might have been. The originator of these rumours was a master-baker of Halle on the Saale, Heydrich's birthplace, who stoutly declared that Heydrich's grandmother Sarah, whom he had known personally and who later died in Leipzig, was a full-blooded Jewess, and that his father, a teacher of music, was therefore himself half a Jew. Heydrich took the master-baker to court and won his case, which, thanks to official instructions issued to the Press, aroused little or no public comment. The 'slanderer' had been unable to furnish any documentary proof of his assertions, and when on appeal he demanded that the Marriage and Birth Registers of the town of Halle should be produced in Court, it was found that for some queer and inexplicable reason the entries for March 1904 (just exactly when Heydrich was born) were nowhere to be found!

Again in 1935 and 1937 Heydrich was forced to threaten legal action against two people who declared that he was of Jewish origin; but in neither instance did the case get as far as the Courts. The first man withdrew his accusation unreservedly in a written statement; and the second, who volunteered to produce unimpeachable proof of Heydrich's Jewish origins, disappeared for good into a concentration camp.

What Heydrich had done was ruthlessly simple. He had ordered his trusty henchman, an S.S. Sergeant-Major from the old Hamburg days, to break in and steal all documents and registers which might give any pointer to his father's ancestry, and to destroy them. He quite forgot, however, that in Leipzig there existed a grave-stone with the name Sarah Heydrich. Later, when it did occur to him, he sent the same henchman to obliterate this piece of evidence as well. One night the grave-stone of the Jewish grandmother disappeared; it was removed from the cemetery in a lorry and pitched into a neighbouring river, and, leaving nothing to chance this time, Heydrich replaced it with another stone bearing the discreet inscription 'S. Heydrich'. The bill for this latter was still in existence in Heydrich's personal office in 1945.

Had Heydrich thus succeeded in obliterating all possible traces? The indications are that he had not. In Meissen, where both his father and his grandmother Sarah had lived for a long while, there were plenty of proofs of the Jewish origin of the Chief of the German Security Police, and these, apparently, fell into the hands of his foremost opponent, Admiral Canaris. What use was made of them will be told later.

Heydrich's finest hour was 30th June, 1934, 'the night of the long knives'. It was then that he proved for the first time how indispensable he was to Hitler, and rendered him a service, which could never be forgotten. With that foresight which was characteristic of him he sensed the crucial moment in the tension between the S.A. and its Chief of Staff, Roehm, on the one side and Adolf Hitler on the other, and his keen intellect fully and correctly appreciated its dangers. Far more clearly than Himmler, he realized that Hitler must, under all circumstances, guard himself against the threat of a second revolution, over which he would have no control and which would certainly

rob him of his personal dictatorial powers.   To wait until
Roehm launched the 'second revolution' seemed far too
dangerous. Hitler, thought Heydrich, must anticipate any and
every eventuality.

One day a German court in possession of all evidence relevant
to the 30th June will give its verdict, and this must not be
anticipated here. It is nevertheless permissible to state certain
indisputable facts. On 30th June, 1934 there was no vestige
either of a Roehm revolution or of an S.A. *putsch*. That there
would eventually have been a 'second revolution' is more than
likely; but at that moment neither plans nor preparations had
been made for it. There are but two facts beyond dispute; the
first is that Roehm certainly wished to raise a National Socialist
Wehrmacht—an idea to which the old Prusso-German Reichswehr was opposed; and the second is that Hitler himself viewed
Roehm's intentions with mistrust and misgiving.

All this put together did not, however, suffice to prove either
the necessity for, or the justice of, a paralysing blow against the
S.A., so Heydrich proceeded to manufacture the missing
evidence and deliver the necessary pretexts for preventive
action. Only a small fraction of the accusations made against
his old comrades-in-arms and placed before Hitler was genuine
and correct; the rest was all conjecture or deliberate mis-
representation. It was Heydrich who convinced Hitler that
Roehm was scheming not only to become Minister for War,
but also to suppress Hitler or at least to relegate him to a position
of purely nominal significance. It was Heydrich, too, who
produced 'proofs' of a conspiracy between the S.A. and certain
foreign Powers.

Hitler's disapproval of Roehm's Wehrmacht plans was, it is
true, getting stronger; and it had some measure of professional
justification, for an efficient army could certainly have best
been created with the help of the old, professional Corps of
Officers. But there is no doubt at all that this alone would never
have caused Hitler to take action against the S.A.; he was
provoked to it simply and solely by Heydrich's material. Admittedly, it will now never be known with certainty whether
Hitler really believed Heydrich's accusations against the S.A.
Chiefs or whether he only wanted to believe them, because

they furthered those most secret of his plans, which he had perhaps not yet admitted even to himself. Be that as it may, he gave Heydrich plenipotentiary powers to act as he thought fit.

It was Heydrich who prepared the lists upon which the shootings in both Berlin and Munich were based; and in them, as is well known, he included not only the 'conspirators', but also people who had nothing to do with the faked S.A. revolt, but whom he considered dangerous for one reason or another. Even Goering, who was given executive responsibility for the counter-measures in Berlin, received his shooting list from Heydrich. He was, of course, in no better position to see through Heydrich's machinations than was a yokel like Sepp Dietrich, whose execution squads, drawn from Hitler's personal body-guard, went faithfully about their business according to the lists given to them.

The 30th June was widely portrayed in both home and foreign Press as a victory for the Reichswehr, but Heydrich certainly had no intention of acting as its ally; on the contrary, it was he who was responsible for the shooting of General von Schleicher, one of the most able of the Reichswehr officers and von Papen's successor as Chancellor of the Reich.

Of the prospective victims on the opposition and the Reichswehr sides only one, von Papen himself, slipped through Heydrich's fingers. Heydrich never forgot this, and he did his utmost to rectify the omission. Up to the day of his death, a member of the Secret Service had been given the task of getting von Papen at all costs. Freiherr von Ketteler, who had also escaped the 30th June massacre, was in fact murdered by this man. When von Papen was appointed Ambassador to Austria, von Ketteler accompanied him as special adviser. Shortly after the invasion of Austria, Heydrich's assassins seized him in his house, murdered him and threw his body into the Danube, from which it was some time later washed up on the banks close to the Czech border.

But von Papen eluded even Heydrich's long arm. The possibility that the attempt on his life in Ankara, which was attributed to the Russians, was in reality Heydrich's work is strengthened by one curious fact. Heydrich was wont occasionally to supply his assassins with a 'smoke-bomb'; having executed his task, the man was supposed to shatter his bomb on the ground and make good his escape under cover of the ensuing smoke screen. In reality, these smoke-bombs were ordinary bombs, designed to destroy the user and thus eliminate any danger of his talking in the event of his being captured. Von Papen's would-be assassin had a 'smoke-bomb' of this kind; a cunningly resourceful man, he decided to let loose his smoke screen before going into action and to use his revolver under cover of it. This excessive caution cost him his life—and saved von Papen's. It must, however, be emphasized that Heydrich's connection with the attempt is a conjecture, based upon the smoke-bomb coincidence; whether it is in fact justified will probably never be known.

What was Heydrich's ultimate goal? No one can say with any certainty, for he made no confidants even among his most intimate and closest colleagues; under the influence of drink he would sometimes talk a little, and then it became clear that his great ambition was nothing less than to become 'the foremost man in the German Reich'. He once developed the theory that the posts of Fuehrer and Reichs Chancellor should be separated, by which he meant that the Fuehrer should be relegated to the titular role of a President of the Reich. The Reich Chancellor, on the other hand, would be the man with the real power in his hands, and it was this job that he fancied for himself.

But Heydrich was no mere dreamer. He did not merely toy with such ideas, but calculatingly chose his objective and worked for it with a systematic planning worthy of the General Staff itself. The first step towards becoming Reich Chancellor was, as he saw it, to become Minister of the Interior—a post which would place both the Security Police and the whole of the normal Police Force under his control. Himmler, he thought, could well remain as S.S. Reichsfuehrer; with the police already subordinate to the Ministry of the Interior and with the Waffen S.S.—in war-time at least—in the field orders of the Wehrmacht, it became a position of very minor importance. The Ministry of the Interior was not, however, to be reached in one single bound. First, he felt, he must show that he was a sound and capable administrator of public affairs, and to have the chance of so doing he hit upon the idea of becoming Deputy Reichs-Protector of Bohemia and Moravia.

Accordingly, he submitted a memorandum to Hitler in which he suggested that it was impossible for the Reich-Protector, Freiherr von Neurath, to fulfil his duties single-handed. Hitler, who in any case made a practice of doubling all important posts whenever possible, was easily persuaded, and Heydrich achieved his first purpose.

In Bohemia and Moravia he carried out his duties with cunning skill. It is not true that he instituted a general terror which earned him the hatred of the whole Czech people and the nickname of 'the bloodhound'. On the contrary, he met with very considerable success in his efforts to separate the intellectual upper classes from the workers and peasants, and thus to create a cleavage in the Czech people. His intention was to exterminate —or at least render innocuous—the upper classes, whom he regarded as the protagonists of nationalism, and, by improving the economic conditions of the country, to win the workers and peasants over to the side of the régime. In actual fact, from the material point of view, the Czech peasantry had no grounds for complaint against Heydrich, while among the workmen of the industrial centres his praises were loudly sung—and certainly not with the object of currying favour with any German who might be listening.

This made Heydrich all the more dangerous in the eyes of the Czech leaders. It was not hatred alone, but consideration for the well-being of the State and, if you will, of the nation itself, which caused them to decide that he must be removed. This did not present much difficulty, for Heydrich was foolhardy as well as courageous, and always drove about the country in an open car without police escort; and the exceptionally efficient assistance given by the British Secret Service ensured the success of the enterprise.

The removal of Heydrich, however, was a special case. The mass of the Czech people had little in common with his murderers and did not regard his death as a signal for wholesale sabotage, partisan warfare or anything of that sort. On the contrary, the Czechs worked obediently and well for Germany to the very end. The production target set for Czech agriculture was invariably reached and was above the average production figures of the Reich itself; the Czech industrial workers during the war years were for the most part just as efficient as their German counterparts; and there was hardly any underground opposition until the Czechs were quite sure, both that no risk was involved and that the collapse of National Socialism was certain. Then indeed the Czech people rose—but with less vigour against the German Wehrmacht than against the Germans in their midst, who were driven from the lands of Bohemia and Moravia.

It is as yet perhaps too soon to pass final judgment on Heydrich. He was without doubt an outstanding personality and a leading figure—not only of National Socialism, but of the whole conception of the totalitarian State. Cesare Borgia is perhaps the closest historical analogy that can be drawn. Both men were imbued with the same complete disregard for all ethical values, both possessed of the same passion for power, the same cold intelligence, the same frigidity of heart, the same systematically calculated ambition, and even the same physical beauty of a fallen angel. That Heydrich had his own code of sorts, that he had principles which he disobeyed only with a feeling of guilt is possible, but not probable. Far from possessing any Christian code of ethics, he was devoid even of the most elementary and instinctive moral sense. Not the State, but Power—personal power was his God. He was a type from the Cæsarian age, in which the objects of power were never questioned, and power was regarded as an object in itself. He cared naught for ideologies, gave no thought to their truth or value, but regarded them solely as an instrument with which to sway the masses, and the whole was subordinated in his mind to the possession and enjoyment of power. Truth and goodness had no intrinsic meaning for him; they were instruments to be used for the gaining of more and more power, and everything was true, everything was good, which furthered this object. Politics, too, were, for him, merely stepping stones for the seizing and holding of power. To debate whether any particular action was of itself right appeared so stupid to him that it was certainly a question he never asked himself.

As a result, the man's whole life was an unbroken chain of

murders—murders of people whom he disliked, of competitors for power, of opponents and of those whom he regarded as untrustworthy; and of intrigues which were as bad as murders and often more evilly conceived. The light of human life had no value in Heydrich's eyes, and if it interfered with his striving for power it was ruthlessly extinguished. His wickedness was not the mere evil dishonesty of the opportunist, but the devilish nihilism of an undoubtedly great mind. His crimes were not the outcome of uncontrollable impulse, but the dictates of a superlative intellect, upon which the promptings of the heart exercised no influence at all. Not for nothing had Hitler called Heydrich 'the man with the heart of iron'. *Corruptio optimi pessima*, runs the old saying. An ordinary man could never have reached such heights of iniquity, and only a man of hyper-intelligence could have committed such criminal enormities.

The story of an evil genius exercises a compelling fascination, and any idealization of Heydrich is a danger to be guarded against, for it might encourage others to imitate him. But the danger that he might be idealized is lessened by the fact that his crimes were not committed for the sake of some great cause, but purely for his own personal advantage. He cared nothing for the might of the German Reich; it was only power for himself that he sought. He had no desire to serve the German people, but sought only to satisfy his own lust for authority.

Heydrich's character is not without its pathological aspects. His overweening ambition, for example, might be designated, in the popular quasi-scientific jargon of the day, as a hyper-compensation for the inferiority complex aroused by the knowledge that his antecedents were not irreproachable, by National-Socialist standards. His nordic complex, too, originates probably from the same source. He wished to see around him only people of the purest Germanic type, and in his own personal appearance he was at pains to emphasize what he referred to as his 'glorious nordic physical attributes'. Only the somewhat singularly crooked setting of his eyes was perhaps displeasing. This was often attributed to some drop of mongolian blood in the distant past, and it was only his death mask which clearly revealed whence this slight blemish really originated.

There were pathological aspects, too, in Heydrich's relations

2

with his wife. The daughter of a school-teacher on the island of Fehmarn, she belonged to that type of evil, ambition-ridden women described in Germanic legends. She ceaselessly fanned the already glowing ambition of her husband and impatiently drove him onwards. It is possible that his urge to excel in everything—as a fencer, an airman, a horseman and a Don Juan—arose from the sexual pathological complexes to which his married life gave birth. Some day psycho-analysts may explain all this to their own satisfaction, but the essential judgment on this most terrible of all the leaders of the Third Reich will not be altered thereby.

Heydrich, the amoral cynic, believed in neither friendship nor comradeship. At such sentimentality he sneered often, long and loud. He had no faith in voluntary corporate fidelity, and there was but one tie which he regarded as trustworthy—knowledge of another's secrets. He considered it to be of the utmost importance, therefore, to find out all and any shady secrets in the lives not only of his own immediate colleagues, but of all the leading personalities of the Third Reich. Such knowledge, he considered, would give him actual power over his fellow men and lead indirectly to power and control of political events. He admitted freely that he had copied this system from the Bolsheviks, and he certainly made himself a complete adept in the use of it.

Many of the leaders of National-Socialist Germany knew that Heydrich was making a collection of incriminating material. On that account he was hated and feared, for no one knew what he had found out, and everybody had something to hide. The opportunist type which quickly came to the fore in the Nazi hierarchy after the assumption of power was easily plunged into a state of terror. A small peccadillo, the acceptance of gifts, some insignificant misdemeanour of the past—these were enough to awaken a guilty conscience and make it tremble lest the benevolence of the Party should be withdrawn. The secret files, which Heydrich kept in his own hands, were among the most dreaded documents in the whole of the Third Reich.

Even Hitler himself was not exempt from the attentions of this system. Heydrich, it might well be said, was the first of the 'Hitler Researchers' and did his utmost to find out about every detail of his master's past life. In this he was very successful; for years he had a special confidential agent in Munich, whose sole duty was to gain the confidence of Hitler's cronies and collaborators of the early years. This the agent accomplished and, particularly during the course of a few hard-drinking bouts, extracted from his unsuspecting victims (most of whom hated Heydrich like the plague) some extremely valuable pieces of information. Heydrich's file on Hitler would be worth its weight in gold to any future biographer.

The information came from such people as Max Amann, Hitler's Sergeant-Major in the first world war, Emile Maurice, his closest friend from the earliest days of the Nazi movement until the end of the 1920s, Hermann Esser, an equally close friend, and Hoffmann, his well-known personal photographer, whose connection with Hitler dated from the time when he sat up half the night arguing with a Hitler suffering from insomnia brought on by the death of his niece, Geli Raubal. Then there was Christian Weber, another crony of the early days, and one of the few who were privileged to use the familiar *Du* in addressing him—an honour shared only with Dr. Friedrich Weber, Ambassador Kriebel, the S.A. General Roehm and an old war-time comrade named Schmidt. None of these had any suspicion that their interlocutor was an agent of Heydrich's.

Maurice was the man in whom Heydrich was most particularly interested, for he it was who knew more about Hitler's early days than anybody else. But Maurice was the only one who did not succumb to the tongue-loosening effects of drink. Even so, Heydrich's agent got a lot of most interesting information out of him—how, is not known and most probably never will be known.

Maurice, apparently, did not measure up to Nazi standards of pure Aryan descent, and his father was said to have been a 'half-caste of the first grade'. In spite of this, he was one of the earliest of Hitler's supporters in Munich; he became his chauffeur and—in so far as Hitler was capable of real friendship—his trusted friend. It is not generally known that Maurice was once for a while head of the S.S. before Himmler and that once, on Hitler's orders and much to his own satisfaction, he had the pleasure of dismissing Himmler from the corps on account of his excessively military antics. (When Himmler was later re-instated he promptly dismissed Maurice whom he had never forgiven for the insult.)

Hitler's close friendship with Maurice lasted for ten years and then came to an end over a woman. Hitler was in love with a girl named Geli Raubal, the beautiful daughter of his step-sister. It is probably quite true that this young girl was the only human being for whom Hitler felt a genuine, unbridled and unconditional love. And it was with this very Geli Raubal that the agile Maurice was having an ordinary and rather sordid love affair. That much he admitted to me himself. When Hitler found out about it, he broke completely with Maurice. After the rupture, which also entailed his dismissal from Hitler's service, Maurice had the bad taste to sue Hitler before the Employment Court in Munich. Hitler, usually so vindictive, bore him no ill-will however, and after his assumption of power he even took steps to ensure that a blind eye was turned to the shortcomings in the genealogy of Maurice. The latter, then, certainly had no justification for the vindictive and vicious disclosures he made about Hitler after the collapse of Germany.

In the autumn of 1931 Hitler decided to send Geli Raubal to Vienna to have her voice trained. Her uncle wanted her to become a great singer. For a variety of reasons she had no desire to leave Munich and objected strenuously but without avail against her uncle's wishes. It is more than probable that this enforced departure from Munich was the reason for her otherwise inexplicable suicide. She shot herself—it was not murder. This terrible act brought about a grave crisis in Hitler's life. The shock appears to have had a marked effect on his character; at one time he was determined to take his life and was only with great difficulty dissuaded by his many friends. But the hardening of his nature and his subsequent suppression of all normal human sentiment are undoubtedly attributable to the death of Geli Raubal. It was from this moment that he devoted himself passionately and exclusively to politics; 'henceforth,' he declared somewhat pathetically, but with apparent sincerity, 'Germany alone will be my bride.'

He did not, however, exclude all women from his life on that account; and although his relationships with them were for the most part in the nature of transitory acquaintanceships, there is no truth in the widely-spread and sensational rumours that he was inclined towards perverse practices. He never had the slightest intention of entering upon any serious union, and latterly—and particularly during the war years—he was far too busy to indulge in any sort of private life at all. His most intimate colleagues were therefore all the more astonished when, face to face with the end, he suddenly married Eva Braun on 30th April, 1945.

Heydrich, of course, knew all about Maurice's little ancestral 'indiscretion', for he made a particular point of delving into the antecedents of all the leading personalities of the Third Reich, in the hope of digging out some weakness which he could turn to his own advantage. This was a curious form of activity on his part when it is remembered that he himself was in no position, except by faking, to prove his own pure Aryan descent. Perhaps it was that he was seeking accomplices or people in the same boat as himself.

The case of Dr. Ley, the Head of the German Labour Front, is a good example of Heydrich's methods. He suddenly came across something which gave him good reason to think that Ley was a 'non-Aryan'. Without hesitation he attempted to break in-to the office of Walter Buch, the Chief Justice of the Party, by whom, on Hitler's orders, Ley's personal file was kept. Although he succeeded neither here nor anywhere else in finding any documentary proof, he nevertheless made skilful use of his knowledge against Ley.

Not even his own immediate Chief, Himmler, was immune from his ancestral witch-hunting, and it was a curious incident in the spring of 1933 that set him hot-foot on the trail. Himmler had just been appointed Chief of the Munich Police, when one day a man presented himself at Police Headquarters, saying that he was a cousin of the new Chief and wanted to see him. He proved to be a Jewish cattle dealer from Wuerttemberg, and the first reaction of the police was to lock him up forthwith for his impertinence. The complete self-assurance of the man caused them to hesitate, however, and, as a precautionary measure, to sound Himmler himself, before doing anything quite so drastic.

To the utter astonishment of all concerned, Himmler declared that the man was under his protection and that not a hair of his head was to be touched. Right up to the time of Germany's collapse there existed in the Munich Police Headquarters a G.R.S.-file (*Geheime Reichssache*—A State secret) on the episode in charge of a completely trustworthy official.

What use Heydrich made of this useful bit of information about Himmler is not known in detail; but it may safely be assumed that the very strong influence he exercised over Himmler was due to the hold which this incident had given him.

These few examples of Heydrich's search for personal skeletons must suffice. They are authentic and were obtained from one of Heydrich's personal staff officers, who had a measure of access to the secret files, though even he probably had no idea of how complete and all-embracing this collection of documents really was. Now let us examine some typical examples of Heydrich's activities and methods.

HEYDRICH'S FIGHT AGAINST THE CHURCH

Heydrich had a most bitter hatred of Christianity in general and the Catholic Church in particular. It was almost pathological in its intensity and sometimes caused this otherwise cold and calculating schemer to lose all sense of proportion and logic. He was convinced that Christianity was a disaster for the German people and that there existed a Christian conspiracy, at the head of which stood the Vatican and the Jesuits, whose aim was the destruction of Germany. But he was shrewd enough to see that a direct attack on the Christian Church and an all-out anti-religious crusade in Germany might well shatter the whole foundation of the Nazi régime. He decided, therefore, to try and discredit the Church in the eyes of the people, to destroy its prestige, to weaken it by fomenting internal dissension and, by a series of progressive but cautious measures, to put it on the road to decline and ultimate disintegration.

This plan for the disintegration of the Catholic and Protestant Churches could, he thought, best be initiated from within. He accordingly set up a special section of his own for this purpose at

Headquarters of the Security Services; all the principal members of it were Catholic ex-priests who had been dismissed by their Church, and its Head was a former secretary of Cardinal Faulhaber. This plan of using renegades in the fight against the Church proved, however, to be a bad one. The hatred characteristic of all apostates blinded these people's sense of reality and caused them to commit numerous and elementary tactical mistakes, which contributed in no small measure to Heydrich's failure to put into practice his plan of campaign.

The notorious actions for currency offences and for offences against public decency, brought against Catholic priests in Germany and designed to discredit the Church in the eyes of the people, were founded almost entirely upon evidence which had been faked by Heydrich's orders. The whole idea was a complete failure, and the cases aroused far more mistrust of the judicial system as a whole and of the police in particular, than of their intended victim, the Church.

But Heydrich had another and far more dangerous plan, which, had he but been able to put it into practice, might well in years to come have jeopardized the very existence of the Christian Church in Germany. His idea was that young men, exceptionally talented and of unshakeable National-Socialist conviction, should enter the priesthood and then, when they had attained key positions, should set about the disintegration of the Church from within.

These agents could not, of course, be smuggled into the Church, crudely disguised, as it were, as priests; they would have to go through the appropriate theological colleges and acquire all the rights and the status of duly ordained priests, if they were to achieve the positions and the confidence necessary for the execution of their mission. The powers of deception and the mental discipline demanded of participants in this scheme of truly devilish ingenuity were so great, that Heydrich began by personally selecting a few exceptionally gifted young men from the Hitler Youth. These he intended to send with false names to the various theological colleges and seminaries in Germany and abroad. He elaborated a plan to penetrate the Protestant Church in a similar manner, and he reckoned that within fifteen or twenty years his emissaries would have attained the positions from which it would be possible for them to begin their deadly work of destruction.

Curiously enough, Hitler evinced little enthusiasm for the scheme. When Heydrich asked, in the interests of speed, that the selected young men should be exempted from military service, he bluntly refused. Heydrich, however, did not give up the idea; he regarded it as merely postponed until after the war, and in its place, as an immediate preliminary, he set about the building-up of his spy ring within the organizational circles of the Church. In spite of the inefficiency of his adviser on ecclesiastical affairs, he succeeded in obtaining a deep insight into the innermost activities of the Church. He had informers planted in the highest ecclesiastical circles; there was not a diocese in Germany in which he had not at least one agent in a well-placed position. His secret agents worked close to the Papal Nunciate in Berlin and got into the very Vatican itself; and he received consistent and detailed reports on all the most important ecclesiastical and episcopal gatherings.

His death rid the Church in Germany of its most formidable opponent. Kaltenbrunner, his successor, had very different ideas on Church matters. He was certainly very far from leading a Christian life or confessing to a Christian faith, but Heydrich's deadly hatred of the Church passed his comprehension, and he very quickly dismantled the whole anti-ecclesiastical apparatus which his predecessor had erected.

Kaltenbrunner, as is well known, eventually made his peace with the Church and, having made confession and received Holy Communion, met his death at the hands of the hangman.

HEYDRICH AND THE JEWISH QUESTION

It is psychologically understandable that Heydrich should have been the most implacable of all the enemies of the people from whom he partly derived. By exterminating the Jews he was subconsciously wiping out the blot which he thought disfigured his own ancestry. The Advisory Councils for Jewish Affairs in both the Security Service and the Gestapo were organized according to his personal instructions, and the 'Central Organiza-tion for Jewish Emigration' was his own personal creation.

Whether for reasons of foreign political expediency or whether out of deference for the humanitarian principles generally accepted throughout Europe, the National-Socialist Government had no intention, originally, of solving the Jewish problem by means of physical extermination. Jewish emigration was therefore in no way impeded, and the first mass emigration at the time of the Nazi assumption of power was followed by a second at the time of the Austrian *Anschluss* in 1938. Heydrich considered that these emigrations were badly conceived and haphazardly organized. On account of the exceptionally high State charges, the road abroad was open only to Jews with plenty of capital; but the vast majority of Jews in Germany, unless they enjoyed assistance from some organization or from relatives abroad, were financially compelled to remain in the country. Heydrich hit upon the idea of opening mass emigration to all Jews by the expedient of making the richer Jews pay both the State charges and the emigration expenses of a number, according to the means at their disposal, of their less fortunate brethren.

The organization charged with the execution of this policy was the Central Organization for Jewish Emigration, with orders to encourage, and not to hinder, the departure of the Jews, as had hitherto been the practice in Germany. Those willing to emigrate received every possible assistance in the way of documents, travel tickets and the like; their possessions, of course, they had to leave for the most part, in the hands of the State. By this means, according to Heydrich's plan, Germany and the Protectorate of Bohemia and Moravia would have been cleared of all Jews by the end of 1941. The outbreak of war threatened to defeat this intention; but after the occupation of France, Heydrich fell back on an old Napoleonic plan of sending the Jews to the island of Madagascar, and he obtained Hitler's permission to send a plenipotentiary to discuss the question with the French authorities in Vichy. Owing to the course of the war, however, this plan came to nothing.

When Heydrich realized, after the beginning of the war with Russia, that Hitler was now indeed determined physically to exterminate Jewry, he brought the whole of his organizing genius to bear on seeking a means of implementing this monstrous decision. It was he who devised the scheme for 'The Final Solution of the Jewish Problem'—that most devilish masterpiece of this virtuoso in the black arts of deception and camouflage— and he it was who invented the horrible machinery by which, 'in an imperceptible manner,' millions of people were hounded to their death. The whole procedure was so carefully concealed, that only vague and intangible rumours of Jewish massacres ever reached the ears of the German people, and they, for the most part, were disbelieved. Even people who, thanks to their positions, normally had a deep insight into current affairs, remained ignorant for years of the mechanism of annihilation.

Initially, special squads of the Security Police had carried out mass executions in the Eastern theatre of war, and the former Gauleiter of Vienna, Odilo Globocnik, had, as Chief of the Lublin Police, carried out mass murders of Jews. The wave of horror and revulsion evoked by these massacres might have caused the régime considerable embarrassment, and it was Heydrich himself who persuaded Hitler to supplant these 'crude methods' by his own silent machine of destruction.

The basic principle of his system—a particularly repulsive nuance, typical of Heydrich's inherent wickedness and contempt for all human decency—was that Jews must be employed to destroy Jews, and the first stage of extermination was served unwittingly by Jews under the supervision of a few Security Police. The practice had the advantage that the further the process of liquidation proceeded, the greater grew the number of those in the know who became victims of it. Heydrich used to boast that he had learned a useful lesson from the history of ancient Egypt, where the workmen who constructed the tombs of the Pharaohs were themselves all put to death, so that the secret of the resting places might remain well guarded. The Jewish National Committees in Berlin, Vienna, Prague, Frankfurt and numberless other great cities of Europe were themselves compelled to decide who of their co-religionists were to go to the ghettos of Poland. Only very few knew that the next stage of the journey was also the last—to the annihilation camps of Auschwitz and Maidanek.

Heydrich's organization continued to function smoothly for a long time after his death. The plan for 'Jewish Emigration from Hungary', which was agreed upon by the Governments of Germany and Hungary in the spring of 1944, bore the unmistakable hall-mark of the Heydrich method.

It was agreed, officially, that the Hungarian Jews should be deported to the ghettos of Poland. In order to give the Jews of Budapest no chance of fleeing the city and hiding in the countryside, the deportations began in the provinces. The Hungarian Gendarmerie was given the sole responsibility for the execution of the plan, but the selection of individuals for deportation was thrust upon the Jewish Council of Elders.

Two trains, each carrying two thousand Jews, left daily for Poland. The unfortunate Jews themselves had no idea of the terrible fate that awaited them; unresistingly, they docilely marched in long columns to the railway stations and allowed themselves to be packed into the waiting trains. There were very few gendarmes in charge, and flight would have been an easy matter, while in the Carpatho-Ukraine, where the biggest Jewish colonies were settled, the highly inaccessible mountains and forests would have afforded ideal hiding places for months to come. Yet only a very few seized this last chance of cheating death.

Once the train was loaded, it was generally taken over by a German police officer, who had no idea of its final destination. His written orders were that he and his small guard of German police were to accompany the train to some specified Polish station and there to hand it over to a relief that would be awaiting them. Usually, the train would be halted just short of the given destination and the new escort would be waiting to take it over. Not only the officer in charge, but the guards themselves were also relieved, and then the miserable and bedraggled column of unfortunates would disappear into the forests and on into some subsidiary camp of Auschwitz or Maidanek, where the mills of death awaited them. The empty train itself went on to the next station, where it would be turned round and sent back to Hungary, and none of those concerned had the slightest idea of what became of the people they had so recently uprooted from their homes.

CHAPTER III

HEINRICH HIMMLER

THE Supreme Chief of the German Intelligence Services was, in theory at least, the S.S. Reichsfuehrer Heinrich Himmler.

How came this man, who in both mentality and appearance resembled some petty bank clerk and who sprang from the most humble origins, to rise and become the closest and indeed the most indispensable of all Hitler's collaborators, and as Chief of the S.S., wield a power which made him the most important man in the Reich after the Fuehrer himself?

His rise to power is indeed astonishing. In the days before Hitler's assumption of power there was no Heinrich Himmler among the leaders; he was, admittedly, to be found somewhere in the rear rank, but nobody took him seriously, and he was generally regarded as being a bit of a romantic crank. As a member of a militant free-corps, Himmler was implicated in Hitler's abortive Munich *putsch* of 9th April, 1923 and afterwards automatically became a supporter of National Socialism. For a while he served as the unpretentious secretary of Gregor Strasser, Organizer in chief of the Party. Even his appointment in 1926 as S.S. *Reichsfuehrer* was not of any great significance, for at that time the S.S. was nothing more than is implied in its title of *Schutz-Staffel* (bodyguard)—a body of effective and trustworthy men charged with the protection of Party leaders at public meetings and the like. Until 30th June, 1934 the S.S. was subordinated to the Chief of Staff, S.A., and in the nineteen twenties no one had any idea of the enormous expansion that lay before it.

Himmler, indeed, was once temporarily dismissed from the S.S. on account of his ultra-military antics. He possessed that characteristic, not uncommon among those of inferior physique, of placing an exaggerated value on those qualities in others in which he himself was lacking. Because he could not compare in physique or athletic prowess with the men of his Shock

Troops, because with his poor eyesight he could not shoot and because he was not robust enough to take part in a route march in field service order, he became a military martinet of almost super-Prussian fanaticism. Oafs like Sepp Dietrich, who later commanded the *Leibstandarte* Adolf Hitler (the Hitler Guards) had the bad taste to make fun of him to his face and hold him up to ridicule in front of his comrades; and among the 'old warriors' no one predicted any great future for Heinrich Himmler. A minor administrative post, they thought, would be his just reward when the Party came into power.

To the question—how then did he achieve greatness, there is but one true answer. Heydrich carried him to the top, and it was he who made Himmler the man he became; his, too, was the idea of pushing this inconspicuous, diffident man of mediocre intelligence upwards, until he felt the right moment had come to topple him over and take his place. Himmler's extreme mediocrity remained hidden from the public for so long, only because Heydrich's premature death prevented him from taking the final step in the plan upon which he had decided; and by the time Heydrich died, Himmler had already reached a level from which further advancement was automatic and without regard to personal capability. It would have required a man of Heydrich's stature and intelligence to expose him; the remaining few who saw through him were far too weak for such a task.

It was first and foremost Heydrich who drew Himmler's attention to the possibilities inherent in the position of *Reichs-fuehrer* of the S.S. He, too, was the originator of the plan that, on the assumption of power, the S.S. should as a first step acquire control of the entire existing police system of the country and in this way become the real Police power behind the régime; his again was the idea of transforming the S.S. into the Elite of the Third Reich. He made quite sure that Himmler did not again revert to his somewhat ridiculous military antics with the S.S., but went soberly forward with its systematic and progressive development; and when he died, the whole foundation, upon which the future might. of the S.S. was to be based, was already complete.

In every branch of the Administration, of Industry and of

the Party hierarchy senior officers of the S.S. held important positions, and were, of course, under Himmler's orders. Heydrich had indeed succeeded in making this scheme of dual sub-ordination into a practical, working reality, and in expanding the S.S. into a State within the State. But Himmler had not the intelligence to make full use of the possibilities thus placed in his hand; the practice of conferring high rank in the S.S. on the incumbents of all the most important key positions in the National Socialist régime, by which means Heydrich intended to make them at the same time real subordinates of the S.S., degenerated under Himmler into meaningless, formal and honorary appointments, which none of those thus 'honoured' regarded as any serious obligation. Individuals like Ribbentrop and Martin Bormann, for example, both of whom held high rank in the S.S., would have been profoundly astonished, had Himmler suddenly assumed the role of their Commanding Officer and issued orders to them; and they would undoubtedly have repudiated his right to any such presumption with the ut-most energy and indignation. Such crises, however, never materialized, for Himmler never made the slightest attempt to influence either the activities or the opinions of his highly-placed honorary subordinates. Even the Generals of the Waffen S.S., the purely military formations of the organization, did not bother their heads very much about their Supreme Com-mander. They had other worries to think about and preferred to take their orders from their superior officers in the Wehr-macht; and the remainder, the ordinary S.S., from which prac-tically all men fit for active service had been called up, played a completely insignificant part in war-time.

Himmler's real power, then, was not nearly as great as it appeared to outsiders. With Heydrich's death the expanding movement of the S.S. power-tentacles came to a halt; and, as with many other things, here also a halt was but another word for a withdrawal. Heydrich himself would never have allowed things to come to such a pass, even with a fictitious semblance of power in his hands he would still have succeeded in in-fluencing the policies of the Third Reich. But Himmler merely lapsed more and more into passive lethargy.

Even so, to regard Himmler as the most powerful man in

the state after Hitler is no mistake. The key positions which he held—Supreme Chief of the German Police Forces and Intelligence Services, and later Minister of the Interior and Commander-in-Chief of the *Ersatzarmee*—a species of second-line, Home Guard Army—made him potentially so and gave him the opportunity for decisive participation in the fashioning of German policy. All this, however, remained in the realms of potentiality, and in the great events that mattered Himmler made no practical use of his position. In the opposite direction, in the exercise of his power downwards from above, he was a very different man; in the lower grades of the Party hierarchy and among the broad masses of the ordinary people he manfully played his part as the arbiter of their fate and the master with powers of life and death. But of opposing Hitler and gaining his point—if indeed such an idea ever entered his head —he was quite incapable.

In this recital of the powerful positions which he held, the most important has still to be mentioned; it is his 'strong position' *vis-à-vis* the Fuehrer. Did Hitler ever see through his S.S. *Reichsfuehrer*? Did he recognize him for the weak and insignificant personality that he really was? For a long time, probably, Hitler failed to realize of what poor stuff Himmler was made, for he was an indifferent judge of men. Later he must have realized that Himmler was nothing more than a puppet of Heydrich, and he began more and more to draw the latter directly to his side. It would have been only a matter of time before Heydrich completely outclassed Himmler in the Fuehrer's eyes and stepped into his shoes; but the silent struggle between the two men was brought to a final conclusion by Heydrich's premature death.

No second Heydrich appeared on the scene, and Kaltenbrunner neither possessed the necessary personal drive and initiative to oust Himmler from his privileged position with the Fuehrer, nor for a very long time did he evince the slightest desire to do so.

And so Himmler retained his position, and Hitler saw no reason to dismiss him. He had in the meanwhile made himself indispensable to Hitler and had won his personal affection. Unlike the generals, the diplomats, the industrial leaders and many other Party members, who, in the early phases of the dictatorship, were sometimes inclined to make things difficult for Hitler, Himmler from the very beginning followed the basic principle of never contradicting the Fuehrer. To him, no plan suggested by Hitler was impracticable, and when all the others raised objections he agreed with neither thought nor compunction. Hitler did not realize that it was Heydrich, still at that time very much in the background behind Himmler, and not Himmler, who so often achieved the impossible and who made such frequent use of the dangerous phrase—'nothing is impossible'. Even had Hitler realized this, it would probably have made little or no difference, and after Heydrich's death Himmler continued successfully to play his part of the confirmed yes-man; and by that time Hitler seemed to attach less importance to this theoretical agreement being transformed into a practical success than to the fact that he had not been confronted with a pig-headed 'no'.

Himmler was not only weak, cowardly and insignificant; his character abounds with definite pathological traits. His hatred of the Church was pathological in nature, and his abhorrence of renegades amounted almost to a disease. For Himmler came of a middle-class and devoutly Catholic family; his father had been a royal tutor at the Bavarian Court, while his uncle, the honoured and revered member of the family, had been a Canon of the Chapel Royal. When Himmler rose to power, he compelled his uncle to leave the Church and place his vast experience at his disposal for use in his campaign against Christianity. The unfortunate man, to whom Himmler gave the rank of Lieutenant in the S.S., could find no roots in the new world into which he had been thrust. After the collapse of Germany he was first interned and then brought to Nuremberg as a witness for the prosecution. He died in captivity, literally of a broken heart, but at least reconciled and at peace with his Church.

As a youth, Himmler served as an acolyte at Mass, and as long as his father remained alive he did not dare to leave the Church and openly admit the hostility which he undoubtedly already felt towards it. It was only after his father's death that he made public renunciation and became a violent oppressor of Christianity and, in particular, of the Catholic Church. He regarded the Christian faith as a menace to the German people, and he accepted at its face value the grotesque idea of an alliance between the Vatican, World Jewry and Free Masonry for the destruction of the German nation in general and the National Socialist régime in particular. A psychologist, however, will doubtless have no difficulty in showing that Himmler's hostility to the Catholic Church had no intellectual basis, but was merely the expression of a hatred towards his father.

A similar, though much more complicated, trait was his boundless fear of Free Masonry. He was convinced that the Lodges constituted a terrible source of danger for the German people, and he succeeded in persuading Hitler more and more to his own way of thinking. There was hardly an operation which turned out badly for the Reich, hardly an accident which claimed a highly-placed Nazi as its victim, hardly an unexplained death, which Himmler did not immediately ascribe to the Free Masons. He surrounded himself with a host of similarly minded 'experts', who further strengthened his phobia of Free Masonry. In his 'Chief Adviser on Free-masonic Affairs' this *idée fixe* was exaggerated to a persecution mania of such proportions, that in the end he scarcely dared to leave the Gestapo building, for fear that some Free Mason was lurking, intent on taking his life!

Himmler's craze for the Germanic cult became a regular mania. He was a romantic bureaucrat. If he had been able, he would dearly have loved to put the German people, or at least his own S.S., back into the old Germanic epoch. Symptomatic of his craze were his ordering the use of ancient Germanic symbols, runes, architectural styles and the strange, but by no means harmless, idea of re-establishing the biological purity of the nordic race in the S.S. by an officially imposed process of selective breeding. If he had had his way, the ancient Germanic religion would have returned and ousted the hated faith of the Christians.

Bound up, presumably, with this Germanic complex is yet another strange peculiarity which cannot be lightly dismissed as mere romantic lunacy, but which in all probability was an inhibition in the language of the psychiatrist. Himmler in all earnestness believed himself to be a reincarnation of the German King Heinrich I, around whom he built up a pathetically romantic and spurious cult.   In the eleventh century Prince Henry the Fowler, of the Salic family, had suddenly risen to lead the German peoples. Himmler fancied that destiny had something similar in store for him.

His predilection for the occult sciences also went far beyond the confines of a harmless hobby; it can with truth be said that all his major decisions hung upon the advice given to him by his clairvoyant and other, more obscure than occult, advisers.   It sounds incredible that the S.S. Reichsfuehrer and Chief of German Police should have had self-professed alchemists working for him in the cellars of Gestapo Headquarters! This was known to many in the administrative branch of the S.S. as early as 1936.   The task that Himmler had set them was to produce, with the aid of formulæ from some ancient alchemist scripts, the gold with which he proposed to free Germany from the clutches of the capitalist Powers of the West. It is perhaps superfluous to add that these experiments cost lots of money, but produced no gold and were wound up by 1938.

Another scientist who received hundreds of thousands of marks for his experiments, worked for months on the perfection of a 'thunderbolt', a secret weapon that was to destroy all Germany's enemies at a single blow! But when the explorer Dr. Schaeffer, a serious-minded scientist of high repute very different from the crooks and cranks who enjoyed Himmler's support, returned to Germany from his expedition to Tibet, Himmler set him the task of breeding a strain of 'winter-hardy Steppe horses'! There was some method in Himmler's madness. He had an idea of occupying the whole of the Eastern Territories as far as Siberia with his S.S.; they were to live in so-called strongholds, rather in the manner of the military communities of the ancient German Orders of Chivalry, whence they would rule over the surrounding country and its conquered and enslaved inhabitants. But these strongholds, according to Himmler's idea, were to be made absolutely and completely independent of all modern machinery, which would be replaced by the 'winter-hardy Steppe horse'. This latter would serve not only as mount and beast of burden, but would also be required to furnish flesh, milk and cheese for the stalwart S.S. warriors guarding Germany's frontiers along the Ural Mountains!

Himmler was in deadly earnest about all this; in the midst of war thoroughbred bloodstock was procured from all over the world and placed at Dr. Schaeffer's disposal, and as late as 1944 Himmler found time to visit his stud in the Austrian Alps to see what progress was being made.

All these peculiarities, exaggerated almost to the point of lunacy, could have been dismissed as of little account, had Himmler kept this world of abstruse phantasy strictly apart from the world of politics, and shown some real sign of political genius. But this was not the case; on the contrary he mixed his phantasies and his political activities inextricably. A document which has survived contains the text of a speech, not for publication, delivered by Himmler in October 1943 to an audience of senior S.S. officers. At a moment when Germany was being thrust violently back on all fronts, when even a peace without victory but by negotiation was being regarded regretfully as unattainable, Himmler was still obsessed with his ideas of a gigantic newly-won empire, stretching to the far Ural mountains and governed by his beloved S.S.! The speech is so full of the most striking imbecilities, that his astounded listeners, who, from the high positions they occupied, had a fairly shrewd idea of what was really happening, came away with the impression that their Commander was a case for a mental specialist.

This man, then, who in normal times would have been put into a nursing home, if not a sanatorium for nervous diseases by his family, was the right-hand man of the Head of the German State. The devastating effect of the knowledge that this was so, that Himmler the foremost man after Hitler in the German Reich was beyond any dispute mentally deranged is in no degree lessened by the assertion that 'Himmler was a man, whose hands were clean'. Money and riches to a man of this type, obviously, meant nothing; he never dreamt of leading a life of luxury, of building himself ostentatious villas or of posing as a great figure in a new renaissance. Property could have no attraction for a man who lived in the crazy world of his own illusions. But apart from corruption in its elementary and primitive form, born of mere greed for wealth and luxury, there is also that moral corruption, which is far more subtle and far more insidious, and from this Himmler could not hold himself immune.

He was not mad in the sense that his thoughts and actions were senseless contradictions. His mind functioned perfectly logically. There was no visible symptomatic disturbance of the nervous system. For his official and political activities he must undoubtedly bear the full moral responsibility.

He of all people might justifiably have been expected as *Reichsfuehrer* S.S. to serve as a model of that upright character and decency, which the S.S. claim so vociferously. He was far from doing so, as is convincingly shown by the disreputable part he played in the events of 20th July, 1944. Himmler had been introduced by his trusted colleague and Chief of his personal Staff, S.S. General Wolff to the Berlin lawyer, Dr. Langbehn, who was an intimate friend of Dr. Popitz, the former Prussian Finance Minister, and like him a conspirator. It must not be assumed that Langbehn informed the *Reichsfuehrer* of all the details he knew of the plot. Neither Himmler nor Wolff could have failed to realize that Langbehn was not speaking on his own responsibility, but on behalf of an opposition group, which was ready for action and with which he was in contact. Like Schellenberg, Langbehn regarded Himmler as the appropriate man to set the German ship of State on a new course and bring her to the haven of peace with the Western Powers. After a talk with Wolff and Himmler, cautious in wording but quite unmistakable in intent, he must have gone away with the impression that Himmler agreed with him and was willing to play the part assigned to him—otherwise, surely, as Chief of Police he would have had Langbehn arrested on the spot. Instead he negotiated for months on end with Langbehn and even granted him facilities for a journey in 1943 to a neutral country for the purpose of trying to establish contact with the Western Powers. In the summer of the same year he had another secret meeting with him and Wolff on an estate in East Prussia. When Langbehn was arrested a few weeks later by the Gestapo and was subsequently executed in October 1944, he did not at any time lift a finger to help him; nor did he do anything for Popitz, beyond summoning him from prison to a very confidential *tête-à-tête*.

Himmler's willingness to negotiate with Langbehn may perhaps be regarded as a cunning police ruse to get on the trail of the whole conspiracy; but even if it were, it is still a shabby trick. Nor is this the only example of Himmler's double dealing. The question has often been asked how it was that the otherwise so efficient Gestapo did not discover the July plot in good time? The question does not arise; the Gestapo were well aware of the existence of the plot, and, although they had not discovered exact details about the participants and their intentions, they knew quite well who the leaders were. By the end of June 1944 so much evidence had been collected that according to all the rules of normal police and criminal procedure, the Gestapo should have forthwith arrested both General Beck and Dr. Goerdeler. But as neither Kaltenbrunner nor Mueller, the Gestapo Chief, was prepared to issue a warrant for the arrest of two such distinguished persons, application had to be made to Himmler himself. In spite of at least two urgent reminders, the latter took no action. Indeed, it was only in the early days of August, when the Gestapo was in the midst of the turmoil stirred up by the events of 20th July, that the application was returned, and then it was marked: 'Application for warrant refused'—and it was dated 17th July!

Although the Gestapo were well aware both of the existence of the plot and of the general lines of intended action, the actual day found them, from the professional point of view, astonishingly unprepared. The only weapons at Gestapo Headquarters, for example, were a round dozen light automatics. The moment that the first reports were received, at about two in the afternoon, Kaltenbrunner immediately set off by air for the Fuehrer Headquarters; he told Mueller what had happened and ordered him to take all necessary measures of precaution. At half-past four a senior official of the Gestapo asked Mueller's permission to leave Berlin, as he wished to go and collect his laundry which he had left elsewhere. Mueller, who normally was the very reverse of considerate towards his subordinates, readily agreed. The incident would have been without significance but for the fact that the applicant for leave was none other than the official in charge of the personal files of the known and suspected conspirators. It seems incredible that Mueller should give leave to the one man whose specialized knowledge would be of the utmost importance within the next few hours. It was also not until late in the evening of 20th July that Mueller asked for a section of Waffen S.S. to strengthen the Guard over Gestapo Headquarters.

It is still too soon to say with any authority how much Himmler and Mueller knew of the plot and what their intentions really were. It is, however, fairly certain that Himmler, who already had Langbehn's promise that he would become Head of the State after Hitler's overthrow, decided to wait and see what would happen, and that Mueller followed his Chief's lead. Only after several hours had elapsed, when it had become clear that with the failure of the attempt on Hitler's life the whole conspiracy was doomed, did Himmler and Mueller decide to throw the full weight of their organization into the struggle against the conspirators.

Himmler's behaviour in the final phases of the war was, if possible, even more dishonestly contemptible. As has already been said, Schellenberg had been doing his utmost to persuade him that it was his duty to make peace with the Western Allies and that to do so he must first seize plenipotentiary powers within the Reich. Any means, in Schellenberg's opinion, were justified, which would gain his ends. From Hamburg he produced an astrologer, by name Wulf, with orders to serve up a horoscope which would give Himmler the necessary courage and convince him that he was destined by Fate to become the Fuehrer and the saviour of the German people; further, he won over Himmler's personal masseur, Felix Kersten, to his side. This latter, an obscure character, worked on the basis of a Finnish degree in medicine. In all his utterances he combined fact and fancy in a masterly fashion, but he was most certainly a first-class masseur. He relieved Himmler of the very severe neuralgic pains from which he suffered, and as a result he exercised more influence over him than all the S.S. and Police Chiefs put together. Himmler trusted him absolutely and believed every word that he said.

The combined and strenuous efforts of Schellenberg, Wulf and Kersten gradually succeeded in bringing Himmler ever nearer to the conviction that he really was destined by Fate to be Hitler's successor and that he must take immediate steps to replace him. But again and again he drew back at the crucial moment. On several occasions he asserted firmly that now he was ready to take decisive action and seize power; then his old blind faith in the Fuehrer would suddenly overcome him, he would hesitate, retract and finally vehemently reject all Schellenberg's proposals and pleadings. On one occasion he said that for the sake of the German people he would act—and in the next breath protested that he could never bring himself to do murder against his old Leader. It was not Hitler's death, Schellenberg retorted, but merely his removal from political power that was required; but it was all in vain, and Himmler remained adamant in his hesitancy.

His vacillations became all the more violent in April 1945. Not content with astrologers and masseurs, Schellenberg enlisted the help of medical specialists in his efforts to goad Himmler to action. He persuaded his good friend, Professor de Crinis, the well-known psychiatrist, to tell Himmler that Hitler was suffering from Parkinson's disease—a diagnosis which he got Professor Brand, a former personal physician to the Fuehrer, to confirm; at the same time Dr. Stumpfegger, Brand's successor, stated that he also suspected a disease of the mind. Stumpfegger asked de Crinis to give him certain medicines for Hitler; the latter agreed and had the prescriptions made up in his own clinic. But the drugs were never called for.

The last meeting between Hitler and Himmler took place on 20th April, when Himmler called to express his good wishes for the Fuehrer's birthday. At the same time he had a long talk with Stumpfegger, a very old friend of his school-days. No one was present, and what passed between them is unknown; but Schellenberg asserts that Himmler tried to persuade his friend to get rid of Hitler by means of an injection—an assumption which subsequent events do nothing to refute. On 23rd April Himmler was again in Berlin, inspecting the battery of his personal bodyguard. He was expected at the Reich-Chancellery, but did not go there. This in itself is most significant; communications were already so badly disorganized that a visit to the city was surely a golden opportunity not to be missed of having a personal interview with the Fuehrer; it was, indeed, the only satisfactory means of communication which remained. Nor had the breach between the two men yet occurred; it was on the night of 24–25th April that Himmler made his notorious statement to Count Bernadotte that Hitler had at the most two or three days more to live. On what did he base this? Hitler's state of health was not such as to warrant it, nor was the military situation yet so critical that the end could be foreseen within so short a time.

Schellenberg considers that there is a connection between the Himmler-Stumpfegger conversation and the statement to Bernadotte, and that Himmler had Stumpfegger's promise to give the lethal injection within that specified period. Immediately after the meeting with Bernadotte, Himmler had a long telephone conversation—with Stumpfegger in Berlin. All this is, of course, circumstantial reasoning and not proof; but it does lend colour to the theory that Himmler was thinking of getting rid of Hitler by poison. Why the idea was not carried out—for that Hitler died by his own hand is beyond dispute—will now never be known, for all the actors in this grim, shabby drama—Himmler, de Crinis, Stumpfegger—have themselves since committed suicide.

CHAPTER IV

HEYDRICH AND HIS RIVALS

THE portrait of Reinhard Heydrich then is that of a cruel, brave and cold intelligence. His colleagues were not all of the same sort. Perhaps that is why he was quite unable for any length of time to maintain even tolerable relations with the most trustworthy and gifted of them, S.S. General Werner Best. To such a man as Heydrich colleagues were also rivals.

Best was an idealist. I knew him as a well-established lawyer and administrator, elegant, sensible and soft-mannered. When he decided to collaborate in the organization of a new Secret Service as an instrument of the National Socialist State, he did so with no egoistic aims or ambitions for his own advancement. He realized what sort of man Heydrich was and whither his activities must lead. So he broke with him early in the war even though he knew that to break with Heydrich was a dangerous thing to do. Best took refuge under the ægis of the Wehrmacht, and was appointed Chief of War Administration Services in Paris.

Heydrich harboured a deadly hatred against his renegade colleague. His agents in Paris watched every step, every action that Best took, and not for a single moment was he ever safe from the Gestapo murder-gang. It would certainly only have been a matter of time before Heydrich decided to strike; what he had in mind is not known, but that his blow would have been a quite fatal one is certain. Best was lucky that Heydrich was murdered before he thought the time and opportunity were ripe. It saved Best's life, and his case is the most convincing proof that no man of upright character was safe in Heydrich's entourage.

Later Best was appointed Reich Protector in Denmark. The post confronted him with certain problems, his solution of which caused him later to be charged with a breach of International Law. But the fact that, on appeal, the Danish judges reduced his

punishment to one of five years' imprisonment is a tribute both
to the man and to his character and qualities.

Of a totally different kind was his relationship with S.S.
General Heinrich Mueller, the Chief of the Gestapo. A man
with an imposing head and sharp features, curiously disfigured
by a thin gash of a mouth that had no lips, he had risen in life
from modest beginnings in the Bavarian police. In him Heydrich
had found a worthy partner, ready at all times to co-operate in
any and every sort of villainy. It was he who perfected
Heydrich's spy system by supervision, based on the principle of
charges against public decency. Mueller's model had always
been the Soviet Secret Political Police, and he certainly succeeded in setting up an organization worthy of his ideal. Thanks
to his activities the backbone of the German people was broken;
not only did he stifle at birth any vestige of an opposition movement, but he maintained so rigorous and oppressive a grip on
Party members, that no one felt safe from the attentions of the
Gestapo.

His great ambition was to build up a central card index, with
an individual card for every living German and, of course, with a
precise note on any 'dubious episode' no matter how trivial.
Before 1939 he had not been a Nazi, nor did he ever become one,
in spite of his formal admission to the Party. The principles
by which he judged men were not those upon which the judgment of the Party were based. The decisive factor, in his opinion,
was whether the individual unreservedly and unconditionally
obeyed the State, or whether he showed any tendency towards
independent thought or action. He recognized no law other
than that of the omnipotence of the State. His narrow, policeman's mind was content to seek no further. He regarded as an
enemy anyone who was suspected of even intellectual resistance.
People who know Mueller well declared that it was the rigid
State discipline inherent in it that attracted him towards National
Socialism, and that the ideological conception meant nothing to
him at all. Just as he had served the Bavarian People's Party
until 1933 and the National-Socialist Party until 1945, he would
be quite prepared to serve as a faithful police hound any régime
that employed him.

Some of Mueller's associates assert that he was already in

touch with the Russians in 1944 and that on the collapse of Germany he succeeded in deserting to them. This is by no means a fantastic idea. The Gestapo had a special section, whose function it was to continue to operate the wireless sets of captured Soviet agents as though the original operators were still at liberty. In this way misleading information, which often caused them to take disastrously wrong decisions, was frequently passed on to the Russian High Command. The name given to this section was 'The Wireless Games Section'; it was a section of considerable size, and by 1944 contained something like three hundred members. It is by no means impossible that Mueller should have used one of these numerous and confidential lines to get into touch with the Russians—even to give them genuine information—before the final collapse.

At all events it has been definitely established that certain former German Gestapo officers have appeared on the scene in Eastern Germany, after, it is said, having been 're-educated' in Russia by Mueller. It is true that as a faithful subordinate Mueller had always been a zealous persecutor of Communists, and he was responsible directly for the deaths in the concentration camps of many thousands of them who sincerely believed in the aim of a world union of Soviet States. But the Bolsheviks, as is well known, have no petty-minded hesitation in pardoning people who might—temporarily at least—be of use to them, and of Mueller they could certainly make excellent use. A man who for years was the Head of the German Secret State Police and who, with the vast extension of German domination, had ruled practically the whole of Europe with his police force, had one most valuable thing to sell to the Russians, namely, his immense knowledge. Mueller was famous for his phenomenal memory; he could give at once and out of his head the name of even some unimportant agent in a small town abroad, and there is certainly no other police expert who possesses so wide a knowledge of personalities and who, at the same time, has so deep an insight into political events, a detailed knowledge of which is still important to this very day.

It may therefore well be that Mueller is now working for the Russians, although, as yet, there is no actual proof of it. It is, however, known that after Hitler's death he disappeared from

the Chancellery with his trusted friend Scholz, and that neither
has ever been heard of since; and this Scholz was the very man
to whom Mueller had entrusted the running of the 'Wireless
Games Section'.

Mueller was a character without any subtlety and easy to
describe. The same cannot be said of S.S. General Arthur Nebe,
the Chief of Branch V of the Reich Security Central Office, who
was a most complicated character. His participation in the 20th
July plot gives the false impression that he had followed the
leadership of Himmler and Heydrich under compulsion and was
in reality an opponent of National Socialism. This is by no
means true.

Nebe was undoubtedly a clever man. He came of a family
prominent in the civil service of Prussia. But his political
prescience was limited to the purely tactical. There is little doubt
that he joined the Nazi Party because he realized that it was
the Party to which the future would belong; that this was
destined to be a future lasting only a few years he did not at first
foresee. In 1932 Prussian officials were forbidden to become
members of the Party; Nebe, who was then serving in the
Prussian Criminal Police, enrolled under a false name in an
isolated regional group. His calculations proved to be correct,
and after Hitler seized power, he was one of the very few police
officers who could prove that he was a member of the Party, and
so qualified at once for a high appointment.

As he was in fact a first class police officer, unlike many of the
new men who rose and burst like bubbles at the time, he
thoroughly justified his appointment. He never disassociated
himself from Heydrich's methods; on the contrary, there was
hardly an operation of any importance in which he did not play
his part, and he did his utmost to foster and deserve the reputation of being one of Heydrich's trustworthy collaborators. After
the beginning of the Russian campaign Nebe took command of a
so-called *Einsatzgruppe*—a sort of police commando—and
was responsible for the shooting of tens of thousands of human
beings.

His ambition and foresight—the same characteristics which
had led him into the National-Socialist fold—caused him, as
the position gradually deteriorated on all fronts, to seek a position

of safety to which he could retreat in the camp of the opposition. He was an old friend of Dr. Gisevius, of whom mention has already been made, and he had a very shrewd idea that the latter was in touch with the underground opposition movement. He approached his friend and through him was in fact introduced into the circle of organized resistance.

Nebe anticipated that, if the Nazi régime collapsed, Gisevius would be given an important position in the police service, and his idea was to commend himself to his friend's attention as a suitable expert adviser on criminal police affairs. Obviously, he could not get out of the set-up in which he was then working; and to have done so would have greatly diminished his value to the conspirators, who had great need of men in key positions in the machine of Government. Skilful as he undoubtedly was, he managed to play his double role for a long time and at the same time to avoid exposing himself in any way. I do not believe from what I have heard of the interrogations of these people that the information he passed on to General Beck, the Chief of the General Staff, Dr. Karl Goerdeler, the former Lord Mayor of Leipzig and other opposition leaders was of any real import-ance. If one of the secret opposition ever got into any difficulty, Nebe invariably regretted that he was in no position to be of any assistance. A word at the time from Nebe would undoubtedly have led to the release of Admiral Canaris' colleague, Dr. Dohnanyi, who was arrested as early as the spring of 1943. Nebe's stake in the great hazard was therefore comparatively insignificant, and he would probably have survived the events of 20th July, if he had not suddenly lost his nerve and fled from his office.

When suspicion arose that Count Helldorff, the President of the Berlin Police, was in some way implicated in the plot, Kaltenbrunner asked Nebe, whom he knew to be a friend of Helldorf, to 'phone the Police President and ask him, on some excuse or other, to come and see him. Nebe immediately jumped to the conclusion that Kaltenbrunner had seen through his in-trigues, and he incontinently took to his heels and fled. In actual fact, Kaltenbrunner never had the slightest suspicion against Nebe. He attributed the flight of the Head of Amt V to the fact that he was unwilling to betray a friend in this manner, and he reproached himself bitterly for having placed his trusted sub-ordinate in so difficult and invidious a position. He even did his best to get in touch with Nebe to beg him to return and accept his apologies, and it was only very much later that he was con-vinced that Nebe's flight had not in any way been actuated by feelings of friendship and loyalty.

The story of Nebe's flight, if ever it came to be written, would make an excellent sensational film. Thousands of his former policemen were on the trail of their late Chief, but again and again he managed to slip through their fingers, and, with his intimate knowledge of police methods, he would probably have eluded them for much longer had he not been betrayed by a woman. There was hardly a disreputable house in Berlin before which his big Mercedes, parked for the night, was not a familiar sight, and his well-known weakness in this respect proved fatal to him.

Nebe must not be put on the same plane as the other members of the July plot: he was merely an opportunist, who was not in the least worried by Heydrich's criminal methods as long as all went well, but who, with the minimum possible risk to himself, changed camps when things threatened to go badly.

The youngest and at the same time most interesting of Heydrich's Sectional Chiefs was undoubtedly the Chief of Amt VI, Overseas Political Secret Service, S.S. General Walther Schellenberg. As a young man of just over thirty he took over charge of the then not very important Amt VI from S.S. General Jost, who had shown more zeal than efficiency in the execution of his somewhat difficult task. Four years later, having in the meanwhile risen to become Chief of the whole German Secret Service and shown himself to be one of the most striking per-sonalities of the National Socialist régime, he made his exit from the political stage.

Only a man endowed with gifts of the highest order could thus successfully have filled a post, which in war-time placed the almost intolerable burden of an unending series of demands upon him. Schellenberg had originally been regarded as just one more of Heydrich's creatures, no different from the majority of the Chiefs of the Central Security Office. His courage in sticking to his own opinions even in the face of Heydrich's opposition very quickly exposed the fallacy of this assumption. In the struggle against Heydrich which such an independent attitude rendered inevitable, he naturally got the worst of it, and Heydrich clearly and ominously let it be known that the attitude of his young Sectional Chief no longer found favour in his eyes.

Heydrich's premature death was a stroke of luck for him, which freed him of a grave threat and gave him the chance of making his own position impregnable. This latter he accomplished for the most part during the months when Himmler took personal charge of the Central Security Office; he then strengthened his personal ties with the S.S. *Reichsfuehrer* to an extent which enabled him later to use Himmler for the furtherance of his own plans, and by the time Kaltenbrunner took over, his position was so assured that he could have been unseated only at the cost of a very severe internal conflict.

From 1943 onwards, the defeat of Germany was, for Schellenberg, a foregone conclusion, and he felt that only a separate peace with the Western Powers could save the country from complete annihilation. But his position was not strong enough to allow him to influence the course of political events in any decisive way; to strengthen it, therefore, he set about uniting all the branches of the German Secret Service into one corporate entity under his own control. After a bitter struggle he finally achieved his aim when, at the beginning of 1944, the Military Intelligence Service, until then directed by Admiral Canaris, came under the command of the Reich Central Security Office.

At the same time he felt that it was essential to have the support of some leading personality of the Third Reich, and his choice fell upon Himmler, over whom he exercised so powerful a personal influence. But Himmler as the executive Head of a Peace Party—and therefore an opponent of Hitler—was obviously a most unfortunate choice, and this was the great tragedy of Schellenberg's career. He devoted his whole energy to remoulding Himmler into the tool of his political objectives; at times he seemed within an ace of success, but at the last moment Himmler would invariably hesitate and then revert to his former babblings about 'final victory'. All his plans were wrecked by the political vacillations and the personal weakness of the S.S. *Reichsfuehrer*, and his independent, desperate eleventh-hour effort to conclude a separate peace through the intermediary of Count Bernadotte was his final and irretrievable failure.

Whether he would have had any greater success had his choice fallen upon some other leading personality—Goering, for example, whose friendship he was said to enjoy—is admittedly problematical. Germany's attempt to make peace with the West came far too late, and only after the Allies had announced their firm determination to demand unconditional surrender. Schellenberg, it may be objected, as Chief of the German Intelligence Service, should have known how determined President Roosevelt was on the subject of his 'unconditional surrender' formula. But even Schellenberg could not imagine that the President never for a moment even thought of giving the Germans a chance, albeit under the harshest possible conditions, of coming to terms with the West and thus saving themselves and the whole of Europe from a triumphant Bolshevik advance against the West. Nor could he imagine that anyone could really believe, as Roosevelt obviously did, that the Bolsheviks were loyal and co-operative and would remain faithful to their treaty obligations. His failure to reach such flights of fancy cannot be held as a reproach against Schellenberg.

That he was absolutely sincere in his desire to achieve a peace by negotiation is proved by his attitude and his actions in many incidents which had nothing directly to do with his duties as Chief of the Political Intelligence Service. As soon as he heard in late summer 1943 that Germany was contemplating the invasion of Switzerland, he intervened at once; he did his utmost to persuade the German Government that from the military, political and economic points of view, the step would be a great mistake; and at the same time he informed his Swiss colleague Colonel Masson, the Chief of the Federal Secret Service, what was afoot. There is some evidence that the Military Intelligence Service of Admiral Canaris was pursuing a similar policy. In doing so, Schellenberg's object was to force the Swiss to take defensive precautions, so that he could use the fact as an argument against Hitler's intended onslaught. His action helped to convince Hitler that the plan should be abandoned.

In 1944 Swiss neutrality was once more threatened by Germany. A German pilot testing a new aircraft fled with it to Switzerland, where he himself was interned and his machine confiscated. Hitler, fearing that the secrets of the aircraft would find their way via Switzerland to the Western Powers, gave orders that steps were to be taken for its immediate destruction. The task was entrusted to the famous liberator of Mussolini, Otto Skorzeny; it was only when all arrangements had swiftly been made, and Skorzeny was but awaiting Hitler's personal order to go, that Schellenberg heard of the plan. Again he intervened and, by volunteering to settle the matter satisfactorily without violence, he obtained a postponement of the operation. Then, with the assistance of his Swiss colleague, he arranged for the destruction of the machine on the spot at Duebendorf aerodrome by the Swiss themselves, and promised them ten new Messerschmitt fighters in return. It was touch and go, and only a question of hours, and the citizens of Zuerich were very nearly given the opportunity of seeing for themselves a *coup de main* on the lines of the rescue of Mussolini from the Gran Sasso.

Ernst Kaltenbrunner, who was the Chief of the forbidden Austrian S.S. before the German invasion of 1938, was a close collaborator of Heydrich. And he was to succeed him when Heydrich was assassinated.

After Heydrich's death on 24th June, 1942, Himmler was determined at all costs to avoid appointing as his successor any man who could be as dangerous to him personally as Heydrich had been. The prize went to a complete outsider, the S.S. and Police Chief of Vienna, Dr. Ernst Kaltenbrunner, whose chances, as he possessed neither the professional police qualifications nor the personal pull which was an essential prerequisite for the appointment to high office in the Third Reich, had not been fancied by anybody.

This young lawyer from Linz had only once attracted attention, and then fortuitously, when, in 1936, following the sudden arrest of all those senior to him, he found himself at the head of the illegal S.S. in Austria. As such he later automatically became the Head of the S.S. and Police in the so-called Ostmark—a purely subsidiary post of little or no importance. His appointment to a post which, thanks to the activities of his predecessor,

3

had now become one of the most important in the whole of the Third Reich, came as a complete surprise, particularly to those behind the scenes.

It is neither possible nor appropriate to try here to give a final verdict on Kaltenbrunner, There is, however, no doubt that the Allies over-estimated the influence he exercised in Germany. He died as a substitute for Himmler, who succeeded in evading his responsibilities by committing suicide; and in so doing it might with justice be said that Kaltenbrunner was paying the penalty for the crimes of his predecessor, Heydrich.

Kaltenbrunner had had no previous experience of police work of any kind; he had therefore to rely to a great extent on the guidance of his professional collaborators. Mueller and Nebe, Chiefs of the Gestapo and the C.I.D. respectively, were able to do practically as they liked under him; but they were cunning enough to obtain his sanction for all important decisions and in this way to foist the entire responsibility on his shoulders. Kaltenbrunner himself was less interested in the detailed working of the organization under him than in the opportunities which, as he rightly thought, the control of Home and Overseas Intelligence Services gave him of intervening in political events of the highest importance. The instrument was indeed ready to his hand, but he himself did not possess the necessary personal attributes to use it to its full advantage; further, Schellenberg, fearing that Kaltenbrunner might well seek to oust him, clung even more tenaciously to Himmler's side and caused a certain tension to spring up between the two men.

Kaltenbrunner assumed office at the time of the Stalingrad catastrophe. He had even then no illusions about Germany's plight; Schellenberg's reports, those of his own subordinates and the direct information given to him by personal friends among the officers of the Intelligence Services all combined to strengthen his conviction that victory was no longer possible and that the conclusion of a peace by negotiation with the Western Powers was the only right and feasible objective to pursue. Yet in spite of all efforts to galvanize him into some decisive action in this direction, he remained a lethargic and passive failure.

Why was it that Kaltenbrunner persisted in his hesitation to

lend his powerful support to a peace move until it was too late?
The reason can doubtless be found in his personal devotion to
Hitler. Here was no case of reasoned loyalty alone. To the very
end Hitler's personality held an almost mesmeric fascination for
him; he sincerely worshipped him, and he had unbounded faith
in what he regarded as his inspired foresight and vision. He
mistrusted both himself and his own innermost convictions when
they whispered that the war must be brought to an end—at all
costs and, if necessary, even against Hitler's wishes; and so he
continued to sway from side to side. Only in the very last phases
of the war did he see, clearly and beyond any further doubting,
that Hitler was leading Germany to inevitable annihilation; and
then only did he join in an effort to secure peace. But by that
time it was far too late.

His personal devotion to Hitler was undoubtedly an obstacle,
insurmountable in his eyes, to the use of his power to bring
about any alteration in the internal state of affairs in Germany.
In many directions, as in his successful efforts to modify the
policy of oppression against the Church, his actions were laudable
and justified. But to a regular, all-embracing intervention for
wholesale reform he could not bring himself. His personal
tragedy was that while he was not guilty of the abysmal wickedness of his predecessor, he was equally not possessed of his great
ability and character.

Seldom has a figure of historical importance been judged with
so many contrasting verdicts as the small, silent, eccentric figure,
Admiral Wilhelm Canaris, the Chief of the German Military
Intelligence Services. Abroad he was widely regarded as the
sinister *deus ex machina* behind all the crimes of the National
Socialist régime; his friends profess to see in him the spiritual
leader of all the opposition movements against Hitler and a
martyr in the cause of the fight against National Socialism. A
large section of the German people, on the other hand, agree
with neither of these verdicts, but condemn him simply as a
traitor to his country and the man largely responsible for
Germany's defeat. How much truth do these contradictory
verdicts contain?

The Canaris family are of Greek origin settled for many
generations in Northern Italy before migrating to Germany. In

the first war young Canaris was an officer in the German cruiser *Dresden*. When the *Dresden* was scuttled in Cumberland Bay in the spring of 1915, he and the rest of the crew were interned by the Chilean authorities in the Juan Fernandez Islands. After a few months of captivity, Canaris made an adventurous escape over the Andes to Valparaiso; he had acquired a Chilean passport in the name of Reed Rosas, and with it he succeeded in getting back to Germany on a Dutch ship via Plymouth and Rotterdam.

In the summer of 1916, still using his Chilean passport, he slipped through the British blockade to Spain. Attached to the office of the German Naval Attaché in Spain, he rendered outstanding service to the German Naval High Command in organizing the supplies for German U-Boats from Spanish bases, and in observing and reporting Allied shipping movements, particularly to and from Gibraltar. On his way back to Germany to take command of a submarine he was arrested at the Italian railway station of Domodossola. The Italians decided to hand him over to the French as a German spy, but when Canaris disclosed his identity as a German officer to the captain of the ship taking him to France, the latter put in to Cartagena instead of Marseilles, and from there Canaris was picked up by a German submarine and so eventually reached German territory. He was then given command of a submarine operating in the Mediterranean and based on Cattaro. At the time he had a large number of intimate friends in the Austrian Navy, and he also possessed a deep insight into Austrian mentality.

With these experiences of the first war, Canaris seemed a particularly suitable officer to take over the organization of the new German Military Intelligence Service which the Reichswehr had started to build up in the late nineteen twenties. The Service was originally of very modest proportions, and it was not until the second war that it expanded into the vast organization which, under the name of *Abwehr*, became as well known throughout the world as the Intelligence Service of Britain and the Deuxième Bureau of France.

The actual organization and expansion of the *Abwehr* was not, however, Canaris' own work. This he left largely in the hands of his subordinates, while he himself turned to what he called 'Intelligence politics', by which he meant the using of the information obtained by his organization as a political weapon; and in this sphere he was a complete master. It is doubtful whether any Intelligence Service can cut itself off entirely from politics and exist, as it were, as a means and an end in itself, and Canaris had never the slightest intention of trying to achieve such a schism. He realized that knowledge—not only of military, but also of political secrets—and most particularly of the secrets of opponents was the seed of potential political power, and he was determined to use this knowledge as a means of influencing unobtrusively the political and military policies of the Third Reich.

Due, probably, to this lack of interest on the part of its Chief in the purely organizational side of his duties, the *Abwehr* grew in time into an exaggerated and top-heavy structure, in which the Administrative Branch was swelled out of all proportion to the Intelligence scope and aims of the Service. In particular, the subsidiary *Abwehr* formations attached to the various Military Districts were of a size, in both men and means, which bore no relation to the services rendered and transformed the Military Intelligence into an over-staffed and bureaucratically clogged machine. The various Military Headquarters protested frequently and vigorously against this uneconomic and inefficient expansion, but for the most part their protests were in vain. Equally good results could undoubtedly have been obtained with a smaller and less cumbersome organization; but it would be an error to say that, on the whole, the Military Intelligence was not efficient. All the Admiral's immediate collaborators, and in particular the Chiefs of his three most important Sections, Generals Piekenbrock, Lahousen and Bentivegni, were, without exception, experts of the highest order.

Canaris himself was a complex character, by no means easy to understand; and in judging him, even solely in his capacity as Chief of the *Abwehr*, it must be borne in mind that he was of the type who, as an almost naïve matter of course, brand their official activities with the stamp of their private personality. He was undoubtedly a true German patriot. He welcomed the resurgence of Germany under Hitler to the status of a Great Power, and he was proud of his high position and the contribution he made towards this political development of world-wide importance. But he was an equally convinced and determined opponent of the National-Socialist system. These two conflicting view-points governed his whole behaviour and explain the many contradictions in his actions which caused him to be regarded as equally unreliable by friend and foe alike.

Canaris' rejection of National-Socialism was based perhaps even more on æsthetic and ethical grounds than on the score of pure reason. He had a nature, hyper-sensitive to a degree which was quite incompatible with his choice of the career of an officer and which caused him to regard force and any expression of force with horror. So strong was this aversion that he looked with distaste upon that soldierly type which was the ideal of the Wehrmacht—and indeed of every Army—the courageous, dashing and thoroughly efficient officer or soldier. The sight of a decoration immediately evoked his resentment, and any officer who appeared before him wearing the ribbon of the Knight's Cross could be quite sure that his proposals were already as good as rejected. Later, while still observing all the external formalities when on duty, he developed a strong dislike of uniform and military trappings of any kind, and he much preferred mufti and the modest demeanour which goes with it.

This æsthetic antipathy, which may well be sympathetically regarded as a protest against the exaggerated esteem in which all things military are held in Germany, caused him very often to give preference to people whose anti-military attitude was the result of a defective character rather than of any sincere conviction—and sometimes to get into difficulties in consequence.

His inherent goodness and his readiness at all times to help his fellow men were boundless. It was common knowledge in Germany that the persecuted could always find asylum in the bosom of the *Abwehr*, and this fact was very often abused. It was not only people persecuted by the régime on political or racial grounds who sought and obtained Canaris' help; a host of bad characters, swindlers and professional tricksters of all kinds had but to claim police persecution to be sure of *Abwehr* protection, with the attendant advantages of being able to avoid the inconvenience of military service or to obtain some post useful in the furtherance of their private interests.

This great and often wrong-headed magnanimity on the part of Canaris, who was no profound judge of character, frequently made things very difficult for his colleagues, and it is a high tribute to the efficiency of the latter that they were able, in spite of the mass of dubious material thus foisted upon them, to bring the *Abwehr* to that height of proficiency which it undoubtedly attained. A Secret Service inevitably attracts people of doubtful character and men who from choice prefer to live only just within the law, and this natural attraction became, in Germany, all the stronger, thanks to the human weaknesses of the Admiral. Under him, many a thoroughly bad character succeeded not only in securing a key position in the *Abwehr*, but also in exercising very considerable influence on its Chief; scandalous corruption, black market and mal-practice were constantly coming to light, but the Admiral refused to countenance any proper investigation and did his best to hush up the incidents. While he succeeded in a large measure in thus avoiding any public scandal, the numerous enemies of the Military Intelligence, notably in the Nazi Party, the Gestapo, the Security Services but also in the Wehrmacht, found ample discreditable material to add to their collection of accusations against 'Canaris and his Closed Shop'.

In spite, then, of his professional qualifications, Canaris was more a burden than an asset to the Military Intelligence, and particularly so as his lack of interest in organization began more and more to be replaced by a general stirring-up process, as meaningless as it was violent. His tours of inspection came to be dreaded by his subordinates; at them he was wont to turn everything completely topsy-turvy and to leave a chaotic mess in his wake. His Sectional Chiefs, aware of this idiosyncrasy, made it a rule to send an officer close on the Admiral's heels, with orders to tidy up the mess and put everything in order again, regardless of any instructions or directives which the Admiral might have given. This could be done without undue risk, for Canaris never bothered to find out whether his instructions had been obeyed; he was content as long as he himself was in motion and active.

This urge to be up and doing developed later into a dynamic obsession, which found its outlet in never-ending journeys.

Canaris could not bear to sit still, and this passion for travelling became stronger as he grew older. He hastened like one possessed over all the territories under German domination and seized any pretext to rush across half the continent from one capital to another. In this he showed not the slightest consideration for his family, although both his wife and his daughters were devoted to him; even occasions like the Christmas holidays found him far afield, without any real reason for the journey.

This feverish restlessness is in keeping with his characteristic lack of interest in human relationships. The man who, regardless of his own interests, made a habit of helping worthy and un-worthy alike, was himself unconscious of any need for human affection; but he worshipped his dogs. The dachshunds of the Admiral were the terror of his entourage. Their state of health was his greatest concern, and they meant much more to him at all times than any human being; a minor indisposition of one of his beloved pets caused him to suffer from the most acute depression and seriously affected the efficiency of his work. Wherever he was, in Germany or abroad, he invariably tele-phoned each day to ask about the dogs, demanding to know the most minute details of their menus and their natural functions; on one occasion the Chief of the Spanish Secret Police received the surprise of his life when a recording of a telephone call of the Admiral's from Tangiers to Berlin was placed before him. He had hoped to gather some interesting tit-bits of political informa-tion; instead he received a detailed report on the natural motions of an ailing dachshund! Only a minor portion of the call was devoted to official business, and here Canaris expressed himself with such skilful reserve that an outsider could make nothing of it.[1]

He had, naturally, no social truck with people who were not animal lovers. Even the most zealous Intelligence Officers bring-ing the most important information could get nowhere with him, if it had come to Canaris' ears that they had at some time spoken disparagingly about dog-lovers; and when attending official ceremonies or conferences he refused to stay at an hotel

[1] The German police attaché in Madrid related to Schellenberg the details of this incident in a private conversation, which Schellenberg repeated to Kaltenbrunner and myself.

in which dogs were not welcomed. These peculiarities are mentioned because, as subsidiary characteristics, they shed considerable light on the personality of this strange man.

Intercourse with the thugs of Hitler's entourage must have aroused a feeling of physical repulsion in a man of Canaris' character. It was thanks solely to his powers of dissimulation and his gift for diplomacy that he did not betray himself and succeeded in preserving his position in the hierarchy for so long. He rejected National-Socialism absolutely, and was ready in spirit to do anything to bring about Hitler's downfall; but he had a horror of any act of violence, his sincere patriotism caused him to fear that a *coup d'état* in war-time against Hitler would react unfavourably on Germany's war effort, and these two considerations combined to restrain him from any decisive action to sweep away the Nazi régime. And so, he remained hesitant to the end. He was by no means the head of all the various conspiracies against Hitler, but he was initiated into nearly all of them and he supported them, primarily by throwing the protective mantle of the *Abwehr* over their members. Even so, never once did he place the whole weight of his personality, his position and his power into the scales in the favour of such an enterprise.

This hesitancy, this lack of ultimate decisiveness brought down on him the most bitter reproaches of the men of 20th July, and particularly of Count Claus Schenck von Stauffenberg, who declared with repeated vehemence that the Admiral was primarily responsible for the long delay in any decisive action against Hitler and that with his eternal vacillation and his unceasing misgivings he had crippled the *élan* of every enterprise plotted against the Fuehrer. This forthright condemnation of Canaris by von Stauffenberg is admittedly an expression of the strongly contrasted ideologies of the two men, which were poles apart; Stauffenberg, in his desire to defeat the Western Powers, would probably have been ready to make tactically common cause even with the Russians, while Canaris, profoundly and utterly Western in his outlook, would never for an instant have considered such a possibility.

Although Canaris did not place his own person unreservedly at the disposal of the 20th July conspirators, he did give them the

powerful assistance of his office. In particular, he found a post
in the Military Intelligence for one of the most zealous members
of the plot, Major Hans Oster, who later became his Deputy with
the rank of a Major-General. As Oster had no gift for Intelligence
work and little interest in Secret Service activities, except in so
far as he could make political capital out of them, the Admiral
created a post for him in the so-called Central Section, which
technically placed the whole apparatus of the *Abwehr* at his
disposal. The two men, however, were far from being brothers-
in-arms in the plot against Hitler. For that they were too
different in both character and outlook; they might work
uneasily side by side, but they could never have become trusted
friends. Canaris always firmly maintained that the fight against
Hitler should be waged by constitutional and morally acceptable
methods, and that no crime of the régime could justify a similar
crime on the part of its opponents. Oster, on the other hand,
asserted that the end justified any and every means, and he was
prepared to go to any lengths to get rid of Hitler and his friends.

If ever an authoritative account of the German resistance
movement comes to be written, it will certainly arrive at the
conclusion that General Oster was no great acquisition to the
ranks of the active opposition. He was certainly of the conspiratorial type, but he lacked character, and the fury and blindness
of his hatred impaired his judgment and made him really
dangerous; he believed what he wanted to believe and what
was in accordance with his picture of National-Socialism, and
he rejected everything which did not fit into this framework.
General Erwin Lahousen, who knew them both well, summed
up this tendency in Oster by saying to me that if Oster were
told Himmler had ordered that every S.S.-man should daily
have a roasted enemy baby for his breakfast, he would believe it
literally and without question. Oster was responsible for the
fact that although the conspirators received a lot of information
that was genuine, they received a great deal more that was not,
and which misled them into taking faulty decisions; in this way
he undoubtedly made a decisive contribution to the failure of
the enterprise. He was quite incapable of any constructive
action, as would have been fatally proved, had he ever risen to a
position of authority.

Canaris himself was also impassioned in his hatred of Hitler and National Socialism. He was convinced that every war success of Hitler's was a tragedy for the German people, for, from the very beginning, he never for a moment doubted that Germany would eventually lose the war. Each new German victory, therefore, filled him with the most petulant dismay, for in his opinion it was prolonging the war and enlarging the extent of the inevitable final catastrophe. When Field Marshal Rommel gained his outstanding successes in North Africa, Canaris was reduced to tears of vexation at the news, and was only comforted when someone proved to his satisfaction that, taken as isolated incidents, these very victories themselves contained the seed of ultimate defeat.

When Hitler went to Prague in March 1939, Canaris followed him in order to witness the armed resistance of the Czechs. His disappointment when the passivity of the Czechs enabled Hitler to make a bloodless and triumphant entry, was boundless, and he spoke it aloud to General Lahousen. He realized that this success would but goad Hitler further along his fatal path. It was his constant endeavour to circumvent at its inception stage any plan of Hitler's which he thought would end in catastrophe— but always only with such German means as lay to his hand.

Admiral Canaris was ready to commit high treason, but he was not prepared to betray his country.[1] In this respect he was at loggerheads with both Oster and Gisevius, who maintained that this was a distinction without a difference. Be that as it may, Canaris was certainly not the complete traitor, for which so many people held him. I think it improbable that he himself divulged military information to Germany's enemies.

It seems astonishing that Canaris should have succeeded in retaining his position until as late as February 1944, in spite of the facts that his political views remained by no means unknown and that his organization had been so widely discredited in the eyes of the Nazi régime. He had the strong personal influence

---

[1] There was a distinction in the minds of Canaris and many other officers between 'high treason' (Hochverrat), which covered all conspiracies and offences against the régime, including plots against the life of the head of the state, and 'treason against the country' (Landesverrat), which meant betrayal of secrets to the enemy. Whereas a large number of German officers were prepared to commit the former, only few would even countenance the latter.

of a brilliant and flattering intellect over the simple-minded
Chief of the German High Command. Field Marshal Keitel
shielded him many times and often against his better judgment.
That is a partial, but not a wholly, adequate explanation. It does
not explain why the Gestapo and the German Secret Service, his
most implacable enemies, held their hands, in spite of the fact
that they had more than enough evidence to bring about his
downfall. The 'G.R.S.'[1] papers on Admiral Canaris in the
Gestapo archives ran into several volumes, for everything unsatis-
factory in the eyes of the Gestapo which occurred in the *Abwehr*
organization was debited to the personal account of the Admiral.
Yet no use whatever was made of this abundance of incriminating evidence, and when Canaris was finally deposed at the beginning of 1944, it was on the flimsiest and most obvious of pretexts.
A few *Abwehr* agents in Turkey had deserted to the British,
and Canaris, accused on this account of bad leadership, was
dismissed in consequence.

On his appointment as Chief of the Security Police in 1943
Kaltenbrunner, having studied the Canaris files, approached
Himmler, confident that with the evidence he had just examined,
he would secure the immediate dismissal of the Abwehr Chief.
To his great astonishment, Himmler declared that he was well
aware of the contents of the files, that he had for good reasons
nevertheless refrained from taking any action against Canaris,
and that any future action by Kaltenbrunner on his own initiative was undesirable!

Kaltenbrunner naturally asked himself what the explanation
of this most curious attitude could be, and what reason the S.S.
Reichsfuehrer and Supreme Chief of the German Police could
have for shielding a man who was demonstrably guilty of plotting
against the régime? After much cogitation he came to the conclusion that Canaris must be in possession of some sort of incriminating evidence against Himmler himself, and it was only
much later that he discovered that the victimized person was not
Himmler, but Heydrich. This, however, did not affect the issue,
for anything that threatened Heydrich was equally a menace for
Himmler.

According to Kaltenbrunner, documents proving the partially

[1] *Geheime Reichssache* or State Secret Documents.

Jewish origin of Heydrich had come into Canaris' hands. Previous mention has already been made of the three Court cases which Heydrich had instituted in this connection; in one of these cases the defendant had succeeded in finding certain papers in Meissen, where Heydrich's Jewish grandmother had lived for years, and proposed to produce them in Court. At that moment the great coup of 30th June, 1934 against the S.A. took place. The defendant, a lawyer and at the same time an officer of the S.A., was high up on Heydrich's list for arrest and execution; although arrested, he successfully smuggled a letter out of prison to Hitler himself, who intervened on behalf of this old comrade of the struggle period and ordered his immediate release. He thus escaped with his bare life, and in order to avoid further persecution by Heydrich, he begged Canaris for asylum and was taken into the Military Intelligence Service.

This much Kaltenbrunner was able to prove. Whether the man in question then handed over the incriminating papers to Canaris and the latter deposited them safely in Spain, informing Heydrich at the same time that he had done so, is a matter of conjecture. But this would certainly explain the reluctance of both Himmler and Heydrich to take any action against Canaris; nor must the fact be overlooked that when proceedings eventually were taken against the Admiral early in 1944, they were initiated not by Himmler, but by Kaltenbrunner and largely on his own responsibility. But the papers Canaris is said to have deposited in Spain have never been found, those who know the truth are no longer alive, and the secret will probably remain buried with them for ever.

Yet although he was dismissed, no actual Court proceedings were taken against Canaris, in spite of ample evidence, either at the time of his dismissal or after the events of 20th July. When finally he was arrested, he showed an astonishing calmness and lack of preoccupation, as though he knew quite well that he would never be brought to trial.

In his interrogation, whether under torture or whether as the result of the seizure of his note-book with lists of names and notes against which no denial was of any avail, Dr. Goerdeler gravely compromised both the Admiral and many other members of the conspiracy; and still Canaris was not accused in Court.

He may well have hoped that he would survive to see the end of the régime. But he overlooked the fact that to those in power it was of vital importance to close for ever a mouth which would unfailingly testify against them, to destroy a man who would rise before the whole world with irrefutable proof of their crimes in his hand, and to consign irretrievably to the depths an unparalleled knowledge of their evil deeds and their wickedness.

Canaris, with many other prisoners, was executed by secret order in Flossenburg Concentration Camp, immediately before the entry of the American troops, and many secrets of his life were scattered with his ashes.

CHAPTER V

HOW FORGERS MURDERED A SOVIET MARSHAL

HEYDRICH's interests were not confined to the German scene alone. From the very beginning he was at pains effectively to link his Secret Service with foreign political events. His most successful intrigue was in connection with the Tukhachevsky affair.

On 11th June, 1937 the Soviet News Agency, Tass, caused a world-wide sensation by announcing that on the orders of the Commissar for Internal Affairs eight senior Generals of the Red Army, among them the former Deputy Peoples' Commissar for Defence, Marshal of the Soviet Union Tukhachevsky, had been arrested and brought before a Court Martial. The course of the trial itself brought no very special surprises to light. The Soviet legal system was already familiar to the world at large, and that travesty of justice, the farcical proceedings against the Trotsky opposition in 1936, with all its paraphernalia of incredible confessions by the accused, was still fresh in people's minds.

No one, then, was surprised when Tukhachevsky and his confederates duly confessed in their turn that they had organized an underground opposition movement, that they had been in contact with the military High Command of a Power hostile to the Soviet Union and had passed on information about the Red Army. Nor was the conviction of the accused and their summary execution unexpected.

That the proceedings, under the Presidency of Ullrich, the Supreme Commissar for War and with Vyshinsky, the Attorney-General, as public prosecutor, should have been conducted *in camera* occasioned very considerable comment. No one, however, had any idea of the events which had led up to the conviction of Tukhachevsky, and no one later placed any credence in the disclosure that the Chief of the German Security Service had played a decisive part in the case.

Heydrich started to set up his secret organization against the

Soviet Union in 1935. Initially he had but meagre funds at his disposal for the purpose and had to content himself with second-hand information obtained from abroad and particularly from Russian emigrants, living in Germany. The *émigrés* in Germany were in close touch with the Paris emigrant colony, which, together with that in Belgrade, was the most important in Europe. Heydrich was thus able, through his own agents, to get into contact with the Central Committee in Paris. Here his representative got into touch with the former White Russian General, Skoblin, whose wife was the famous Court Opera singer, Nadyeshda Plevitskaya. This couple occupied an important, though somewhat equivocal, position in Parisian *émigré* society, where they were regarded as not wholly trustworthy. Heydrich's agent found out that Skoblin maintained excellent relations with the highest circles in Moscow. This in itself was astonishing, for in no other case had the *émigré* Secret Service succeeded in penetrating into the upper branches of the Soviet hierarchy. In the course of his subsequent dealings with Skoblin, the German agent further discovered that, like his notorious fellow country-man, Evno Asev, who alternately betrayed revolutionaries to the Czarist Police and vice versa, the General was working for both sides—for the Soviet Union and against it.

Skoblin's double-crossing activities seemed to Heydrich to be no good reason for refraining to make use of him, and Skoblin for his part was quite prepared, at a price, to add the German Secret Service to the list of his employers. From him Heydrich received information, towards the end of 1936, that Tukhachevsky was planning to seize power with the help of the Red Army and to get rid of Stalin and the whole Bolshevik régime. Whether this information was true must remain an open question, for the G.P.U. Chief, Yessov, who provided Vyshinsky with the evidence against Tukhachevsky, himself very shortly followed the 'Red Napoleon' to the gallows. Of the witnesses for the prosecution, hardly one is still alive, and that Vyshinsky, Marshal Voroshilov, who played an important part, or Stalin himself should ever speak was too much to expect. The question has in any case but little bearing on the issue. The only query that is of any importance is whether the evidence produced to prove that Tukhachevsky was plotting against Stalin was faked in the same way as was the evidence proving his traitorous liaison with a foreign Power.

When, exactly, Heydrich first conceived the idea of the monstrous intrigue which was destined to bring about the downfall of Tukhachevsky cannot be precisely determined. But the idea was probably born even before a decisive conversation with Hitler and Himmler, just before Christmas 1936, when he first told his colleagues about Tukhachevsky's ostensible intention to seize power. Both Hitler and Heydrich, presumably, appreciated the chance that this split in the Soviet system would offer Germany for a decisively crippling blow at the U.S.S.R. There were two possible courses of action. Germany could either support Tukhachevsky and by so doing assist him to liquidate Bolshevism; or she could betray Tukhachevsky to Stalin and by so doing cripple the military strength of the Soviet Union. Each seemed to be equally rich in potential reward. On the one hand it was obviously easier to bring about the downfall of Tukhachevsky than to support him in the more hazardous undertaking of trying to overthrow the masters of the Kremlin; on the other hand German participation in the destruction of Tukhachevsky and the consequent crippling of the Red Army would necessitate a reversal of the policy of co-operation between the Armed Forces of Germany and the Soviet Union which had hitherto been pursued.

Russo-German military co-operation began in 1926, when Colonel General von Seeckt, the Chief of Staff of the Hundred-Thousand-Man Army, sought and obtained technical assistance from the Russians. Von Seeckt's two successors, Generals Hege and von Hammerstein Equord, each followed the same policy, with the full support of the parliamentary Reichs-Minister of Defence. Behind this co-operation there was no political plan, such as the formation of a Russo-German *bloc* against the Western Powers. To assume that the Prusso-German Generals regarded this liaison with the Red Army as part of a wider political conception is to credit them with a political acumen which, with the possible exception of von Seeckt, they none of them possessed. All they desired was technical military assistance, and particularly training facilities for officers with armoured fighting vehicles, aircraft and other weapons denied by Treaty to the Reichswehr; and in return they were prepared to place the experience of the German Officer Corps and their knowledge of the basic principles of military leadership at the disposal of the Red Army. The Russians, on the other hand, may well have regarded this as the starting point for future political *rapprochement*, but no practical results were ever achieved.

When Hitler became Chancellor of the Reich, the situation immediately changed. There is no doubt that from the very beginning he regarded an ultimate struggle to the death with Bolshevism as inevitable—a political outlook which precluded the possibility of any further military co-operation between the armed forces of the two countries. Less understandable are his reasons for not seizing the opportunity of crushing, or at least of severely crippling, the 'Bolshevik World Enemy' by supporting, actively or otherwise, the *coup d'état* which Marshal Tukhachevsky was reputed to be preparing. The difficulty, already mentioned of affording any practical assistance undoubtedly influenced him; but it was certainly Heydrich's intervention which swayed the balance. He was convinced that the traditional leaning towards a Russo-German alliance still survived in the Prusso-German Officer Corps, and he so overestimated both the political significance of this factor and the potential results of any continuation of the military liaison, that he regarded the combined whole as a very real and pressing danger.

Nothing could undermine the relationship between the two armed forces more effectively than the proof—for public consumption—that it was in reality a cover for espionage and treason. This could be staged either way, in Germany or in Russia, with German Generals or Russian Generals as the accused, as might seem more expedient, and Heydrich had no qualms against framing 'charges of treason' against some German General or other.

All round, however, it seemed to him better to choose Moscow as the place and Tukhachevsky as the victim; the Soviet system offered exceptional facilities, whereas the staging of a case in Germany might be much more difficult. Further, by staging the case in Moscow and against the partner of the Wehrmacht, it would be possible to strike an indirect blow at the leaders of the latter, and there is no doubt that for Heydrich this latter was a very desirable, if subsidiary objective. Since his ignominious dismissal from the Navy, he had cherished an almost pathological hatred against the Chiefs of the Armed Forces, and he never missed a chance of striking some wounding blow against them. The Tukhachevsky affair certainly gave him an excellent opportunity.

After a great deal of very confidential discussion, he managed to persuade Himmler and, more important, Hitler to his way of thinking. In the internal quarrels of the Soviet Union, Germany would come out on the side of Stalin, Tukhachevsky and his associates would be exposed as traitors, and the indignant Red Army, incidentally, would be robbed of the services of some of its most able officers. All that had to be done was to supply Stalin with evidence of Tukhachevsky's treasonable dealings with the German High Command; evidence of his intended *coup d'état*, to complete the picture, could safely be left to General Skoblin to discover (or fake).

The whole operation was prepared with the utmost secrecy. It lasted from 1936 to 1937. Heydrich briefed only his immediate Chiefs, and them only to the minimum necessary to enable them to play their parts. I was told later by General Behrens how he had arranged the technical details. Other than Himmler and Heydrich himself, the only man admitted to the full secret was Behrens. I got to know him very well during the war when he was Chief of German S.S. and Police in Belgrade. (Later, in 1946, Behrens was handed over to Tito and executed for war crimes.)

At first, Heydrich tried to draw his great rival, Admiral Canaris, Chief of Military Intelligence Service, into the plot. He asked Canaris to let him have any documents in his possession which had been exchanged between the German High Command and the Russians on the subject of military co-operation, and particularly any original letters from Tukhachevsky and other senior Soviet officers. But Canaris, who knew Heydrich only too well and immediately suspected some sort of foul play— and who, in any case, had no such documents in his keeping— made some excuse and refused. Nevertheless Heydrich—or rather Behrens—succeeded in getting what he wanted without

Canaris' help. How this was done is not quite clear; but once at least Behrens is known to have broken in and burgled the archives of the German High Command.

Having obtained the specimens he required, Behrens started off in April 1937, in an isolated basement of Gestapo Head-quarters in Berlin, to prepare the necessary forgeries. For this purpose he set up a laboratory complete with all the requisite technical appliances and himself took personal charge of the security measures. The laboratory was completely cut off from the rest of the building, only those directly employed there were permitted to enter, and a specially selected guard was mounted. Heydrich also enlisted the services of two G.P.U. agents who had been captured some months previously and whom he 'invited' to assist him, while a third Russian agent, who had volunteered for service with the Berlin Gestapo, was employed in helping to prepare the forgeries.

As regards this third individual Behrens had ideas very different from Heydrich; and he went so far as to assert that it was the Russian Secret Service, and not Heydrich at all, who had conceived the idea of faking a case against Tukhachevsky, and that Heydrich was, in reality, the unconscious tool of the G.P.U.

What is certain is that an exchange of letters, covering a period of some twelve months, between Tukhachevsky and his asso-ciates on the one side and senior German Generals on the other, was forged in the Gestapo basement in the Prinz Albrecht Strasse, and they suggested that Tukhachevsky had succeeded in obtaining a promise of support from the German Wehrmacht in his attempted *putsch* against Stalin. The documents were rapidly prepared, and in a very few days, at the beginning of May, Himmler was able to place the dossier—a quite bulky file—in Hitler's hands. Apart from the actual correspondence, the dossier contained a variety of documents, including receipts from Russian Generals for very considerable sums of money, said to have been received from the German Secret Service in return for information given.

The alleged letters from Tukhachevsky and his confederates bore all the marks of authenticity; the initiallings in their margins, denoting that they had been seen and read by von

Seeckt, Hammerstein, Canaris and a number of other Generals, were reproduced with complete fidelity, and the carbon copies of the letters written by the German Generals to the Russian conspirators were included in the file. Finally, in order to implicate Canaris in the plot, Heydrich included a forged letter in which Canaris thanked Tukhachevsky and one or two other Generals for their information about the Red Army. Hitler expressed marked appreciation of the way in which the material had been prepared and gave his assent to its being played into the hands of the Russian Secret Service.

The original plan had been to pass on the forged documents via the Czech General Staff, who were known to be in close contact with the Russians. Liaison having been established through an agent, Behrens went to Czechoslovakia under an assumed name to make the necessary preparations. The Czechs refused, however, to disclose the channels through which the documents would be sent on to Stalin, and there seemed therefore to be no guarantee that they would not fall into the hands of some friend of Tukhachevsky en route. Heydrich rejected the idea as too risky and preferred to approach the Soviet Embassy in Berlin direct. He got into touch with an Embassy official, whom the Gestapo knew to be in reality a member of the Russian Secret Service, and quite openly placed the information at his disposal. The Russian immediately flew to Moscow, whence he shortly returned accompanied by a special representative of Yessov, the Chief of the Russian G.P.U., who declared that he had Stalin's personal authorization to negotiate for the purchase of the documents.

It had certainly never occurred to Heydrich to enter upon any official dealings with the Soviet authorities, and still less that he would be able to sell his forgeries to them; but with great agility he modified his tactics and demanded a sum of three million roubles. The same night he informed Hitler of his intentions and received his assent to the transaction. The next day Behrens handed over the file to the Soviet representative and received a bulky package containing notes to the value of three million roubles in exchange.

Heydrich placed these notes at the disposal of the Russian Section of the Secret Service. By chance, however, three German agents, who made payments in Russia with some of them, were immediately arrested by the G.P.U. In the course of my duties I learned that these agents had been lost. It had to be assumed that the Russians had paid either with forged notes or with genuine notes marked in some way as to render them readily identifiable, and the issue of further notes to agents was immediately stopped. That the Russians had paid with faked coin for his good forgeries infuriated Heydrich for years to come. It was, so to speak, a reflection on his artistry that all but robbed him of the satisfaction of his success.

Heydrich's machinery functioned with deadly infallibility, and Marshal Tukhachevsky and his confederates were promptly arrested. The case against them opened at ten o'clock on the morning of 10th June. By nine o'clock the same evening it was all over. The proceedings started with a speech by Voroshilov on military treason, and this was followed by the interrogations of the accused. According to Soviet reports, the accused, overwhelmed by the mass of evidence against them and confronted with the letters in their own handwriting to the German High Command, broke down and confessed their guilt. Vyshinsky's summing-up lasted a bare twenty minutes. He demanded the expulsion of the accused from the Red Army and the imposition of the maximum penalty. Within a few minutes the verdict was given and the sentence of death passed. The accused were forthwith stripped of their army insignia and decorations, and within twelve hours they were executed. The execution squad was commanded in person—at Stalin's order, it is said—by Marshal Bluecher, who, a few years later, himself became a victim of Soviet Justice. Indeed, with the exception of the two Marshals, Voroshilov and Budenny, all the members of the Tukhachevsky Court sooner or later lost their own lives.

Heydrich had arranged a special wireless link-up, so that he could follow all details of the proceedings direct from Moscow. Brief and summary though these were, they sufficed to convince him of the efficiency of his measures, and he was proud to think that his forgeries had played a decisive part in bringing about the condemnation of the Russian Marshal. To the day of his death, he remained convinced of the value of what he had done.

General Behrens, however, was by no means so sure. He had begun by being a ruthless man like Heydrich, but as the Russian army rolled ever nearer to Belgrade in 1945, he told me of his misgivings. His own forgeries haunted him. The decisive defeat that Germany was suffering at the hands of the Russians was making him wonder whether it would not have been better to support Tukhachevsky's efforts to overthrow Stalin. Tukhachevsky's downfall, he declared in 1944, delayed the build-up of the Russian Army only for a very short while, and the Bolshevik régime had remained untouched and unchallenged. Stalin's energy and flair for organization had quickly made good the slight setback in Soviet armament which the Tukhachevsky affair had caused. A live Tukhachevsky,[1] he thought, would be worth more to Germany than ten Vlassovs; even if active support of Tukhachevsky's alleged plans for a *putsch* had proved impracticable, because Skoblin had already betrayed them, Germany should have done her utmost to save the Marshal's life and get him out of the country.

OPERATION BERNHARD

But not only documents were forged by the German Secret Service. We forged money too, and ran an undertaking known as 'Operation Bernhard'.

Initially, the German Secret Service had very little money. Because of a general shortage, the Finance Ministry placed a strictly limited amount of foreign currency at its disposal and in 1939 the Chief of the Technical Branch of the Foreign Secret Service felt compelled to try and finance the Overseas Intelligence Service with forged Bank notes. This was no original idea; the Secret Services of other countries, particularly that of Soviet Russia, had already used the same means to a considerable extent. Only the forgery of sound and universally acceptable currency, of course, was worth while, and this restricted operations to the dollar and the pound sterling.

---

[1] Vlassov, a Red Army General, was captured by the Germans in 1941 and worked for them as the Commander-in-Chief of a force of Russian P.O.Ws. and deserters. Captured by the Allies in 1945, he was extradited to the Russians and sentenced to death.

The usefulness and the drawbacks of this undertaking first became clear under Kaltenbrunner in the famous case of the spy 'Cicero' in Ankara who received enormous payments in forged notes. While Germany was not yet at war with the United States, Hitler would only sanction the forging of British pound notes. Although the actual forging presented no very serious problem, the technical difficulty of producing the exact paper used in Britain proved to be very great; at last, however, such good forgeries were produced that they were accepted as genuine by Banks throughout the world, and only the Bank of England itself detected that they were forged.

It was not until 1943 that any large-scale use could be made of these notes. In order to shield them from the economic chaos which would inevitably have followed such procedure, the Reichs-Minister for Economic Affairs succeeded in preventing any wholesale distribution of the forged notes in countries under German domination, and operations were therefore confined to enemy territories.

A host of agents, carrying very large quantities of false pound notes, was sent to Italy with the task of distributing their wares in these districts, the occupation of which by the Anglo-American Forces appeared to be imminent. They found particularly ready purchasers among the anti-German civilian population, who were only too eager to get rid of their dubious liras and receive in exchange the currency of their prospective liberators. With the liras thus obtained, the Germans purchased gold and genuine currency—scrutinized, in the circumstances, with the utmost care—in the Black Market, and in 1943 and 1944 the German Secret Service had acquired a very large capital at a very small cost.

The agent in charge of the Italian operation hit upon one very subtle idea. The Germans knew that the British and Americans were supplying the Italian partisans, by submarine and parachute drops, with large quantities of small arms—exactly the weapons which the Germans themselves needed urgently for their struggle against the local insurgents. It was soon found that many of the partisans were willing to sell the arms thus acquired, but refused to accept liras, partly because they regarded them as of dubious value, but particularly because they were fairly certain that Trieste and district would fall to the Yugoslav forces. British pounds, on the other hand, were readily acceptable, with the result that a truly paradoxical business, probably without parallel in the history of war, was built up, in which the German Secret Service bought from the Italian partisans arms which had been supplied to them by the British and the Americans —and paid for them in forged British pound notes! Nor were these transactions piece-meal in nature. They were not even confined to waggon loads of arms; entire trainloads were bartered in this way, and the arms were then used by the German Secret Service to fight the very partisans who had sold them!

By no means all the Italian partisans indulged in this grotesque business, and the whole purchase transaction was often very dangerous. On one occasion the German director of operations, who invariably accompanied his lorries into partisan-occupied territory, all but lost his life; his driver was killed, and he himself only escaped by feigning death. This, however, did not prevent him from putting through some highly satisfactory deals a few weeks later in very much the same districts.

The Bank of England suffered enormous losses as the result of these forgeries, so the Allied interrogation officers told me after the war. This no doubt accounts for the fact that at the end of the war all British notes of five pounds and over were withdrawn from circulation and replaced by fresh issues.

It was a very long time before the German Secret Service succeeded in producing good dollar-note forgeries. A series was printed in 1943, but the blemishes were so palpable, that the agents entrusted with their distribution refused to accept the notes. It was only immediately before the end of the war that a second series was produced, which in the opinion of experts was equal in standard to the forged British notes; and by then it was too late to make any great use of them.

On the collapse of Germany, the notes, machinery and plates were all destroyed. A transport column, taking the material from the Ebensee Concentration Camp, where the forgeries had been made, to the Tyrol, was prevented by the congestion on the roads from reaching its destination. The contents of the lorries were therefore dumped straightway into the Traunsee lake. But the cases quickly disintegrated at the bottom of the lake, their contents rose to the surface, and very soon the lake was bedecked, like a lotus garden, with hundreds of thousands of forged pound notes!

CHAPTER VI

PLANTING A BOMB

On 8th November, 1939, a bomb exploded in the Buerger-braeukeller in Munich soon after Hitler had left the traditional anniversary celebrations held there to commemorate his first abortive coup in 1923. Many foreign observers regarded this 'plot' as a fake, and evidence since disclosed by a senior Police official who served on the investigation committee appointed immediately afterwards, tends to support this belief, although conclusive evidence may never come to light.

When the alleged perpetrator, Georg Elser, was arrested at the German-Swiss frontier on the evening of 8th November, 1939, and handed over to the Committee of Investigation, none of the experienced experts on the Committee believed that he was in fact the man they sought.

Elser was said to have placed the infernal machine in the pillar behind the speaker's rostrum with quite astonishing cunning, resolution and skill; and yet one was asked to believe that this man, who had given such ample evidence of his foresight, determination and resourcefulness, had to all practical purposes, been almost at pains to supply proof of his complicity. He carried with him a post-card of the Buergerbraeukeller and some bomb detonators; in the back of his overcoat he had clumsily concealed a badge of the Rotfrontkaempferbund (A militant Communist Formation in pre-Nazi days), and he had sidled round the little German frontier customs house with such conspicuously secret intent as to ensure attracting attention. He was already in possession of a genuine pass for local transit to and from Switzerland, he had already used it a few days before, and he had merely returned to assure himself that the clock-work of his bomb was functioning properly. Having done so, he had only to use his pass to leave Germany in the normal manner. For what possible reason, then, did he take the risk of an illegal crossing of the frontier?

There can be but one explanation—Elser was determined to ensure at all costs that he would be arrested. But had he been that type of fanatic who, for the sake of the publicity value to his cause, desired to stand and admit his deed in open court, he could quite easily have given himself up to the police immediately after the explosion. Instead he elected to stage this complicated farce of an attempted flight, the main purpose of which could obviously be interpreted only as a deliberate intention to force his arrest at the frontier.

The assumption that Elser was a man suffering from so strong a pathological desire for notoriety that he was prepared to purchase it even at the cost of his own life is perhaps a little more plausible. In that case, his behaviour at the frontier, designed to ensure his arrest, makes some sense, and the crude proofs he carried would compel the Police to charge him with having committed a deed, the responsibility for which he had, in reality, merely usurped for the sake of the notoriety it would bring him.

The C.I.D. officials, who at once started their investigations during the night of 8th November, at first deliberately refused to interrogate Elser, preferring to follow what appeared to them to be a much more promising line of inquiry. Suddenly, however, a telegram arrived from Mueller, the Chief of the Berlin Gestapo, ordering the Committee forthwith to interrogate Elser. At this point Elser had not yet confessed, and the meagre result of the Munich C.I.D.'s preliminary investigation was the only material available. Is it possible that the Berlin Chief of the Gestapo was already aware that Elser was the perpetrator—or at any rate was destined to be branded as such?

Apart from this, there were other suspicious features which hinted darkly at men behind the scenes of some really big drama, in which Elser was but an incidental piece of stage property. Normally, the Buergerbraeukeller was always kept under Police supervision for a full week before the traditional annual celebrations, which Hitler invariably attended. In 1939, curiously enough, this supervision was restricted, on the orders of the Deputy Chief of the Munich State Police (the Chief himself was absent on duty in Poland) to the single night of 7th–8th November. The official who had previously always been em-

ployed for this duty was moreover replaced this time by a
Commissar of the C.I.D., who was the holder of the Golden
Badge of the Nazi Party. None of the responsible officials
was subsequently punished; the Deputy Chief of Police who,
by restricting supervision to the one single night, had laid himself open to a charge of grave dereliction of duty, was actually
promoted and appointed to a Police Directorship in Central
Germany; and finally the relevant higher command of both S.S.,
Police and Security Service escaped without reprimand.

All this was very contrary to normal procedure. Usually in
a case of this nature, even the officials remotely connected were
called to account, and, particularly in the case of the Police
Service, any failure was immediately followed by a series of
punishments from top to bottom. In this case, however, in
which, according to the official account, the life of the Fuehrer
himself had been spared by a hairsbreadth, nothing of the sort,
most astonishingly, was done. The Chairman of the Investigation Committee, on the other hand, was transferred abroad and,
later, charged with some petty misdemeanour which would
normally have earned him a reprimand; he was flung into a
concentration camp, where he remained until the end of the
war.

Nor is this all. S.S. Major-General Schellenberg, later Chief
of the German Political Overseas Secret Service, with a small
group of collaborators had got into touch with the British Intelligence Service. Posing as German officers hostile to the régime,
he and his colleagues succeeded eventually in establishing contact with highly placed British officials and interesting them in
the alleged conspiracy. His object was to penetrate ever higher
into the hierarchy of the British Government. Hitler had given
his formal approval to the idea, and Schellenberg had just been
assured by his British contacts that a senior British official
would come over to Holland in the immediate future to meet
him. This fact was also known to Hitler. Suddenly, in the early
afternoon of 8th November—a few hours, that is, before the
explosion of the Buergerbraeukeller bomb—Heydrich gave
orders that the secret negotiations with the British Intelligence
Service were to cease and that the British liaison officers were
to be seized and brought across the frontier into Germany.

This was the well-known Venlo action of 9th November, in which the two British agents, Stevens and Best, were taken prisoner.

Now why should Heydrich have given this sudden order which, contrary to all that had been agreed upon, put a premature end to a most promising enterprise on the very threshold of success? Later official Press communiqués tried to give the impression that Stevens and Best had been implicated in the Buergerbraeukeller plot, and that it was they who had employed Elser and furnished him with the materials for his attempt. Assuming for a moment that this was correct, how was it, then, that Heydrich ordered the capture of these two Britons several hours *before* the bomb exploded? Did he know about the plot they were hatching? And if so, why did he not prevent the explosion of the infernal machine?

Satisfactory answers to all these questions can be found if the assumption is accepted that it was Heydrich himself who arranged the whole affair. This would explain:

1. Why Headquarters of the Munich State Police changed their normal procedure of surveillance at the Buerger-braeukeller.
2. Why none of the Police Officers was punished for dereliction of duty.
3. Why Heydrich ordered the capture of Stevens and Best before the event, which, through them, he wished to impute to the British authorities behind the scenes.
4. Why Elser was at such pains to ensure his own arrest—because he had received instructions to do so.
5. Why the Investigation Committee was given a specific order by Mueller to turn its attention to an individual, who, from the viewpoint of criminal investigation, hardly deserved even suspicion of any complicity.
6. Why the alleged perpetrator was never brought to trial.

Elser was put into a concentration camp, where he enjoyed the preferential treatment usually reserved for prominent personalities such as Schuschnigg and Pastor Martin Niemoeller.

How otherwise can it be explained that the man, who had

attempted to assassinate the Supreme Head of the German State and had succeeded in assassinating eight of his oldest and most trustworthy supporters, should have had his every wish fulfilled in the concentration camp, even to the extent of being given a wireless set and a work-bench at which to practise his hobby of carpentry? It was only in April 1945, by a special and secret order given to the Commandant of the concentration camp, that Elser was shot. And that shot, it may safely be assumed, was fired—not at Elser, the would-be assassin, but at Elser, the man who knew too much.

But, it may well be asked, if indeed he did so, why did Heydrich organize this elaborate plot? There are several good reasons.

On the evening of 5th November Himmler had had a conference with Hitler. The latter was still under the influence of the after-effects of a violent argument, which he had just had with General von Brauchitsch, the Commander-in-Chief of the Army, concerning the date for the attack on France. Brauchitsch had strongly opposed Hitler's demand that the offensive should be launched that very autumn of 1939, and had produced many telling arguments to prove that the German Armed Forces were not in a position to do so. Hitler had reacted violently and had ordered the attack for 12th November, in spite of the Commander-in-Chief's protests. (A few days later Hitler cancelled this order, and, after a series of postponements, the offensive was finally fixed for the spring of 1940.) Hitler had told the S.S. Reichsfuehrer about this argument and had complained passionately at the state of unpreparedness of the Army High Command and its failure to be ready to implement his plans. His primary preoccupation, apparently, had been lest the German people should lose their faith in him as their Fuehrer. This preoccupation was probably his reaction to Brauchitsch's assertion that there was little sign among the people of any enthusiasm for the war or of any desire to see an offensive launched against the Western Powers.

Himmler had arranged for a conference with Heydrich immediately after his talk with Hitler, the obvious object of which must have been to give him a detailed exposition of the views Hitler had expressed. Is it possible that Heydrich's desire was to rid Hitler of his anxiety about the morale of the German people and their continued faith in the blessing of his leadership? If so—a plot of this nature, skilfully exploited by subsequent propaganda, would go a long way towards doing so. The impression could be given that the Fuehrer had had the narrowest of escapes, that but for the miraculous intervention of Providence he must indeed have been killed and that the miracle was certainly a sign that he was God's chosen instrument for the high office to which he had been called. The Western Allies, and particularly the British, could be denounced as the instigators of a cowardly crime, and the public hatred and indignation, which were the necessary precursors to any large-scale military operations, would thus be fully roused against them. In short, the necessary enthusiasm in support of Hitler's autumn plans could be evoked by this means. Not only that, but Holland could also be compromised, for Schellenberg's negotiations with the British had proved that the Dutch General Staff had been collaborating with Germany's enemies to a degree which was quite incompatible with a state of neutrality. That the subsequent court case, at which all this would have been served up to the German people, never materialized, is due probably to the postponement of the offensive against France. With it disappeared also any necessity for a sensation, and by the spring of 1940 German public opinion had completely changed.

The above consideration would have furnished an ample motive. Whether Hitler was aware of Heydrich's intentions cannot be established with certainty. The most significant fact in favour of such an assumption is his sudden and premature departure for Berlin, which saved him from becoming one of the victims of the plot. The reason for his departure, in view of the importance which he is known to have attached to the traditional ceremony, is flimsy in the extreme. A military conference at ten o'clock on the morning of 9th November at Berlin could surely have been postponed for a few hours!

But there are equally some aspects which support the assumption that Hitler was not an accomplice before the act. It is unlikely in the extreme that Himmler would not have been fully informed of any such project, and he undoubtedly believed that the plot was genuine. He was the driving force behind the investigation, and he did his utmost to get on to the track of the people who were behind Elser. He was for ever seeking new minds, like the Head of the Vienna Gestapo, to help grapple with the problem; after Elser's confession, he ordered a "further and more rigorous" interrogation, with a view to finding out who his employers were, and generally showed the keenest personal interest in the case.

On the whole, it is more probable that both Hitler and Himmler were ignorant of Heydrich's intentions, and that the latter found some still unknown reason with which to persuade Hitler to leave the Buergerbraeukeller in good time.

The most difficult skein to unravel is that of the relationship between Heydrich and Elser, and this must remain a matter of pure guesswork. The most likely explanation is that offered by a member of the Munich State Police who was *au fait* with part of the background story. Elser, he maintained, had no idea either of the part he was being called upon to play or of the fact that he was acting as Heydrich's cat's-paw. He had, in fact, planned the whole thing himself, but had been discovered by a member of the Gestapo. This latter had posed as the leader of a Communist opposition cell and had encouraged Elser to continue his preparations, in the hopes of finding out for whom he was working. Heydrich must certainly have been informed of Elser's activities both by the Deputy Chief of the Munich State Police and by Mueller, the Chief of the Gestapo in Berlin. He took no action against Elser—originally, no doubt, from the purely police motive of holding his hand until he had found out all that there was to be learnt—and removed all obstacles such as the nightly watch from his path. When, on the night of 5th November, he heard of Hitler's plans and anxieties, it presumably flashed through his mind that he could make good capital out of Elser's plot in the way that has already been described. This would remove the objection that Heydrich would never have had time himself to organize from Berlin so complicated a plot in the brief period between the night of 5th November and 8th November; he had no need to do so, for Elser made him a present of a ready-made plot, and all that Heydrich had to do was to use it to his own ends, to see that no obstacle was put in

4

Elser's path and to ensure that Hitler left the cellar in good time.

The fact that the plot would of necessity cause the death of at least some old and trusted members of the Party carried no weight with Heydrich; and that the bomb might explode too soon and kill Hitler himself likewise did not worry him unduly. Whoever Hitler's successor might be, he, Heydrich, was quite sure to keep his job as the mighty Chief of Police.

This explanation rings for the most part true; nor does the preferential treatment later accorded to Elser in the concentration camp detract in any way from its verisimilitude. He was, after all, only an unconscious pawn in a big game, and even the conspiracy did not remain solely his to the end.

THE DISMISSAL OF BLOMBERG AND FRITSCH

On 5th November, 1937, Hitler held a conference in the Reich Chancellery with the Commanders-in-Chief of the three Armed Services—Colonel General von Fritsch, Admiral Raeder and Reichsmarshal Goering—the War Minister, Field-Marshal von Blomberg, and the Foreign Minister, Baron von Neurath. Hitler's adjutant, Colonel Hossbach, also attended, and his notes, a copy of which was captured by the American forces at the end of the war, were later used as evidence by the International Military Tribunal at Nuremberg. They contain details of the discussion which took place on that important occasion.

It was at this conference that Hitler divulged for the first time his innermost thoughts on the future of Germany to his immediate Service collaborators. The essence of his discourse was that a war was inevitable, and that the only question which could not yet be answered was when it would begin. The subsequent course of the conference came as a bitter disappointment to him; with the exception of Goering, all the Service Chiefs disagreed radically with both his conceptions and his intentions; and even Goering was very reserved in his opinion.

Shortly after the conference Hitler received S.S. Reichsfuehrer Himmler and informed him of what had been said.

He had come to the final conclusion, declared Hitler, that with military and political colleagues of this kind he could never attain his object of restoring Germany once more to the status of a Great Power by means of a war. Himmler, of course, immediately passed this on to Heydrich.

The situation now confronting Heydrich was similar in every way to that which had faced him in the early summer of 1934. At that time, by trumping-up for him an alleged conspiracy in the S.A., he gave Hitler the opportunity of ridding himself, with one devastating blow, of those of his old colleagues who threatened to jeopardize the success of his plans. Now he found himself faced with a very similar task. Blomberg and Fritsch must be got rid of; but the real reason for their dismissal, namely, that they favoured the pursuit of a policy of peace by Germany, must never become known. On this basis Heydrich set to work with his customary methodical skill.

One of Heydrich's favourite methods of getting rid of awkward people had always been to impute to them a leaning towards perverse practices, and this, he thought, would be a particularly appropriate method in the case of the unmarried and very reserved General von Fritsch. In the course of his unceasing search for embarrassing information against leading personalities of the Third Reich he had some time ago filed the statement of a Berlin guttersnipe, in which the latter had asserted that General von Fritsch was a 'client' of a certain 'clique'. At the time he had made no use of the information, but now he turned it up again and sent for the informer, a youth by the name of Schmidt.

This young blackguard, who had been sentenced more than a dozen times on charges of unnatural offences and blackmail, was next briefed, on Heydrich's orders, as a Crown witness against General von Fritsch, accusing him of immoral malpractice. The youth declared that, with others of his kind, he had discovered the General's habits in 1934 and had been blackmailing him ever since.

For the preparation of his case, Heydrich employed his most trusted colleague, Criminal Director Meisinger, who was known to stick at nothing, however despicable, to attain his ends. Meisinger 'groomed' Schmidt so perfectly as a witness for the prosecution that Heydrich had no hesitation in producing the youth before Hitler himself, though how the latter could have allowed such a person to be brought into his presence passes comprehension.

With the General himself, however, Meisinger failed completely. All his efforts were in vain, and even when confronted with Schmidt in person, the General remained master of the situation. Further investigation and numerous intensive interrogations brought nothing new to light, but they gave Hitler an excuse to dismiss von Fritsch. An alleged request from him to be allowed to retire for reasons of health was granted.

The verdict of the Military Court of Honour set up to investigate the facts was not yet available at that time. The principal hearing, which had been fixed for 10th March, 1938, with Goering as President, had to be broken off shortly after it had begun, because the senior Wehrmacht Officers who formed the Court were required for duty in connection with the invasion of Austria. It was only on 17th and 18th March that the proceedings could be brought to a conclusion, and then they proved the complete innocence of the General beyond any shadow of doubt. It was Goering himself who, though initially he had believed that the accusation had some basis of truth, eventually brought about the downfall of the witness Schmidt. His pointed questions pierced the armour of lies with which Meisinger had surrounded his witness, and the latter was forced to confess that his whole story was nothing but a pack of lies.

For General von Fritsch the clearing of his honour came too late. He was given command of a regiment, but was never restored to his original position. His fight against the monstrous slander had shattered his deepest feelings. At the outbreak of war he volunteered for service at the front and on 22nd September, 1939, he was killed at the head of Artillery Regiment 12 in the Warsaw suburb of Praga. There is no doubt that he sought this soldierly end of his own free will.

The Reich War Minister, Field-Marshal von Blomberg, could not be 'got' on a charge of homosexuality. This sixty-year-old officer had for a very long time had a close liaison with a young woman named Eva Gruhn, who was well known to Heydrich's sleuth-hounds. As he was able to find no discreditable episodes in Blomberg's own career, Heydrich concentrated his attention on the Field-Marshal's young woman. His investigation squad succeeded in unearthing information according to which Eva Gruhn's mother was said to have been the proprietress of a so-called massage salon and had been in trouble with the authorities on more than one occasion as a procuress and brothel keeper.

Meisinger said at the time that all this was well known to Heydrich in 1937, and that this proved that Himmler and Heydrich were in a position to restrain the Field-Marshal from the step he was contemplating—or at least to warn him of the inevitable grave consequences. The Field-Marshal had always had the intention of marrying Eva Gruhn, and on January 12th, 1938, he did so, and Hitler and Goering were his witnesses.

Himmler and Heydrich had let the Field-Marshal 'drop into it'—to use the disgusting jargon of the Nazi leaders for describing such intrigues—and they found it most convenient that the two most rigid sticklers in the whole Reich should be embarrassed when it became known that they had acted as witnesses at the wedding of a woman who came not only from a lowly, but also, in the eyes of the Corps of Officers, from a notoriously unsavoury family.

Even this did not satisfy them. A bare fortnight after the wedding, on 21st January, 1938, a criminal record sheet was placed before the Police President of Berlin, Count Helldorff, which showed that Blomberg's bride had for years been under supervision by the public morals branch of the Police and had frequently come into conflict with them; that files on her immoral activities were kept in five large cities of Germany, and much more besides. How came this criminal record sheet to find its way on to the desk of the Police President? According to all accounts hitherto published—by pure chance. A Berlin Inspector of Police, it is said, having heard rumours about the War Minister's young wife, decided in a burst of zeal to have a look at the files on public morality and had come upon the record sheet in question.

This version is quite untrue. It has since been proved that a record sheet bearing the name of Eva Gruhn was seen some days before in the hands of Meisinger, and that he, with the assistance of an official of his section, made certain additional entries on it. Meisinger's intervention was undoubtedly ordered by Heydrich. What cannot be ascertained is whether there ever really was a genuine record sheet of Eva Gruhn in the archives, or whether Heydrich had simply caused one to be faked and planted there; of the two possibilities, the latter is the more probable. But all that can be proved is that Meisinger added false entries to an existing sheet.

A record sheet for Eva's mother almost certainly existed, and this fact made Heydrich's task much easier; but absolute proof of Heydrich's complicity could only be obtained if Meisinger's assistant, who, as far as is known, is still living, were to come forward and testify. (Meisinger was later executed in Poland as a war criminal.)

When the evidence against the wife of the War Minister was laid before Hitler, he succumbed to one of his dreaded paroxysms of rage. Blomberg was forthwith dismissed. His fate is particularly tragic, for he was one of the few senior Officers of the Wehrmacht who were truly devoted to Hitler and the National-Socialist cause. Since 1933, his great ambition had been to bring about a fusion between the revolutionary spirit of National-Socialism and the Prusso-German soldierly tradition, or at least to help Hitler to the achievement of this aim. Hitler's decisive action against the S.A. had only strengthened Blomberg's conviction that Hitler was the man for the task. Even later, when he began to see through Hitler's real intentions, he still adhered to his dream of seeing the ancient military tradition wedded to the revolutionary spirit of progress under the aegis of National-Socialism. This great ambition estranged him more and more from his comrades-in-arms of the Wehrmacht, the majority of whom repudiated him, because they thought he was delivering the Wehrmacht into the hands of Hitler.

He was for these reasons all the more deeply stricken by Heydrich's foul blow, and he never recovered from the shock of his dismissal and the social ostracism which accompanied it. His most bitter complaint was that Hitler, for whom he had sacrificed everything, had betrayed and forsaken him. He was quite convinced that when Hitler and Goering acted as witnesses at his wedding, they were already in possession of the evidence that Heydrich had brought against him, that it was their deliberate intention, by their apparently innocent presence, to increase the enormity of the scandal and make any chance of his surviving it impossible.

The one thing he never regretted, however, was his marriage to Eva Gruhn. Shortly before his death in Nuremberg prison, General Glaise-Horstenau said to him: 'Herr Field-Marshal, do you know that you sacrificed the German Wehrmacht for a woman?'

I heard the reply of Blomberg. He answered curtly:

'I could not help myself. She was the great passion of my life.'

CHAPTER VII

SMASHING THE CZECH STATE

OF those countries that Hitler over-ran after subversive work in minority groups, the case of Czechoslovakia is of special interest. There some three millions of German origin lived along the Sudeten Mountains, and these Sudeten Germans were to play an important part in Hitler's conquest. Yet neither the Sudeten Germans nor their leader, Konrad Henlein—a sports instructor by profession—were National-Socialists from the beginning. On the contrary strong differences marked their early relations with Hitler, even if Hitler's rise in Germany did give a fresh impulse to the Sudeten German movement and to their resistance to the Government in Prague. This was at first hampered by the Party politics in that region, especially the split between the two Right Wing Parties, the German Nationalist Party and the German National Socialist Workers' Party (the D.N.S.A.P.)

It is only natural that the mighty National-Socialist Party in Germany should have had a powerful influence on the independent and previously founded German National-Socialist Party of the Sudeten area. The latter did not attain an importance comparable to that of the N.S.D.A.P. in Germany; and early in 1933 it strove to increase its activities and reform itself on the Nazi model. But the Czechoslovak Government immediately intervened and met with little opposition; the Peoples' Sporting Association—which had been modelled on the German Storm Troops—was disbanded, and its leader condemned to several years' penal servitude. With the object of anticipating any similar action, which they feared with some justification, the German Nationalist Party and the D.N.S.A.P. went into voluntary liquidation.

On 1st October, 1933, Henlein's appeal for the formation of an all-Party Sudeten German Home Front appeared in the Press. This was not a cover organization for the old Parties. The promoters came from the Youth Movement, and its leader, Henlein, decided to launch his appeal only after attempts at unifying the Sudeten Germans with the help of the old Parties had failed.

The response was terrific. In the first few weeks the new Home Front attracted so mighty an influx of supporters, that the Czech Government, after hesitating, felt constrained to allow the new organization. Shortly afterwards it ordered the arrest of nearly all the leaders of the Sudeten German Home Front. Such repressive police methods merely enhanced the prestige of the Party and swelled the stream of recruits to it. Moreover the arrest of so many of Henlein's most important followers was not without internal repercussions; Henlein, compelled to seek new collaborators, turned for the first time to the various leaders of the old disbanded D.N.S.A.P., of whom Karl Frank was the most prominent. Frank took advantage of the imprisonment of the leading functionaries of the Sudeten German Home Front to strengthen his own position and that of adherents, and by the time the original leaders were released, Henlein could no longer get rid of his newly acquired interim supporters.

In spite of all this, Frank's group exercised no particular influence over Henlein during this period. In a great political speech at Leipa on 21st October, 1934, for example, he declared that the Sudeten German Home Front was separated by fundamental divergencies from the Nationalists and would certainly never renounce the principle of the liberty of the individual. In this he was quite sincere, for he repeated exactly the same sentiments in the intimate circle of his friends and at Party Executive conferences, where he had no reason to hide his true opinions. His efforts to limit the co-operation of his own movement with the German Nazis was viewed in Berlin with surly annoyance. Up till then the leaders of the Nazi Party had watched the growth of the Sudeten German Home Front with the greatest sympathy. Afterwards, particularly in the Himmler-Rosenberg groups, Henlein came to be regarded with the deepest mistrust. Hitler himself also made many unfriendly references to Henlein, when some of the anti-Nazi utterances of the Sudeten German Home Front leader were brought to his notice, and from

4*

that moment a sharp watch was set on Henlein by the German Security Services. Most of their information came from members of the former D.N.S.A.P. whom Henlein for the same ideological reasons which governed his attitude towards the German Nazi Party, was treating with the utmost reserve.

Henlein had by no means succeeded in uniting all the Sudeten German Parties into one all-Party organization. As his own Home Front was not strictly speaking a political Party, he realized that he must transform his movement into a Party if he wished to exercise any political influence. Accordingly, in the new parliamentary elections on 26th May, 1935, the Sudeten German Home Front canvassed under the name of the Sudeten German Party. At this first attempt it obtained more than two thirds of the total Sudeten German votes cast and became the strongest individual Party in the new Parliament. Indeed, according to the rules of procedure the Sudeten German Party should by rights have nominated the President of the Czechoslovak Republic!

This admittedly would have been absurd from the practical point of view; but the Czechoslovak Government would have been wise if it had recognized in this success an unmistakable sign that the time was more than ripe for an understanding with the German minority. There was never any question of such a revision of Czechoslovak policy; on the contrary, the Government proceeded with methods akin to those of a Police State against the representatives of the Sudeten people, elected according to the strictest democratic principles, but without steeling itself to deprive them of their basic democratic rights. Despite this, the Sudeten German Party sought to gain its ends by strictly constitutional means. It introduced a bill for Sudeten German autonomy worked out to the last detail. The Czech majority flung out the bill.

Had the Prague parliament acceded to the demand for equality of rights guaranteed by this measure of autonomy, the wind would have been taken out of the sails of Hitler's policy towards the Czechoslovak Republic, and even after the seizure of Austria an internally contented Czechoslovakia would not have offered so tempting a morsel to Germany's policy of aggressive expansion. With the rejection of the bill by the Czech majority the way was opened which led, via the Munich agreement, to the occupation of Prague.

It was later asserted that the Sudeten German Party was not in earnest when it introduced its bill and that it had only done so because it knew full well that the bill would be forthwith thrown out by the Czechs. This is not true. At that time Henlein's attitude towards the N.S.D.A.P. was, as has already been shown, one of the greatest reserve, and his policy was completely independent and in no way dictated by Berlin. The leaders of the Sudeten Germans certainly did not in the early thirties envisage incorporation of their land into the German Reich. Even in their most confidential conferences such a possibility was never even discussed, and the vast majority of the Sudeten Germans themselves had no desire to return 'home to the Reich'.

By making very small concessions then the Czechs could certainly have reached a settlement, and it was their failure in this respect which was responsible for the radical attitude adopted by the Sudeten Germans, and which led to the birth of a genuine movement in favour of absorption by Germany. Benes and his colleagues played right into Hitler's hands and paved the way psychologically for the execution of his plans.

Nothing could have been more opportunely helpful to him than this intransigeance on the part of the Czech Government, which sooner or later would be bound to give the pretext for forcible intervention which he desired. Nothing was more awkward for him than Henlein's sincere policy of reconciliation.

Hitler's mistrust of Henlein was aggravated by Heydrich's reports, which were based on secret intelligence from the Sudetenland. In May 1936 Henlein expelled from his Party a number of former leaders of the D.N.S.A.P., among them Rudolf Kasper, who in the German Sudeten Party had for some time been Chairman of the Party Labour Council; and when he did this, it became clear to both Himmler and Heydrich that he had set a definitely anti-Nazi course.

A separate Intelligence Section was set up to watch Henlein under the direction of a Special Adviser at the Berlin Headquarters of the Secret Services. This section expanded rapidly, and its director had great influence on Hitler's policy and the

Sudeten question. It was he who was responsible for maintaining Hitler's distrust of Henlein and for persuading him to reject as a menace to Germany the suggested compromise with the Czechs, which would at least have assured for Henlein and his Party a strong say in Sudeten affairs for a long time to come, and might well have postponed the 'final solution' which Hitler had already secretly planned.

In Heydrich's own entourage two men, Herr Rutha, an engineer, and Dr. Walter Brandt, were particularly determined opponents of any such 'final solution' and of the annexation of the Sudetenland. They bore the brunt of the fight, which was waged with any and every means available. It ended with the suicide of Rutha and Dr. Brandt being flung into a concentration camp, where he remained till the end of the war.

Hitler regarded with particular misgiving the attempts of the Sudeten German Party to influence world opinion and to inform foreign Governments of their aspirations and keep them *au courant* with the situation. Henlein was well aware of this, but he did not let it turn him from his purpose. He and his colleagues did their utmost to interest the League of Nations and other international bodies in the Sudeten problem. They sent representatives to the European Congress of Nations—a species of parliament composed of the national minorities of all States, they played an active part in the affairs of the League for Unity and International Understanding, to the committee of which leading members of the Sudeten German Party were accredited. They set up their own Foreign Policy Council to keep the various diplomatic representatives in Prague constantly informed on the situation. All these activities, unfortunately, brought but little success. It was only when Hitler's massive pressure on Czechoslovakia began—and it was then already too late to achieve any solution by negotiation—that the world really faced up to the problem. Had it done so earlier, the results might have been very different.

The one exception to this general attitude of indifference was Great Britain. The Sudeten German Party had been particularly anxious to interest Britain, for they knew that British policy aimed at a peaceful solution and stability in Central Europe. In 1935 Henlein had been introduced by Count Karl Khuen to

Colonel Graham Christie, a prominent member of the British Intelligence Service. He was said at that time to be the head of the Central European Section and a close colleague of Sir Robert Vansittart.

Henlein made two visits to London, in 1935 and in October 1937, and on the second occasion had talks with Sir Robert Vansittart, Mr. Winston Churchill and other men in politics. It was largely due to the impression made by Henlein that the British Government began to ask for direct reports on the Sudeten German question to compare with the official reports reaching London from the Prague Government.

The connection between Christie and Henlein became at once of very great political importance, for it had a decisive effect on the development of Sudetenland affairs. Admittedly the constructive plans which they drew up for a solution by negotiation were never put into operation; but that they could not foresee. Their hopes ran high; Henlein in his optimism hoped with Christie's aid to prepare the ground for a general Anglo-German discussion to settle all outstanding differences and bring about a real understanding between the two Great Powers, which would ensure peace for many years to come. He remained factually and consistently faithful to his 'British line' of policy, even when faced with the tempting possibility of closer co-operation with Italy; and when Mussolini asked him to come to Rome, he immediately consulted the British and at their request declined the invitation.

This very success of the Sudeten German politicians, particularly in Great Britain was being observed with acute and growing displeasure in Berlin. Henlein's conception of a peaceful settlement with the Czechs was of itself alone sufficiently contrary to Hitler's real intentions to arouse resentment, and this was further aggravated by the Fuehrer's mistrust of the activities of the leading negotiators. Dr. Brandt, like Rutha and Dr. Sebekowski, was known in Berlin to be an admitted opponent of National-Socialism, and he was as unpopular with Hitler as were those Czech aristocrats of German origin, who placed their connections with London and Paris at the disposal of the negotiators. Hitler's dislike of the aristocracy in general and of the old Austrian aristocracy in particular is well known. It is not therefore surprising that he paid increasing attention to Himmler's and Heydrich's whispered accusations of a betrayal of the Reich by the Sudeten Germans. To these was added the growing concern expressed by Ribbentrop, at the time Ambassador in London, over the activities of the Sudeten German Party in Britain. Apart from his creeping desire to tell his master the sort of things Hitler wished to hear, Ribbentrop was actuated by motives of jealousy and wounded vanity. Dr. Brandt had carefully avoided any contact with the German Embassy in London, and this Ribbentrop could not forgive.

Anti-Henlein information did not reach Berlin from London alone; a lot was supplied from within the ranks of the Sudeten German Party itself by the National-Socialist wing of the Party, which had been steadily strengthening its bonds with the Reich since the beginning of 1937. Some of the information from this source was deliberately calculated to stimulate anti-Henlein feeling in Berlin. At the end of 1937 Heydrich decided that the time had come to strike against Henlein. In a memorandum to Hitler he suggested that Henlein and his friends should be deposed by means of an internal revolt within the Sudeten German Party and should be replaced by others acceptable to National-Socialism and the German Government. As suitable new leaders he suggested the so-called dissident group, which was in reality the National Socialist wing and whose newspaper was *Der Aufbruch*.

But Henlein must have received warning of these intended moves. He still felt himself strong enough to oppose the clearly recognizable wishes of German foreign policy, and he at once expelled from his Party a number of members of the dissident group, among them Rudolf Kasper, who had been ejected once from the Party but had been allowed to return. At the same time he warned the rest of the group that any deviation from the official Party line would be punished with disciplinary action. These measures prove conclusively that the Sudeten German Party was then no Fifth Column for the German National-Socialist Party in Czechoslovakia; on the contrary Henlein pursued a policy which was entirely independent and was very much at variance with the aspirations of the Third Reich, and was often directly opposed to its intentions.

The invasion of Austria, however, changed the whole situation fundamentally, and it was this alone which brought about the co-ordination of policy between the Sudeten German Party and Berlin, the last phase of which was characterized by the events of the Munich conference.   After the invasion of Austria, Czechoslovakia's encirclement by Germany was complete. A year before Hitler would have had to accept the granting of autonomy to the Sudetenland as a solution of the problem.   Now he would not even consider such a compromise, and he had his revenge for the mistaken appreciation of relative strengths which had stiffened the Benes Government.   Up to the end of 1937 Hitler was not yet clear in his own mind whether to settle with Austria or Czechoslovakia first.   He decided to intervene in Austria, and when the 'Anschluss' was accomplished with such smoothness and without any serious opposition from the Western Powers, he became more firmly convinced than ever that a complete clearing up of the Czech question could be undertaken without further delay.   The crux of his plan was the incorporation of Bohemia and Moravia into the German Reich.   The racial aspect, absorption of some three million Sudeten Germans into the population of Germany, was of secondary interest to him.   The factors which fascinated him above all were the great industrial potentialities of the two provinces and their vitally important strategic position.   He regarded both as essential to the furtherance of his plans for the domination of Europe by power.

Not only for the Czechs, but also for the Sudeten Germans themselves, this decision of Hitler was a turning point.   A complete metamorphosis took place in Henlein himself.   He found himself faced with a grave decision, which was at the same time personally and historically of the utmost importance.   Until that moment he had been unable to bring himself to accept Hitler's conception of National-Socialism and to lead the Sudeten Germans into the fold of the German Reich.   He and his colleagues were averse to National Socialism of the Hitler type. Henlein's fundamental policy had always been to achieve equality of status within the framework of the Czechoslovak State.   He had been quite sure that British and German pressure would cause the Czech Government to give way, and that the Sudetenland would be given full territorial and cultural autonomy. Now suddenly, on the very threshold of success, he saw all his work and plans shattered. What ought he to do? Should he retire from the political stage or by going abroad disassociate himself finally and publicly from Hitler's intentions? Or should he remain at his post, and participate in the inevitable? After a bitter internal struggle he decided to throw his old principles overboard. He accepted Hitler's conception that autonomy for the Sudetenland must now be regarded as out of date and that every effort must be made to attach it to the German Reich. With this decision the independent policy of Henlein himself and of the Sudeten German Party came to its end.

A conference was held in Berlin on 29th March, 1938, attended by Ribbentrop, Under Secretary of State von Mackensen, Baron von Weizsaecker, the German Ambassador to Prague Ernst Eisenlohr, a few other diplomats, the Chief of the Liaison Office for German Minorities Abroad S.S. Colonel Lorenz, Professor Haushofer the geopolitician, and finally Henlein, Frank and other leaders of the Sudeten German Party. The instructions given to Henlien by Hitler were repeated to all. The expression 'instructions' was literally used at the conference. It was the first time that Hitler found himself in a position to give orders to the leaders of the Sudeten Germans. Ribbentrop stated that the Sudeten German Party must draw up a programme of minimum demands, the ultimate goal of which was to be the absolute independence of the Sudeten German people. It must not accept mere promises by the Czech Government, as this might give the impression abroad that a solution had been accepted which only partly satisfied Sudeten German demands. In their negotiations with the Government the Sudeten German Party should increase their demands step by step while keeping them abstract. Finally he instructed Henlein to keep in the closest touch with him and with the German Ambassador in Prague.

Details of this conference were obtained from a document found later in the German Foreign Office by the Russians and published by them.

When Henlein returned from his talks with Hitler and Ribbentrop he gave his immediate colleagues a precise résumé of the situation. The future path of the Sudeten German Party was now evident. A programme based on Hitler's orders was drawn up, and in April 1938 the details were made public by Henlein in a speech at Karlsbad. This 'Karlsbad Programme' became the basis of all subsequent negotiations with the Czechoslovak Government. The acceptance of its demands would have secured complete autonomy for the Sudeten Germans; and it would also have necessitated radical changes in the structure of the Czechoslovak State.

Henlein's Karlsbad speech, which denoted a complete acceptance of Hitler's instructions did not however, suffice to stifle the mistrust of his enemies in Hitler's entourage. Heydrich in a memorandum to Hitler said that it was significant that Henlein's first real adherence to Nazi Germany had come only after the invasion of Austria and after receipt of very precise instructions from Hitler, that Henlein would support German policy only under pressure and never from conviction, and that Frank, a man of very different views and character, had made a much better impression at the Berlin conference than had Henlein.

Thus it was that Frank became more and more an opponent of Henlein, not as the result of any intriguing on his own part, but simply because he had been recommended to Hitler as the only man who could be really trusted to support and further German policy. Heydrich indeed suggested at the time that after the solution of the Czech problem Henlein should be side-tracked to some high and honorary appointment and the authoritative power be vested in Frank.

In the spring of 1938 the situation in Czechoslovakia became more critical than ever. The Czech Government showed no desire for conciliation and increased its pressure against the Sudeten Germans, who closed their ranks more firmly in response. The Bund der Landwirte (The Farmers' Association) and the Deutsche Christlichsoziale Volkspartei (The German Christian Social Peoples' Party) amalgamated with the Sudeten German Party, and only the Social Democrats were missing from a completely unified front. The various other minorities in the State also began to coalesce. Representatives of the Sudeten German Party were, it is true, sent to Rome to ask the Vatican to advise the Slovak Catholics to make contact with their German co-religionists; but the actual collaboration between the Party and the Slovaks was brought about by direct negotiation. The readiness of the minorities in Hungary and Poland to co-operate required, on the other hand, instructions from Budapest and Warsaw before it could be translated into action. The initiative was taken by the Sudeten German Party, and in particular by Rutha, who had ambitious visions of a new National Federation of Central Europe, which would not, however, entail the dismemberment of the Czechoslovak State; he was strongly supported by Ernst Kundt and by Frank himself. Through the intermediary of friends in Vienna the protagonists of the Sudeten German Party's programme made contact with Count Istvan Bethlen and Kalman Kanya, the Foreign Minister in Budapest. Through the good offices of Jan Gavronsky, the Polish Ambassador in Vienna, they likewise established touch with Warsaw. Henlein also had a personal meeting with the latter at Count Khuen's estate near Znaim. Complete success was achieved; the Hungarians and Poles in Czechoslovakia agreed to participate at once in common consultation and action; the unity of the minorities was complete.

In spite of the incorporation of the Sudeten German Party into the N.S.D.A.P., Henlein went once more to London to establish contact with leading British statesmen. On his return he was subjected by Heydrich's men to the most vigorous interrogation to find out whether he had committed himself in any way to any sort of undertaking. Nothing, apparently, could allay Himmler's and Heydrich's distrust of Henlein. Again and again they warned Hitler against the possibility that he might break away and with Britain's help even now come to an agreement with the Czech Government hostile to the interests of the German Reich. Impressed by these repeated warnings, Hitler decided in the summer of 1938 personally to initiate unofficial Anglo-German talks and thus to short circuit Henlein.

The originator of this idea was a woman. She bore the name of one of the oldest and most respected noble families of Europe —the Hohenlohe, although she herself, née Richter, was a commoner. When Stephanie Hohenlohe first met Hitler she was some forty years of age, intelligent and full of ambition. The introduction was effected by Hitler's A.D.C. Captain

Wiedemann, who, as a Staff Officer of the List Regiment, had been Hitler's superior officer during the first war. Stephanie Hohenlohe's dream was to play an important part in high politics through her connection with Hitler, and there is no doubt that for a time she did exercise a measure of influence on his outlook on foreign affairs. She had good connections with the noble families of Europe and with the aristocracy of Great Britain. She was thus able to furnish Hitler and his closest colleagues with many most valuable contacts. From the moment that she arranged for Lord Rothermere to visit Hitler she became a favourite adviser.

At that time Hitler held her in great respect. As residence he told Wiedemann to place Schloss Leopoldskron, Max Reinhardt's castle near Salzburg, at her disposal, and there she lived in great style. For a while the Leopoldskron became a sort of elegant ante-chamber to Hitler's own Berghof, and many and important were the meetings held there. On one occasion she had the hardihood to have the local Gauleiter flung out of the Castle. Contrary to all expectation she received Hitler's support and approbation in her subsequent defiance of him.

Heydrich, however, was watching the growing influence and the restless activity of the Princess Hohenlohe with distrust and not a little jealousy. It did not take him long to gather 'material' against her. But during the summer of 1938 she still retained a great influence over the Fuehrer. She persuaded him that the best method of paving the way for the desired talks with Britain would be to send someone, wholly unconnected with the diplomatic world, as the private representative of the Head of the German State. She said that the man best qualified for the job was Wiedemann.

Had Hitler really been in earnest on the subject of Anglo-German talks, even an inefficient underling could doubtless have succeeded in preparing the ground. But the whole idea suffered from one fatal weakness; it did not fit in with Hitler's real intentions, but was simply the result of a whim conceived under the skilful influence of Stephanie Hohenlohe. The failure of his mission cannot therefore be attributed to inefficiency on his part. Even so Wiedemann's visit in conjunction with the activities of the Sudeten German Party in London, caused

Britain to go a step further in the Czechoslovak question and send Lord Runciman to Czechoslovakia.

This was as pleasing to Henlein and his moderate wing of the Sudeten German Party as it was displeasing to Hitler and his immediate advisers. An interesting light on the German attitude is shed by a report which Lipski, the Polish Ambassador, sent to Beck of his conversation on the subject with Goering, and which the Russians later published. In this conversation Goering is reported to have said that he and the German Government did not believe that Runciman's mission would achieve any success and were therefore of the opinion that the Czech question could only be settled by force. The report then went on to describe a talk with the American Ambassador in Berlin, who had just returned to his post from a visit to Benes. Benes had told him in confidence, Lipski reported, that far from being willing to grant the Sudeten Germans any measure of autonomy, he was averse even to giving them any status as 'Staatsvolk' (Lipski used the German expression). And this—just a few short weeks before Munich! These statements bear eloquent witness to the grotesque and quite unintentional inter-play between the policies of Hitler and Benes. For different reasons, both seemed to work against a peaceful solution.

The British Government was kept well informed by its excellent intelligence service of the contrasting attitudes of the Sudeten German Party and Berlin towards the Runciman mission, but was not sure of the line Henlein would adopt. Colonel Christie was accordingly instructed to try and find out what his real opinion and intentions were. Henlein agreed to a meeting, but was compelled to postpone it several times. At the end of March he had given his allegiance to Hitler, and he felt therefore constrained to get new and precise instructions before seeing Christie. At the end of July 1938 he had his chance, when he attended a big German Sports Festival at Breslau, at which he was able to have a long and unfettered conversation with his new master.

The outcome of his conversation became immediately apparent when Henlein finally met Christie in Zurich at the beginning of August. Dr. Walther Brandt, lieutenant of Henlein, told me what happened at this meeting. His moderate attitude was gone, and he declared at once that the Sudeten German Party could wait no longer, that the Czechs must cede forthwith, and that Hitler, his patience at last exhausted, would not hesitate to use force if necessary to achieve a swift and final decision. So the independent leader of the Sudeten German Party became Hitler's mouthpiece.

Christie appears to have been taken completely aback at this new Henlein, and in his report to Vansittart he declared that Britain now had little or no time in which to achieve a peaceful settlement.

On 15th September Chamberlain flew to Berchtesgaden, and events followed each other in rapid succession. Henlein interpreted the visit of the Prime Minister—rightly, in theory—as a sign that the British were about to give way to German demands. He now saw the way clear for the fulfilment of the task imposed upon him, and on the same day, in a speech to the Sudeten German people, he launched his slogan 'Heim ins Reich' (Back to the Reich!). Czech reaction was instantaneous. The Sudeten German Party was declared illegal, and a warrant was issued for Henlein's arrest. These measures were quickly modified into an order for the cessation of all activity by the Sudeten German Party and proceedings against Henlein under the Defence of the State Act. The mobilization of the Czech army and the calling up of several classes of reservists were countered by Henlein with the formation of a Sudeten German Volunteer Corps. At the same time the leaders of the Sudeten German Party did their utmost to prevent clashes between their own men and the Czech forces, which might have led to immediate war. Whether this forbearance on their part met with Hitler's approval is very questionable.

Kundt issued an earnest appeal in the name of the Sudeten Party for calm, pending the results of the Chamberlain-Hitler talks. But after Godesberg many responsible leaders of the Sudeten German Party could not overcome their concern lest the policy followed might still result in a general catastrophe. Berlin on the other hand feared a settlement. The previous attempts to reach a settlement led the Nazis to squeeze Henlein and his supporters out systematically. His appointment as

Gauleiter of the relatively unimportant *Sudetengau* was recognition of a kind but his closest colleagues were all swept aside, and some of them, including Dr. Brandt, were flung into concentration camps. Hermann Frank, on the other hand, who had slavishly followed Hitler's orders and opposed Henlein, now reaped the reward for his services. He was earmarked for high office; and when the Czech State had been finally liquidated, his appointment as German Minister of State made him, next to the Reichsprotector, the most important man in the land.

Many contemporary observers regarded the Munich agreement as the greatest German triumph in foreign affairs since the time of Bismarck. Not so Hitler; there is no doubt that in September 1938 he had already decided to 'solve' the Czech problem by seizing the whole of the Czechoslovak Republic, and Munich was therefore nothing more than a compromise. It has been repeatedly asserted that a group of German officers, encouraged by their conviction that the German people did not want war, planned to seize Hitler's sabotage of the peaceful solution as a pretext to organize a *putsch* and overthrow him, and that their enterprise was only foiled at the last minute by the decision of the British to give way and by Chamberlain's visit to Munich. Churchill himself, as can be seen from his memoirs, believed seriously in the possibility of some such action.

It would be premature to try and pronounce a final verdict on the German resistance movement now, while the knowledge of their activities and intentions still remains far from complete. But it can be said that this alleged officers' plot of September 1938 need not be taken very seriously. First mention of it is made by Gisevius in his book *To the Bitter End*. It attracted considerable attention abroad and has been very greatly exaggerated. I have spoken to responsible individuals alleged to have been party to the plot or who would certainly have known about it. I am satisfied that no plot with any serious chance of success ever existed. It is true that men like General Ludwig Beck, the Chief of the General Staff, and other German Staff Officers were horrified at the frivolous gambling which characterized all Hitler's political activities and which was quite incompatible with their conception of the attitude of a responsible statesman; but Beck had resigned a month before, and his successor, General

Franz Halder, was not the sort of man who would have plotted from the very beginning to get rid of Hitler. It is not possible to imagine him as the head of any conspiracy. Brauchitsch, the Commander-in-Chief, and other senior Generals equally never had any earnest wish to depose Hitler by a military *putsch*. Gisevius' assertion was supported in 1945 by certain staff officers; but this they did merely because they thought that by portraying their senior officers as pillars of the opposition against Hitler they would be rendering the Wehrmacht and themselves a service. Many of them retracted when they realized that participation in a plot of that kind was no recommendation in British or American eyes. In the interest of historical accuracy it must be categorically asserted that at the time of the Czech crisis no serious plot against Hitler existed either in the Wehrmacht or anywhere else. Senior military officers certainly disapproved of Hitler's policy and in the privacy of their own circle undoubtedly expressed their disapproval. Equally certain it is that many regarded Hitler as a fatal menace. But any idea of removing him forcibly did not get beyond the stage of secret discussion at that time. To discern the real activities of the genuine opposition group from those subsequently attributed to it is a task for the historian of the future.

In October 1938 the world at large hoped that peace for many years to come had been assured by the Munich Agreement, and it took Hitler at his word, when he declared that he now had no further claims whatever against the Czech State. In reality, however, Hitler had not the slightest intention of abandoning his real goal, which was the seizure of Bohemia and Moravia. There is no doubt that the occupation of Prague, the subsequent setting-up of an independent Slovakia and the ceding of the Carpatho-Ukraine to Hungary were not improvisations of the moment, but the outcome of a plan long since worked out.

So much has already been written about the annihilation of the remnants of the Czechoslovak State that any repetition here would be superfluous. But one particular incident, which occurred immediately before the entry of the German troops into Bohemia and Moravia, is worthy of mention, for it is both little known and of singular significance. The new Czech Government under the Premiership of Rudolf Beran had been informed by its Intelligence Service, probably about the beginning of February, of Hitler's intention to march on Prague. The Czech Foreign Minister, Chvalkovsky, who previously had been Ambassador in Berlin and was well acquainted with the workings of Hitler's mind, suggested to the Premier that one last attempt should be made to thwart the proposed German action. It was agreed that some special envoy with personal friends in Berlin would stand more chance of success than a highly placed official plenipotentiary, and the choice fell on the Chief Clerk of the Foreign Ministry, Dr. Hubert Masaryk (not to confuse with Jan Masaryk, the son of the President). From a previously held post, Dr. Masaryk knew the permanent adviser to the Czech Section of the German Foreign Ministry, and kept in friendly touch with him. At the end of February having announced his arrival by 'phone, Masaryk called on his friend in the Wilhelm-strasse and asked him straight out what Germany's intentions were as regards Czechoslovakia? The latter could only reiterate that the answer to such a question was beyond both his competence and his knowledge. Masaryk assured him that he fully appreciated that Germany might well feel resentful towards Czechoslovakia; but his Chief, the Foreign Minister, he continued, was nevertheless ready to make a clean break with the past and to seek an understanding on all issues and on the broadest possible basis, to ensure a closer relationship with the Reich. He next went on to elaborate Chvalkovsky's proposals which were—a reorientation of Czech foreign policy to conform with that of Berlin, the conclusion of a Customs Union, far-reaching legal rectifications and the appointment of a German Military Mission as a safeguard against Czech aggression.

The German diplomat pointed out that discussion of such questions was far outside the province of his competence and that the proposals should be brought to the notice of the Foreign Minister or of Hitler himself; and this he was prepared to arrange as quickly as possible. Masaryk replied that he, too, was authorized to negotiate with Ribbentrop or Hitler on the subject.

The Councillor then conferred with the Under-Secretary of State, Dr. Weizsaecker, who without delay passed on a detailed report incorporating the Czech proposals to the Foreign Minister, with the request that he should himself receive Masaryk and conduct any further negotiations deemed desirable. Ribbentrop's reply was: 'The Councillor will kindly have the goodness to throw Masaryk out.' Even so, the Councillor did not give up. In conjunction with some other members of the Foreign Ministry he prepared a second report, in which all the advantages inherent in the Czech proposals were described at great length, and sent it, with the approval of the Under-Secretary of State, once more to the Foreign Minister. Ribbentrop, of course, had one of his customary paroxysms of rage when he found that his orders had not been instantly obeyed. But then he thought better of it and, fearing probably that the case might be brought to Hitler's notice through some other channel, he capitulated to the obstinacy of his subordinates and submittted both memoranda to Hitler.

Hitler must have read them about the beginning of March 1939. A week after the occupation of Bohemia and Moravia they were returned by the Foreign Ministry representative in the Reich-Chancellery, Walter Hewel, with the remark: 'The Fuehrer is not interested.' The Fuehrer was, indeed, not interested. He had no desire to see his 'final solution' of the Czech question (which, since Munich, was no longer a question, unless Berlin desired to make it so) spoiled by a dull and inglorious peaceful settlement; and so the hand of conciliation was roughly and frivolously rejected.

It will be remembered that Hitler justified his action against Prague in March 1939 by stating, among other things, that when Slovakia declared itself independent the Czechoslovak State had ceased to exist. What caused this declaration which contributed so largely to the violent end of the Czechoslovak Republic? It has already been shown how the Sudeten Germans' claims had awakened similar aspirations among the other minorities. This was particularly so in the case of the Slovaks who from 1938 onwards had become increasingly active and passionately resented the spread of Czech ideas and customs over Slovak territories. In this struggle they enjoyed the great advantage that the entire people, with the exception of a small pro-Czech and predominantly non-Catholic minority, was united in one single Party, the Slovak Peoples' Party, under the leadership of the Catholic priest, Andrei Hlinka, and they were further strengthened by the support of the Catholic Church. As in Slovakia, learning and intelligence was almost an exclusive monopoly of the clergy. It was evitable that the leaders of the Peoples' Party should be priests of the Catholic Church; apart from Hlinka, Dr. Tiso, who later became President, and nearly all the other political leaders of any importance were priests. This clerical bias in its political leadership tended, of course, to emphasize the undoubted antagonism which already existed between the devoutly Catholic Slovak people and the Czechs with their Hussite traditions and their strongly anti-clerical, free-thinking upper classes.

As a political organization Hlinka's party represented the overwhelming majority of the Slovak people in much the same way as the Sudeten German Party was the representative of the German population of the Republic. While Hlinka and the actual leaders of the People's Party regarded a far-reaching autonomy within the framework of the Czechoslovak State as the goal of their aspirations, a certain radical element, led by Professor Vojtech Tuka, strove to set up an independent sovereign Slovak State. Tuka, who had previously been sentenced to ten years' penal servitude on this very account, had become after his release a particularly implacable enemy of the Czech Republic.

Early 1938 saw the beginning of a close collaboration between the Slovak Peoples' Party, the Hungarian and Polish minorities and the Sudeten German Party. The Karlsbad programme had not been drawn up without consulting the other minorities, and in it the ideas of the latter had received ample consideration. A mixed committee was given the task of preparing by the autumn of 1938 a statute for all nationalities of the State based on self-government and autonomy, which was not only to apply to the minorities in Czechoslovakia, but also to serve as a model for all minorities throughout Europe. But these activities were rendered meaningless by the Munich agreement.

After the Munich agreement, Prague was compelled to grant autonomy to the Slovaks. The first grave crisis which faced the newly-formed Slovak State was a claim by Hungary for far-reaching frontier revision.

Hungary claimed a territory occupied by a million inhabitants and comprising half of Slovakia. Tiso's Government in Bratislava declared itself ready to cede the Gross Schutt island in the Danube, whose hundred thousand inhabitants were predominantly Magyars, but the Hungarians, naturally, were not content with this, and the negotiations continued to drag on. All this placed Germany in an awkward situation. The sympathies of Berlin inclined towards the Slovaks rather than the Hungarians. But the Hungarians were exceptionally stubborn, and their experienced diplomats found little difficulty in persuading Italy and Poland to support their case. As both these countries at the time exercised a considerable influence on German foreign policy, the latter eventually agreed to a settlement by arbitration. The ruling, given on 2nd November, 1938, and known as the First Vienna Award, granted almost all the Hungarian demands.

The Slovak State, however, survived this crisis, and pro-German sentiment in the country was not seriously jeopardized by the Vienna disappointment. But at the beginning of 1939 the crisis once more became acute. Tuka and Sano Mach, the then Propaganda Minister, advocated with increasing vehemence the complete separation of Slovakia from the Czechoslovak Republic.

The Slovak Autonomous Government at first gave no official expression of opinion on the subject, but gave us to understand that it was most anxious to keep in the closest possible touch with Germany. As they had no diplomatic representation in Berlin, the Bratislava Government established contact with the German Secret Service and the Nazi Party centres in Vienna.

The Slovak move for complete independence, as personified by Tuka and Mach, was a most important element in Hitler's planning against the remnants of the Czechoslovak State. The complete separation of Slovakia from the Czechs and the request of the newly-founded State for German protection were to be both the justification for German action and the signal for the march on Prague. Slovak independence, therefore, was a thing Hitler needed, and in order to force the Slovaks to decisive action, he took secret steps of his own.

As secrecy and surprise were essential to the success of his plans, Hitler decided to say nothing to his Foreign Ministry.

He instructed us in the Secret Service, the Secretary of State, Keppler (whose liaison with the Foreign Ministry was purely nominal and who could be relied on to say nothing) and Keppler's assistant, Veesenmeyer, to work out the precise details on which his plan would be based. At the end of January 1939 members of the Secret Service were received by Hitler and ordered so to accelerate matters that by the end of March it would be possible to set up the independent Slovak State. At this conference he stressed that his instructions were so secret that no Ministry or Office of the Reich or Wehrmacht was to be given any information at all.

Immediately afterwards, at the beginning of February, we held a meeting near Bratislava with those Slovak leaders who were to co-operate with the German Secret Service. We agents found the Slovaks eager to fall in with our plans. It transpired that the moderate wing of the Slovak Government had, with few exceptions, abandoned its objections to the complete withdrawal of Slovakia from the Czechoslovak State. This decisive reversal of policy found expression in the refusal by Premier Tiso and practically all his Ministers to attend a conference in Prague on 8th March.

The Czechoslovak Government now had no alternative but to act, unless prepared to sacrifice the unity of the remnant of the State. It removed Tiso and the majority of his colleagues from office and appointed Josef Sivak, a member of Parliament, as Prime Minister of Slovakia. Martial law was declared in Pressburg and one or two other towns, and strategic points were occupied by the Czech army. The Hlinka Guard and the Local Volunteers of the Carpatho-German Party were disarmed, and Tuka, Mach and a number of other Slovak leaders were arrested.

The situation was now extremely involved, and it became more so than ever between 9th March and 13th. There were now two Slovak Governments, each claiming to be the legal instrument. Although the vast majority of the Slovak people was behind Tiso, it did nothing whatever to support him, and this passivity was a great hindrance to Hitler's plans. On Heydrich's suggestion he ordered that a few S.S. Commandos should be sent illegally into Slovakia to try and stir the Slovaks from their lethargy by a series of acts of terrorism. The situation was further complicated by the fact that the initial energy shown by the Prague Government soon waned. No further clear instructions were being isssued. By now it was generally realized that not only the fate of Slovakia, but the whole unity of the Czechoslovak people was at stake.

The Germans decided to use Tiso as a partner. On 9th March the latter had withdrawn to his parish, where he felt himself more secure from arrest by the Czechs. On the night of 12-13th March I was one of two members of the German Secret Service who visited Tiso and suggested that he should get in touch with other Slovak leaders in Pressburg, form a new Government under his own leadership and proclaim the sovereign independence of Slovakia under German protection. Tiso accepted. In the early morning of 13th March he reached agreement with the other Slovak leaders and said that he was ready to proclaim the independence of Slovakia.

In the meanwhile, however, President Hacha and his Foreign Minister, Chvalkovsky, had asked Hitler to receive them in Berlin. This meant that Hitler could not postpone the desired solution much longer. Time pressed. Before Hacha and Chvalkovsky arrived in the Chancellery to hear his decision, the independent Slovakia must be an established fact. If it were not, a vital link in the chain of events would be missing. It was a question of hours. On the morning of 13th March Tiso received an invitation from Hitler to visit him, and with Durcansky he flew at once to Berlin by special plane. Before leaving he had agreed on the action to be taken by the other Slovak leaders. At seven o'clock in the evening—the time arranged for Tiso's interview with Hitler—at a mass meeting in Bratislava the setting up of an independent State would be proclaimed.

A grotesque incident ensued. On 8th March a proclamation prohibiting public meetings in Slovakia had been issued. The Bratislava Police decided to break up the mass meeting. The obedient and placid Slovak people accordingly went their way. At the last second the solemn proclamation of Slovak independence all but came to nothing. There was no bloodshed. German S.S. Commandos were at hand but they were not called upon to act.

On the demand of Tiso and with the sanction of President

Hacha and his Foreign Minister, the Slovak Parliament held a formal session on 14th March at which the Slovak State became independent. Tiso was elected President and Prime Minister.

An independent Slovak State was therefore set up by Germany as a pretext for the march on Prague. Hacha and Chvalkovsky were not received by Hitler until 14th March, and on the 15th they concluded the treaty by which the Czech people were also placed under the protection of the German Reich. The occupation of Bohemia and Moravia by German troops was carried out without incident, and in a few days the Czechoslovak Republic ceased to exist.

CHAPTER VIII

THE SAPPING OF YUGOSLAVIA

YUGOSLAVIA arose from the wreck of the Austro-Hungarian monarchy. Its three small nations—the Serbs, the Croats and the Slovenes—were ruled by a Serb Royal House, which tried to unite them in a healthy federation. Between the wars the Serbs and Croats in particular lived in a perpetual feud, which culminated on 20th July, 1928, in the murder by a Serb fanatic of Stjepan Radic, the leader of the Croat Peasant Party during a session of the Yugoslav Parliament in Belgrade.

Instead of trying to conciliate the warring nationalities in his realm, King Alexander felt that drastic measures were necessary if the State were to be saved. Accordingly, on 6th January, 1929, he suspended the constitution and proclaimed a royal dictatorship, thereby signing his own death warrant. Croat national feeling immediately became inflamed. A radical group, whose demands exceeded those of the Peasants' Party, appeared on the scene. Shortly after the murder of Radic, a Croat lawyer and Member of Parliament, Dr. Ante Pavelic, founded the Ustase or Insurgents with the object of founding a separate Croat State. Pavelic, a thickset, grim-faced revolutionary and nationalist, had always been an opponent of the Yugoslav conception. As long ago as 1918 he had been fighting against the fusion of the Croats and the Serbs; he was one of the leading members of the Croat Sokol, which, like its counterpart in Bohemia and Moravia, was a nationalist movement with strong pan-slav tendencies. On the collapse of the Austro-Hungarian monarchy the Sokol in Croatia became a cover organization for anti-Yugoslav activities and later furnished the majority of the nationalist leaders from within its ranks. Apart from the Ustase, Pavelic also organized the Croat Home Guard (Hrvatski Domobran), composed for the most part of students and later destined to play an important part in the foundation of the Croat State.

In 1929 Pavelic succeeded in avoiding arrest by fleeing to Germany. He was informed that his presence there was not welcome and went on to Italy in 1930. The Fascist Government received him most cordially and supported him so that he was soon able to organize several training camps for his Croat youth, who had emigrated in large numbers. Similar camps also existed in Hungary. In the old Austro-Hungarian monarchy the Croats had enjoyed a considerable measure of autonomy, and the Hungarian Regent, Admiral Horthy, probably in the hope that an independent Croatia would once again turn towards Hungary, showed great sympathy towards Pavelic's aspirations.

Pavelic himself was anxious to attract world attention to the Croat problem and he decided to try and achieve this end by means of acts of sabotage and terrorism. These tactics had a certain success. The squads trained in the Ustase camps in Italy for this purpose carried out a series of planned and co-ordinated sabotage acts against railways and other Government installations, which caused considerable alarm.

For the furtherance of his objects Pavelic had also concluded a species of agreement with the I.M.R.O. (The Inner Macedonian Revolutionary Organization)—the most powerful secret society ever formed in the Balkans. He was already friendly with many of the leaders of I.M.R.O., for in his capacity as a lawyer he had some time previously defended certain I.M.R.O. members accused in the Skoplje Courts and in the Balkans friendship which has been welded by an action such as this, plays a most important part in the political arena. In addition to all this, a number of other national groups of the most varied character found common cause in the struggle against the King's dictatorship. I have received an account of the events that led up to the Marseilles assassination from Vancho Mihailoff, himself the Leader of the I.M.R.O., who is alive to-day, and leading I.M.R.O. men have been less reserved and told me of their part in planning the actual assassination.

As the crux of all his activities Pavelic desired to remove King Alexander, the symbol of Serbian suzerainty, by assassination. The shock caused by such a deed, he hoped, would immediately raise the Croat question to a position of European prominence. His preparations to this end dragged on for month after month, but action invariably had to be postponed. Finally it was decided to make the attempt on the occasion of the King's State visit to France. At the last moment, however, it was found that the Ustase had at its disposal no assassin sufficiently skilled to undertake the task with any certainty of success. In this dilemma Pavelic appealed to I.M.R.O. for the loan of some of its specialists. I.M.R.O. originally had no intention of taking any part in the attempt but their many years of experience in terrorist activities had left them well supplied with any number of skilled assassins, and out of friendship for Pavelic they readily acceded to his request. The Ustase then carried out its plot with loaned principals, supported by subordinates trained in the training camp at Janka Puszta in Hungary and close to the Yugoslav frontier.

The plot succeeded, and King Alexander and the French Foreign Minister Jean Barthou were murdered on 9th October, 1934, in Marseilles. The expected repercussions focused public opinion and the Press throughout the world on the Croat problem. The politico-economic credit of Yugoslavia sank sharply in Western Europe and the question began frequently to be asked whether after all the Yugoslav State in its present form could in practice be maintained. The efforts of the police to ascertain who were the instigators of the assassination were nullified by Mussolini's refusal to hand Pavelic over to Yugoslavia. The Ustase camps in Hungary and Italy admittedly had to be broken up, and in Italy such trainees as had not already scattered to safety were interned in the Lipari Islands. But the real leaders of the Ustase spread and settled all over Europe and continued their propaganda in favour of an independent Croatia.

From Croatia itself great numbers of Ustase adherents and other Croat nationalist bodies were now compelled to emigrate. Police repressive action, already rigorous, was now sharpened, and very few had the hardihood to stay at home and face it. The most notable among these emigrants were Slavko Kvaternik, an ex-Colonel of the Imperial Austrian Army who later played a leading part in events, Dr. Budak and Professor Lukas. Of the Ustase leaders spread over Europe the most important were Dr. Artukovic, Dr. Lorcovic, Dr. Vrancic and a number of Croat ex-Officers of the Austrian Army who had been in exile

5

since 1918—among them Colonel Percevic, who later became the Head of Pavelic's Military Chancellery.

Shortly before his death King Alexander had decided to modify his rule of dictatorship and to restore a portion of the suspended individual rights according to the constitution, and the Regency Council, consisting of Prince Paul, Dr. Stankovic and Dr. Perovic, adhered to this policy. In 1935 a general election took place. The Yugoslav opposition formed itself into one electoral *bloc*, the Parliamentary Secretary of which was Radic's successor and former secretary, Dr. Macek. Macek was justified in regarding himself as the representative of the Croat people, for his Party, the Croat Peasant Party (H.S.S.) was, as it always had been, by far the strongest Croat group in Parliament. It had expanded into a multi-lateral and powerful organization which stretched into the most isolated villages and embraced practically the whole territory occupied by Croats. In practice there was no Opposition. The Ustase were certainly more radical in their outlook but they did not at that time oppose the H.S.S. and the supporters of a pro-Yugoslav solution of the Croat question were only a minority.

The essential difference between the H.S.S. and the Ustase was that the former represented the broad masses while the latter was a self-contained shock-unit which regarded itself as a *corps d'élite* and therefore the obvious choice for the leadership of the nation. It was composed for the most part of intellectuals, students and a sprinkling of young clergy. The majority of the clergy, however, favoured the Peasant Party albeit unobtrusively. There is nevertheless no doubt that the Catholic Church threw the weight of its very considerable influence into the scales in favour of Croat autonomy. In the few corners into which the Peasant Party had not penetrated there was always a Catholic priest to distribute and propound Catholic brochures and the Catholic Calendar, and even the declaration of Catholic faith was itself in many ways propaganda in favour of Croat national aspirations, for the Serb oppressors were to a man members of the orthodox Pravoslav Church. This was fully realized in Belgrade, and the police measures of the Belgrade Government were directed equally against the Catholic Church and the political organizations of the Croats.

Events in 1938 and 1939 were also a turning-point for Yugoslavia although the country was not itself directly affected. The absorption of Austria, and later of Bohemia and Moravia, into the Great German Reich rendered meaningless the conception of the Little Entente. Yugoslavia's external guarantees were destroyed and a complete re-orientation of policy became imperative. This was undertaken by Dr. Stoyadinovic who had been Head of the Belgrade Government since 1935. He was in no way the Quisling which his opponents have made him out to be—a man willing to sell his country to the Germans for his own personal advantage. His appreciation of the European political situation led this shrewd and most able politician to the conclusion that in the political game his country must put its money on the German card. The astounding docility of the Western Powers as regards Hitler appeared to justify his conviction, and he certainly cannot be blamed if he could see no limit to their supine policy of continual surrender. Even so he did not break the threads of his contacts with friends in London and Paris, while he still maintained deliberately and with great skill good and cordial relations with Germany. Public opinion in Yugoslavia was overwhelmingly in favour of the new policy and when Stoyadinovic was finally overthrown, it was not on account of his foreign policy but because of certain internal events to which he had paid too little attention. The election in December 1938 was a victory for the combined Opposition in Yugoslavia which under Macek's leadership had presented a united front, not excluding the Serb opposition groups, since 1935. It was then that the Peasant Party celebrated its greatest triumph.

Stoyadinovic's successor, Dragisa Cvetkovic, realized that the State could be solidly unified and he himself could remain in power only if he succeeded in reaching an agreement with the Croats. One of his most important intermediaries in his negotiations with the Croats was the Serb politician Mihajlo Konstantinovic. Thanks to his French connections—he had fought as a volunteer for France in the first war—he could be sure of France's blessing on the agreement which was eventually reached. On the eve of the Second World War on 26th August, 1939, Cvetkovic and Macek met at the summer residence of the

Prince Regent in Bled and signed the so-called Sporazum—the treaty of equality which was to be the beginning of a reconciliation between the two peoples. The Croats were given an 'Area of Jurisdiction'—a corporate administrative territory which with the exception of certain parts of Bosnia and Herzegovina and the coastal area gave the Croats everything to which they had laid claim. Within the confines of the Area of Jurisdiction the Croats enjoyed a measure of local autonomy, and in return they solemnly agreed to recognize the Common State and the dynasty.

The Yugoslav policy of *rapprochement* with Germany had one determined and dangerous enemy—the Serbian Corps of Officers. It was difficult for any Yugoslav Government to steer a course which did not meet with the approval of the Officers' Corps. As early as the spring of 1940 General Dusan Simovic, the Chief of the General Staff, appeared on the scene as the spokesman of the strongest group of Serb Officers who were opposed to a *rapprochement* with Germany. Simovic was a Serb imperialist like the majority of his brother officers and like them he too harboured aspirations for Yugoslavia which were quite beyond the capacity of the State to realize. To this was added an at times quite naïve approach to foreign affairs. Characteristic of both these traits are the plans which Simovic propagated in the spring of 1940. The presence of the so-styled Weygand Army in Syria gave him the idea that now was Yugoslavia's opportunity—with Turkish help—to take Bulgaria in a pincer grip and compel her to settle all points at issue between the two countries in favour of Yugoslavia. At the same time Yugoslavia should march against the Italians in Albania and bring that country wholly within the sphere of Yugoslav influence. Simovic submitted these plans to the Prince Regent but with that highly cultured, peace-loving, unsoldierly and somewhat hesitant and cautious personage he had no success. Nevertheless he did succeed in sending delegations of military observers both to Ankara and to Weygand, and in obtaining sanction for a modified trial mobilization of the Yugoslav Army.

This partial success cost him dear. For (masterly though he may have been as a conspirator) Simovic was less than mediocre as a Staff Officer. Through lack of trained Staff officers in the various military reserve Inspectorates the trial mobilization led to an indescribable confusion, and this gave the Prince Regent the welcome excuse to remove Simovic for inefficiency and to give him instead command of the relatively unimportant Army Corps at Sarajevo. In actual fact, the General never took up the appointment. He went on sick leave and with his friend General Mirkovic began at once to lay the foundations of the conspiracy which led to the *coup d'état* in January 1941.

The events which now took place in Belgrade would to-day be called a 'cold war'. The diplomatic representatives of the Great Powers stood aside but the various Secret Services had a battle royal fought out in the dark back-alleys of the political stage. The Intelligence Service, the Deuxième Bureau and even the Italians had a considerable start on the Germans. For many years they had had at their disposal a whole network of agents spread over the entire country, while the German Secret Service only started to organize in 1938, when South-eastern Europe became a new field of activity for German policy. This start could never be overhauled. Right up to the first years of the war the German Secret Service had too little means at its disposal to be able successfully to combat its opponents. And an even greater handicap was the difference of opinion existing between the Secret Service and the Foreign Ministry, particularly Ribbentrop and his immediate advisers. As a result many promising plans of the Secret Service could not be put into operation, and the upshot was not infrequently an inter-departmental tussle which to all practical purposes stultified the whole German activity in Yugoslavia. To offset this, however, there existed a complete identity of view between the military and the political branches of the Secret Service itself.

It is appropriate at this juncture to say a few words about the attitude adopted by the various German leaders towards Yugo-slavia and its problems. When in 1938 it became, as one might say, fashionable in Germany to take an interest in South-eastern Europe and in Yugoslavia in particular, the vast majority of German leaders showed themselves to be pro-Serb. At their head stood Goering who had been given a rousing welcome when he went to Belgrade as German representative at the funeral of King Alexander, and had since then cherished a warm liking for the Serbs. He had also heard a good deal about the brave fight put up by the Serbs in the first war against overwhelming Austro-German superiority, and this had greatly impressed him.

Franz Neuhausen, the German Consul-General whose opinions Goering valued highly, held the same views. When Goering visited Yugoslavia in June 1935, Neuhausen arranged a series of sumptuous receptions and glittering parades in his honour which delighted Goering and made of him a friend for life. Indeed it was Goering who secured his nomination as Consul-General although he had frequently been warned against the man's bad character. Even when the Secret Service produced photographic copies of Neuhausen's conviction in Sofia to five years' imprisonment on a charge of fraud, Goering did not alter his attitude towards the man, and when the British Secret Service distributed hundreds of thousands of copies of this conviction throughout Yugoslavia, it merely added fuel to the fire of Goering's support and caused him to dismiss the whole affair as a 'frame-up and forgery of the British'. In 1944, when Neuhausen was arrested by the Gestapo on a number of charges of fraud, Goering still stuck to his man, forced his release and actually persuaded Hitler to decorate him with the Knight's Cross of the Kriegsverdienstkreuz (The Cross for War Services)! Kaltenbrunner, who had brought his man to justice only with the greatest difficulty, was forced to give way. To-day this same Neuhausen, who was handed over to Yugoslavia in 1946 and condemned to twenty years' penal servitude, is said to be living in a feudal villa on the Topcider and working as Economic Adviser to Tito. If this is true, it is a proof that Neuhausen, as was always suspected at the time, was in fact working for the Communists during the war.

This was the man who in the decisive years of the re-orientation of Yugoslav foreign policy was Germany's most important representative in Belgrade. He had an incomparably greater influence in Berlin than the official representative, the Minister, Viktor von Heeren, who did not stand high in Ribbentrop's estimation, probably because he was a diplomat of the old school. Von Heeren, like Neuhausen, was pro-Serb. In the decisive phase of German-Yugoslav relations before the *coup d'état* in March 1941, he pursued a policy that was not always happy and he frequently found himself not in a position correctly to appreciate the relationship of events in Yugoslav affairs.

A particularly zealous protagonist of the Serbian cause in the German Foreign Ministry was the Chief of the Press Section, Dr. Paul Schmidt. He was no authority on Balkan affairs, but derived his information about the Serbs from the Belgrade journalist, Danilo Gregoric. This latter had supported the new 'Berlin orientation' with great skill in the official newspaper *Vreme*. Schmidt met him quite by chance, and from that moment he became his adviser on Yugoslav affairs. Under his influence Schmidt published a number of pro-Yugoslav articles in the German Press, his primary object being to awaken a sympathetic interest in Hitler and the other leaders for Yugoslavia and, in particular, for the Serbs. He lauded the centuries-old and heroic struggle of the valiant Serbian people against the Turkish oppressor, the military virtues of the warlike Serbs, their chivalrous characteristics and so on, and succeeded in making quite a plausible case for a moral relationship which he professed to see between Germans and Serbs. By this means he greatly strengthened the pro-Serb feeling which already existed among the German leaders. Hitler himself repeatedly declared that he regarded an alliance with the brave and warlike Serbs as an object particularly worth while striving for.

The Croats, on the other hand, had no really influential man in Berlin to plead their cause. It was only in the Secret Service that a few senior officials were to be found who, thanks to their Austrian origins, had a better knowledge of Yugoslav internal affairs than, for example, Dr. Schmidt, and who therefore advocated a higher appreciation of the Croats as potential allies of the Germans.

For the moment, however, Germany's hands were tied. Yugoslavia formed part of the recognized Fascist Italian sphere of influence. Nevertheless it was becoming clearer that the Italian policy being pursued in the country was harmful to the interests of the Reich, and that the Duce was but waiting for the appropriate moment to make his influence absolute throughout the land. The German Secret Service kept under careful observation the various Italian attempts to become the paramount Power in Croatia with the help of Pavelic and his Ustase emigrants. But there was in reality no need to take too serious a view of these efforts for in the first few years after the assassination of King Alexander, Mussolini could not, for obvious reasons, have any official dealings with the instigators of the outrage.

More promising from the Italian point of view was Ciano's relationship with Macek and his Croat Peasant Party. The first intermediary between them was a certain Baron Bombelles, in actual fact an agent of the Belgrade Secret Service. Ciano met him at a shoot given by the Prince Regent and had great hopes that he would be able to bring about the desired collaboration between Italy and the Croat Peasant Party. Macek, however, had never given Bombelles any authority on his behalf. But the conversations between Bombelles and Ciano, including details of the offers Italy was prepared to make to the Croats, were meticulously reported to the Serbian General Staff—and, incidentally, to the German Secret Service which had succeeded in 'tapping' the Serbian Military Headquarters. Eventually Pavelic managed to persuade Ciano that Bombelles was playing a double game and was a traitor, and he was promptly dropped. Mussolini was furious over this comedy of errors. At that time, in 1939, he thought himself to be on the verge of success for Bombelles had promised that provided they could count on Italian assistance the Croats would rise in revolt and proclaim an independent State, with either an Italian Prince as King or a personal dynastic union with Italy. Naturally Bombelles had succeeded in extracting no mean sum of money from Italy for the furtherance of his undertaking.

The second intermediary between Italy and the Croat Peasant Party was an equally dubious character. In March 1939 a Croat of Italian origin named Carnelutti presented himself to Ciano and stated that he was an official delegate from Macek. Ciano saw no reason to doubt Carnelutti's bona fides, particularly as one of his brothers was in the Italian diplomatic service. Having no particular love for the Germans he was further influenced in the man's favour when the latter declared himself to be anti-German in his opinions. On 26th May, 1939, Carnelutti, as plenipotentiary of Macek and the Croat Peasant Party, concluded with Ciano, as representative of Italy, a regular secret treaty which was ratified by Mussolini. The treaty corresponded in every respect to the aspirations of the Fascist Government, for by it the new State of Croatia—still, admittedly, to be set up by revolutionary violence—pledged itself to the closest possible collaboration with Italy. There were to be common Ministries of Foreign Affairs and War and the treaty took note of the possibility of a personal union between the two countries. Ciano declared his readiness to finance Macek's independence movement with a sum of twenty million dinars and this contribution —or at least quite a portion of it—was actually made. How much of the money did, in fact, reach the Croat Peasant Party cannot be ascertained nor indeed is it certain that Carnelutti had been given plenipotentiary powers by Macek and authority to conclude an agreement of such far-reaching implication. Macek never recognized the Rome protocol and refused to ratify it. Thus Italy's second attempt to reach a binding agreement with the Croat Peasant Party failed—and had cost a mint of money into the bargain.

It was apparently only after this second failure that Mussolini and Ciano decided to turn once more to Pavelic. Pavelic later stated that at the beginning of 1940 Ciano sent for him and demanded certain undertakings from him. He had no alternative, he added, but to agree, for as a refugee he had to all practical purposes delivered himself into the hands of the Italians and no support had been offered to him by any of the other Great Powers. Ciano promised him that he and his Ustase should retain absolute power in the new State while the demands made by Pavelic were identical with the undertakings agreed upon in the Carnelutti protocol, namely, an exclusively pro-Italian orientation of foreign and military policy; a close dynastic tie with Italy (which now envisaged the accession of an Italian Prince to the throne, rather than a personal union of ruling houses); and finally—the most fateful and most bitterly contested condition—the cession by Croatia of the greater portion of the Dalmatian coast to Italy. Later, Ciano asserted that Pavelic had definitely guaranteed the whole coastal strip with the exception of a few towns, while Pavelic declared that

5*

he had only agreed to certain temporary bases with the requisite amount of hinterland for the Italian Navy and Army. This controversy played a disastrous part in both Italo-Croat and Italo-German relations, and was the cause of many political difficulties. Nevertheless, for the moment Pavelic could regard himself as the victor. It is true that he had to make concessions to Italy which were harmful to the vital interests of his own country, but against that he was the selected Head of the future new State of Croatia, independent albeit in a measure under Italian suzerainty.

Meanwhile General Simovic had not ceased for one moment to labour at the organization of his conspiracy against the régime of the Prince Regent and his Prime Minister, Cvetkovic. He had established contact with the then Chief of the American Secret Service, Colonel Donovan, and had without doubt received support and assistance from him. He also had one further connection with the United States. While on leave in Planica, a well-known winter-sports resort in northern Yugoslavia, he had made the acquaintance of the Serbian lawyer Radin who had lived in the States for many years and who had now returned to Yugoslavia, apparently on some special mission. Radin told Simovic that he was a friend of Harry Hopkins, President Roosevelt's personal adviser, and that he had been instructed by Hopkins to get in touch with those people who were prepared to do something practical to circumvent the threatened absorption of Yugoslavia by Germany. He appears also to have obtained from Radin both moral and financial support. Nor were the British uninterested in Simovic, who was in particularly close touch with Atherton, a well-connected journalist in Belgrade.

Of greater importance to Simovic, however, was his reappointment to an important military command. General Nedic, who later during the German occupation became the Head of the Serbian State, had prepared and submitted a memorandum in which he stigmatized the political attitude of the Yugoslav government as untenable, and was summarily dismissed by the Prince Regent for exceeding his authority. The new War Minister was General Pesec who had also been a member of the diplomatic service, and he appointed Simovic to the command of the Air Force. Simovic now had at his disposal the means to accelerate his preparations and he immediately appointed a number of the more important conspirators to key positions in the Air Force and found posts for more in the Royal Guards, a unit of vital importance in the execution of a *putsch* in Belgrade. His closest collaborator, the Air Force General Merkovic, was instructed to foster good relations with the British Air Attaché and to try and win him over as an intermediary between the conspirators and the British Government.

At the end of 1940 while Simovic's preparations were still in the preliminary stages a peculiar incident occurred. It appears that among those Officers who were determined to get rid of the Prince Regent and to place the young King on the throne there was no unanimity as to what their next step should be. On several occasions Simovic had emphasized in the confidential circle of the conspiracy that he had been given guarantees of support by the Russians and that later he would use his influence to bring about an improvement in Russo-Yugoslav relations. He probably said this with the object of impressing upon his fellow-conspirators that he had powerful friends behind him and there is no doubt at all that even at that early stage he had established contact with the representatives of the Soviet Union. There were, however, some Officer groups which disapproved of this pro-Russian attitude and one such group decided to get rid of Simovic and his supporters and to carry out the enterprise themselves. The reluctance of the Army Officers to see the proposed *putsch* primarily in the hands of the Air Force was no doubt an additional reason for this decision.

This anti-Soviet group secured the support of a political party which though it had no great following could be of considerable use to display as a kind of protective banner before the eyes of Italy and Germany. This was the Zbor Party under the leadership of Dimitri Ljotic, a relative and friend of the late King Alexander, which as a species of right wing fascist and totalitarian movement could expect to find favour in Berlin and Rome. Since 1918 Ljotic had held that Yugoslavia must pursue a foreign policy friendly towards Germany, and his movement had gained a measure of impetus thanks to the great military successes of Germany and Italy. At the end of 1944 he was killed in a motor accident in Istria. This counter-conspiracy differed from that of General Simovic in that it desired to avoid any rupture with Germany, but equally it did not wish to see Yugoslavia drawn into any close alliance with the Nazis such as would have involved membership of the Three Power Pact. The Prime Minister was to be replaced by a General, the Prince Regent was to be forced to abdicate, and the young King was to ascend the throne. On internal policy there was no difference between the two conspiratorial groups and either would have resulted in a Serbian military dictatorship.

Towards the end of 1940 emissaries of the anti-Simovic group disclosed their plan to an agent of the German Secret Service. They said they desired to give their enterprise the appearance of a move by Germany in the field of foreign policy. This meant that Germany would have to give them a kind of blank cheque, and Heydrich submitted the case to Himmler who hesitated, wavered and refused to commit himself. At first he seemed very taken with the idea and he obviously relished the opportunity of being able unofficially to influence Yugoslav affairs and thus to put a timely end to the anti-German tendencies in that country. Then he conferred with Hitler but was not able to obtain a decision, for the latter still regarded the Balkan situation as too unstable for any immediate and decisive action. This increased Himmler's hesitation. On Hitler's instructions he consulted Ribbentrop who bluntly and forthwith refused to have anything to do with such an enterprise, not because he had any qualms over the moral admissibility of such intervention in Yugoslav internal affairs but because he was already exploring with Belgrade the possibilities of a closer co-operation between the two countries. It was Dr. Schmidt who had urged him strongly to make this attempt because Gregoric had told him that the chances of Yugoslavia joining the Three Power Pact were now particularly rosy. Ribbentrop was therefore convinced that any *putsch* at that moment would be not only superfluous but actually harmful. The conspirators accordingly were given a negative answer, causing them to abandon their plans to circumvent Simovic, for without German support the principal instigators were not prepared to take the risk.

German conversations with Belgrade, official but still tentative and confidential, began in June 1940. Up to that time Cvetkovic does not seem to have had any intention of making any important concessions to Germany except in the economic field. But under the shattering influence of the collapse of France a radical change took place in Yugoslav opinion. No foreign country had ever exercised so strong an influence in Yugoslavia as France. She was the protector and the liberator thanks to whom, after the first war, Serbia was reincarnated and the Yugoslav State founded. She was looked at as a fascinating but inimitable model, and above all her army was regarded as invincible by the Yugoslav military experts. For the Serbs and the Serb ruling circles in Yugoslavia it was a catastrophe when the invincible French Army fell in ruins before the lightning blows of the German Wehrmacht. The support upon which Belgrade still relied, even after the re-orientation of its foreign policy, was gone for ever. And now the Yugoslav Government regarded an understanding with Germany as imperative and unavoidable. The intermediary was Danilo Gregoric. At once in June 1940 he made contact with the German Minister. His conversations with him became increasingly open and straightforward and by November 1940 von Heeren was authorized by Ribbentrop to say unofficially that in return for Yugoslavia's entry into the Three Power Pact, Germany would support her claims to Salonica. Reserved though it was, this statement had a profound effect on the Yugoslav Government for the possession of Salonica had always been an ardent dream of the Serb people. Cvetkovic immediately accepted the proposal and he authorized Gregoric to go to Berlin and continue the negotiations with the object of arranging an official conference as quickly as possible.

Gregoric's visit to Berlin coincided with that of Molotov. As is well known Hitler's negotiations with the Soviet statesman came to nothing and he felt himself therefore more than ever constrained to stabilize the Balkan situation in a manner favourable to the Reich. Pre-requisite to this was an understanding with Yugoslavia, and Yugoslavia had if possible to be won over to an alliance. If Germany were to have a free hand in the East all possibility of friction elsewhere had first to be eliminated.

This explains Ribbentrop's confirmation to Gregoric on 23rd November, 1940, of von Heeren's promise as regards Salonica. Negotiations now entered upon the official phase. Gregoric's place as negotiator was taken by Cvetkovic and his Minister for Foreign Affairs, Cincar-Markovic, and Salonica was practically the sole subject of discussion. Ribbentrop's price was member-ship of the Three Power Pact, while the Yugoslavs tried to get the longed-for port more cheaply. They wanted above all to avoid openly going over to the German side, but were quite prepared to accept the obligations of membership of the Pact and to incorporate them in a secret treaty. Cincar-Markovic in particular was nervous about a dramatic change of sides—for Germany's demands could not be regarded as anything less— and he continued to try and press for further delay.

Eventually it seemed as though a compromise had been found. The German Secret Service had submitted a secret memorandum to Hitler with a suggested modification of the terms of the Three Power Pact which, it was felt, would remove Yugoslavia's hesi-tations. The basic idea of the modification was that there should be two groups in the Three Power Pact of which one would have the right to retain its neutrality. Gregoric was also informed of the contents of this memorandum in the hope that he would be able to persuade the Yugoslav Government to suggest to Hitler the solution which was contained in it. Whether Hitler would have agreed cannot, of course, be known, but at least he did not reject the German Secret Service's note when Heydrich submitted it to him, and it is reasonable to suppose that had the same proposals been pressed from the Yugoslav side he would have accepted them. Curiously enough, Cvetkovic and Cincar-Markovic did nothing to follow up the idea. In the meanwhile German troops had marched into Bulgaria preparatory to the attack on Greece and Hitler certainly anticipated that this move would have an effect on Yugoslav opinion. In this he was quite right for on hearing the news Cvetkovic and Markovic at once withdrew all their previous objections to open membership of the Three Power Pact.

No sooner was the stage set for the official signing in March 1941 of the Pact of Vienna than the widespread opposition thereto in certain leading Belgrade circles made itself apparent.

General Simovic gave the bluntest of warnings both to the Prince Regent and to the Government. He reminded Prince Paul of how in 1903 a Serbian monarch, who had tried to pursue a policy hostile to the Serbian Army, had met with a terrible fate. (He was referring to the hideous murder of King Alexander Obrenovic and his wife, who was a commoner, by the Serbian secret society, the Black Hand.) Gavrilo, the Patriarch of the Serbian Orthodox Church, also took a hand. He had succeeded to the Patriarchate by means of a deal with Stoyadinovic of the most blatant crudity. After much wearisome negotiation Stoyadinovic had concluded a Concordat with the Vatican and had on that account drawn down upon himself the fanatical hatred of the Orthodox Serbian clergy; there were violent demonstrations throughout the country and great difficulties in Parliament and Stoyadinovic would probably have been ousted had not Gavrilo offered in return for the Patriarchate to negotiate with the clergy and put an end to the turmoil. This high dignitary of the Church with his unscrupulous personal ambitions was not exactly the most worthy representative of the clergy of his country, but he did without doubt represent the opinion of a very considerable portion of the Serbian priesthood which was opposed to the Pact, and in view of the influence exercised by the priests over the people this fact was of primary importance.

Up to the last moment the Western Allies too did everything they could to dissuade Yugoslavia from joining the Three Power Pact. Wave upon wave of propaganda by press, radio and pamphlet flooded the country and the King of England himself abandoned his traditional aloofness and sent a telegram to the Prince Regent appealing to his family feelings and imploring him to desist from the proposed step.

But the Prince Regent and Cvetkovic disregarded these warnings, Hitler paid no attention to the anxious reports of the German Secret Service in Belgrade and the Pact was duly signed at the Belvedere in Vienna on 25th March, 1941. Apart from containing Germany's and Italy's promises regarding Salonica the secret clauses also exempted Yugoslavia from certain of the obligations of the Three Power Pact. Provision was made for the free transit of war material and wounded, but not for German troops, and on the economic side Yugoslavia was required to make certain concessions, particularly in respect of the copper mines at Bor.

Simovic struck immediately after the return of the delegates from Vienna, on 27th March, 1941. The carefully prepared plan was put into execution almost without a hitch. Members of the conspiracy occupied key positions in every branch of the State machine, and many prominent people who had not participated in the preparations immediately joined the successful insurgents. A decisive factor in the success of the rising was the absence on the fateful day of the Prince Regent on a visit in Zagreb. On instructions from Simovic the local Corps Commander demanded his immediate return to Belgrade. Probably thinking that the historic hour of the Croat independence movement had struck, Macek offered to place himself at the head of the Croat units and march on Belgrade and crush the rebellion; but after anxious consideration the Prince Regent rejected this offer on the grounds that he did not wish to start a civil war or hazard the Serbo-Croat unity which still remained his most cherished goal. He therefore conformed with Simovic's demand, returned to Belgrade and tendered his resignation. He and his family were then permitted to retire to Greece.

It is worth mentioning that a few days before the former Prime Minister Stoyadinovic had taken the same road. His successor arrested him and his wife and had them escorted to the Greek frontier. In Greece he fell into the hands of the British who interned him for the duration of the war in Africa. (How Cvetkovic was able to reconcile his pro-German policy with this treatment of the supporters of German re-orientation has never been explained.) The remaining two members of the Regency Council also resigned, and only then was Simovic able to approach the young King. The manifestos attributed to the King up to this moment had probably been fabricated by Simovic, but after the resignation of the Regency Council the seventeen-year-old Peter found himself completely in the hands of the new Party in power which was now able to proclaim its association with him without any further risk.

As his Foreign Minister Simovic had chosen Momcilo Nincic, who as an old diplomat *de carrière* immediately recognized that

the new régime's greatest danger was Germany. He therefore
hastened to assure the German Minister that Yugoslavia's attitude towards the Reich remained unchanged and that while the
new Government was ready to honour the signature of its predecessor regarding membership of the Three Power Pact, it desired
to be given a clearer and more authoritative interpretation of the
secret clauses. Von Heeren, the German Minister, who realized
that Berlin would place no value on this assurance, drew the
new Foreign Minister's attention to the recent anti-German
demonstrations in Belgrade and in particular to the destruction
of the German Tourist Agency by a frenzied mob, and he
pointed out that in these circumstances it would be very difficult to convince Berlin that Yugoslavia did not intend to alter
her foreign policy.

Simovic did not, however, leave the direction of foreign policy
during these fateful days entirely in the hands of his Foreign
Minister. He undertook the task of neutralizing Italy, the second
member of the Three Power Pact; he suggested to the Italian
Minister, Mamelli, that Rome should use its good offices to
deter Germany from any military action against Yugoslavia,
hinting obliquely at the same time that the first victim of any
recourse to violence would be Italy herself, as Yugoslavia in that
eventuality would undoubtedly seize the opportunity of ejecting
the Italians from Albania. The manœuvre, however, met with
no success, and neither Mussolini nor Ciano appears to have
reacted in any way to this attempt at diplomatic blackmail.

In his approach to the British Simovic was completely frank.
At the first official meeting he held in his capacity as the Head
of the State with Sir Ronald Campbell the British Minister, he
declared himself quite openly in favour of close co-operation
with the British to whom he apparently offered among other
things military bases on Yugoslav territory. His exchanges with
the Soviet Union, on the other hand, were extremely tortuous
and have never been completely clarified to this day. They do,
however, shed an interesting light on the dubious processes of
Soviet diplomatic method. Immediately after the success of the
coup d'état Lebedev, the Russian Chargé d'Affaires, informed
General Simovic that he had been instructed by Vyshinsky to
suggest a treaty of alliance, the essence of which would be that

the Soviet Union would regard any attack on Yugoslavia as an attack on its own territory. Simovic had written a résumé both of this conversation and the subsequent negotiations in Moscow, and of his talks with Sir Ronald Campbell and these précis were later found in the Yugoslav Foreign Ministry and impounded by the Germans when they marched into Yugoslavia. They were voluntarily handed over by an official of the Foreign Ministry who, as an adherent of Ljotic and therefore an opponent of Simovic, had preserved them from destruction for this purpose.

The German invasion of Bulgaria, which had occurred shortly before these events, aroused great anxiety in Moscow and caused the Russians for the first time to sound, through the medium of the Tass Agency, a disapproving and warning note. Before the invasion the Yugoslav Ambassador in Moscow, Milan Gavrilovic, a politician with somewhat leftish tendencies, found that his attempts to renew the traditional bonds between the two Slav peoples met with little response or encouragement from the Soviet authorities who indeed avoided any serious discussion of the subject. Now, however, Stalin completely changed his mind and Gavrilovic was given a very different reception; so many officials of the Soviet Foreign Office encouraged him to pursue his object that he really thought at last he was to see the realization of his ideas. At this moment, too, an underground propaganda campaign against the signing of the Pact was set afoot in Yugoslavia, directed by the Russians. But neither this wave of propaganda nor the newly initiated cordiality towards Gavrilovic could save the Yugoslav Government from following the course to which it had given its bond and for this reason the possibilities opened by the success of the Simovic *putsch* evoked an even more than normally energetic reaction in Russia. The Soviet Chargé d'Affaires was instructed to express Russia's willingness to conclude an alliance, Simovic sent two of his most trusted colleagues at once to Moscow, and on the night of the 5th April a treaty of friendship was signed. This treaty did not, it is true, go quite as far as the promises Lebedev had given to Simovic but it did at least affirm that the Soviet Union laid great value on the maintenance of the independence, the sovereign rights and the territorial integrity of

Yugoslavia, and pledged itself to a policy of benevolent neutrality.

It must later have been a source of bewildered disappointment to the Yugoslavs that the Russians did not lift a finger—materially or morally—to help them when the Germans attacked. After the German victory, Russia's new ally was never once mentioned in the Soviet Press again. The signing of the Soviet-Yugoslav treaty in Moscow took place only a few hours before the German Stuka attack on Belgrade. A week later Stalin showed the world that he would do nothing for his small ally. The destruction of Belgrade, the partition of Yugoslavia was close at hand.

CHAPTER IX

HIDE-AND-SEEK WITH TITO

I was at this time Inspector of Southern Affairs in Branch VI of the Secret Service, working from our offices in Vienna and Zagreb, and I had tried to support the Croat peasant party of Macek rather than the terrorist Ante Pavelic.

Alfred Rosenberg was Head of the Foreign Policy Office of the Nazi Party. I tried to get him to support my line on Yugoslavia. He replied that Ribbentrop was on the wrong track but that it was too late to alter official policy. This conversation took place in March 1941, just after the revolt of General Simovic. I returned to Vienna and Zagreb, and followed the course of events, which at length led to some remarkable contacts between Tito and the Germans.

On 13th April Stalin appeared unexpectedly at Moscow railway station to bid farewell to the Japanese Foreign Minister Matsuoka. As if to impress his departing Japanese guest, he went up to the German Assistant Military Attaché, Colonel von Krebs, and, putting his arm round his shoulders, pronounced the famous sentence: 'We shall always remain friends, shan't we?'

A month later the Yugoslav ambassador Gavrilovic was called to the Soviet Foreign Ministry. Vyshinsky informed him that the Soviet Union regarded his mission as ended, since Yugoslavia had lost her independence—the same independence, be it noted, which a few short weeks before the Kremlin had solemnly recognized and promised to defend. It was much the same treatment as the defeated Poles had received in 1939.

Stalin obviously never had the slightest intention of allying himself seriously with Yugoslavia. The revolt of the Serbian officers was merely an episode which he saw he could turn to his own advantage. The Belgrade Nationalists themselves later became convinced that the Russians' sole object had been maliciously and in their own interests to goad Yugoslavia to a degree of hostility against Germany which made war inevitable.

With a typical display of cynicism Stalin had delayed the Yugoslav delegates in Moscow until he received definite information from Berlin that the German attack on Yugoslavia was about to begin. The Simovic nationalist group was embittered by what they regarded as 'despicable treachery' and the 'cynical betrayal' on the part of the Russians. This opinion was gradually adopted by the whole of the Serbian people. It is perhaps no exaggeration to see in the shock caused by Russian behaviour at that moment the seeds of that anti-Russian feeling which have now grown into the present policy of Marshal Tito.

Simovic in the situation in which he then found himself had to reach an agreement with the Croats. He tried to achieve this by surprise tactics, announcing the formation of his new Government with the Croat peasant leader Macek as Deputy Prime Minister. He did not even ask him first whether he was willing to serve in the Government. Macek at that time had no intention of entering the Simovic cabinet and contented himself with sending to Belgrade Kosutic, leader of the right wing of the Party, merely to prevent a complete break. Kosutic was instructed to inform Simovic of the demands of his Party—the setting up of a new Regency Council of five to consist of one Serb, one Croat and one Slovene, the Patriarch of the Orthodox Church and the Roman Catholic Archbishop of Zagreb. The new Government must confirm its adherence to the Serbo-Croat 1939 Agreement of Equality; and formally declare its membership of the Three Power Pact.

Simovic must at all costs have the Croats in his Government if he were to avoid dangerous opposition in Croatia. He accepted these conditions without demur. He had no intention of keeping his word. All he desired was to get the Croat leader to Belgrade and to have him for the time being as a member of the Government. Macek, who had thought that his demands would prove unacceptable, was left with no grounds to reject the advances of the Belgrade Government. Berlin had given me no inkling of any alternative support for Macek if he stayed out of the coalition.

German policy towards Yugoslavia during this decisive stage was highly irresponsible. Hitler was completely immersed in his preparations for the Russian campaign. He left the handling of the Yugoslav question almost entirely to his Foreign Minister.

Ribbentrop knew nothing about the complicated Balkan pro-
blems and was in no position to form an independent judgment.
He saw the situation in Belgrade as it was depicted to him by
Dr. Schmidt, his Special Adviser on Yugoslav affairs. Warnings
poured in on him from all sides and particularly from Austria.
He took no notice. He had, in his narrow-minded adherence to
'principle', rejected the compromise suggested by the German
Secret Service regarding Yugoslavia and the Three Power Pact.
With the signing of the Pact he regarded the business as finished.
The fact that the Yugoslavs had signed without reservation was
in his eyes a complete vindication of his uncompromising attitude. At the very moment when Simovic in Belgrade was giving
his final instructions for the *putsch*, Ribbentrop was in Vienna
boasting how lucky it was that he had not listened to the reasoning of 'those compromising Austrians'. Hitler was quite satisfied
and thought that now at last he was free to turn his attention
exclusively to Russia.

His reaction to the Yugoslav *coup d'état* was therefore all the
more violent. His fury was directed against the whole Serbian
people, whom he had been praising a few weeks before. His own
Foreign Minister did not escape. He declared furiously that he
never wished to see Ribbentrop again. The latter did then what
we used to call his 'midnight tango act'. This was the nickname
given to Ribbentrop's habit of shutting himself in his darkened
bedroom. There he remained inaccessible to everyone for days
on end. The Foreign Ministry welcomed these opportunities
for obtaining the signature of the Under-Secretary and Deputy
Foreign Minister to papers which they knew Ribbentrop would
have refused to sign.

This blunder of his Foreign Minister reminded Hitler that
the Nazi Party had a Foreign Affairs Office of its own under
Alfred Rosenberg. He instructed Rosenberg to get in touch with
Macek, without giving him full powers to conclude any binding
agreement. Macek found himself in a most unpleasant situation.
Simovic had robbed him of his last pretext for refusing to join
the Government. The mass of his followers, the majority of the
Croat people, considered a good opportunity to withdraw from
the Yugoslav State had at last presented itself. Only a very few
of his colleagues, among them the Governor of Croatia, Ivan

Subasic, later to become a member of the Government in exile in London, and his own Secretary General, Dr. Krnjevic, were in favour of any sort of compromise with Belgrade. Macek did not possess the character and determination of his predecessor, Radic. He hesitated, hoping against hope that Germany would give an unequivocal indication of her attitude.

Rosenberg had already arrived in Zagreb, but he could not conclude an agreement with Macek or give him any assurances. Karl Freund, the German Consul General in Zagreb, did his utmost to extract some sort of declaration from Ribbentrop. But he was equally unsuccessful. I as representative of the German Secret Service in Zagreb, was in constant touch with Macek. But I could not tell him what Germany's attitude towards Croat independence claims would be. Macek despairing of a satisfactory answer to this vital question decided to go to Belgrade. Although this step committed him deeply he had still not made up his mind to join the Simovic Government. Simovic received him with the greatest ceremony and hoped that he was at last within sight of his goal of a common front with the Croats. Macek, even in Belgrade, sought frantic contact with the Germans in a last attempt to reach agreement with Berlin. But the Minister and the rest of the Legation had already departed. It was only to myself as the German Secret Service representative that he could address his appeals. With no official status, I could do no more than forward his requests to Berlin.

Ribbentrop was about to emerge from his bedroom when he learned that a representative of his rival, Rosenberg, was on his way to see Macek. His vanity prevented him from following his rival's lead. So he cast round for other Croat personalities. His choice fell upon Dr. Ante Pavelic. Up to this moment Germany had shown but little interest in the Croat extremists, whose close allegiance to Italy was well known. Now Mussolini and Ciano suggested to their German ally that Dr. Pavelic was the best leader of a new Croatia. Their object in doing so was obvious. If Germany accepted this man, who was wholly dependent upon Italy, then the loss of influence to Italy that had resulted from German meddling in Yugoslavia would be counter-balanced.

Ribbentrop, eager to thwart Rosenberg and to push his own and Mussolini's solution, made all haste to send an emissary to Zagreb. He selected Dr. Veesenmeyer, who had been employed on similar missions in Austria and in stirring up Slovakia against the Czechs. Veesenmeyer made no attempt to contact Macek or his Party, which still represented the majority of the Croat people. He went straight to Pavelic's representative in Croatia, the former Austro-Hungarian General Slavko Kvaternik. His reports home were optimistic. Veesenmeyer knew what would be pleasing to his superiors. He described the Ustase as a movement closely related to National-Socialism and Fascism, eager to follow the lead of the Rome-Berlin axis. This alone was good enough for Hitler. And it pleased Mussolini. When it became known in Berlin that Macek had at last decided to enter the Simovic Government, Hitler regarded this as the final proof that the policy of trying to reach agreement with Macek had been faulty. He quite ignored the fact that Macek would never have gone to Belgrade had he received the slightest response from Germany.

In the absence of Macek, the other leaders of the Croat Peasant Party were left to their own resources. The alternative was twofold. Either they could go into opposition, or they could try and conclude an agreement with the Italo-German candidate Kvaternik. They chose the latter, and in Zagreb on 10th April, 1941, a few hours before the entry of the German troops, Kvaternik proclaimed the foundation of the independent State of Croatia.

Veesenmeyer, although a secret agent of the Reich, could not resist the temptation of being present at the 'independence' ceremony. He was standing behind Kvaternik and he made it quite clear that it was he who had brought the new State into being. Against the wishes of Macek, who from Belgrade had issued an appeal for loyalty to the new Government, the Croat peasants now went over to the Germans with colours flying and bands playing. These peasant units rendered valuable services in disarming those troops which remained faithful to Belgrade. The peasants were to be most shabbily rewarded for their services.

A few days after the foundation of the new State, Pavelic and the whole emigrant group of the Ustase arrived in Zagreb and assumed control. This group, some 360 strong, took over all the most important posts. Even the Ustase leaders who had sturdily remained in their fatherland had to be content with small appointments. This had a bad effect; but in spite of it morale during the first few weeks was excellent. The Croat people were delighted at gaining their long-awaited independence.

On 6th May, Pavelic returned from his first visit to Hitler with the glad news that the new State was to embrace the whole of Bosnia, Herzegovina, Dalmatia and the coastal territories of Syrmia, Slavonia and Zagoria—all the territories, in fact, to which the Croats had ever laid claim. Enthusiasm knew no bounds. German demands were insignificant. All that they asked in return was that a small force of German troops should be stationed in Croatia for the duration of the war.

But soon Italy formulated her demands, and Germany accepted them. The Rome Protocol of 13th June, 1941, caused the most profound disappointment throughout Croatia. The new State was divided into German and Italian zones of occupation. Worse still, the Italian zone was again sub-divided into primary and secondary zones. In the primary Italian zone Croat sovereignty ceased to exist. In these measures the Croats rightly saw an attempt to prepare for the later annexation of the whole coastal area of Dalmatia into the Italian Empire. Pavelic was blamed for accepting the Italian demands and accused by the Dalmatians of betraying them to Italy. The remainder of the Croats expressed strong disapproval of Pavelic and his Government. Friendship towards Germany also cooled considerably. When finally it became known that an Italian Duke was to become King of Croatia, discontent reached its zenith.

These shortcomings alone would perhaps have sufficed to bring the edifice of the new State down in ruins. But the situation was made worse by the activities of the Ustase leaders. Within a very short time they reduced the country to a state of bloody chaos. Pavelic had nominated Eugen Kvaternik, the son of the General and one of his closest collaborators in exile, as Secretary of State for Security. By so doing he put the whole of his executive at his mercy. Kvaternik junior's first act was to organize a new Police Force led by emigrants which he proceeded to arm, recruiting notorious criminals. Next he disarmed and disbanded the Croat peasant formations, which the new Government regarded as a possible counterpoise to their own policy.

Thus the men who, as members of this truly national organization, had contributed so much to the foundation of the State while Kvaternik and his friends were sitting safely in Italy now found themselves confined to their barracks. They were encircled by machine-guns and compelled to surrender their arms and disband. It was a real betrayal of allies. Feelings were bitter in the extreme. Large numbers went over to the opposition, and this was undoubtedly one of the main sources of the valiant Partisan movement that began to form and fought on to the end.

The hatred of the Ustase leaders was directed primarily against the Jews and the Serbs, who were officially outlawed. The worst of the Jew murderers was the Secretary of State, Kvaternik, although his mother was the daughter of the one-time Croat nationalist leader, Frank, who was himself a Jew. The wife of 'Poglavnik' (Head of the State) Pavelic was née Lovrencevic. She was of Jewish origin, but still could do nothing to help her persecuted compatriots. Far more numerous than the outrages against the Jews were the mass murders of the Serbs. In the summer of 1941 these atrocities reached terrible proportions. Entire villages, entire districts, were mercilessly put to the sword or their inhabitants driven destitute across the Serbian border. By ancient tradition the Croats and the Roman Catholic Church on one side and the Serbs and the Orthodox Church on the other enjoyed equal rights and status; but now, the 'Croatisation' of the country assumed the form of forcible conversion of Orthodox believers to the Catholic faith.

General Glaise von Horstenau of the Wehrmacht, an ex-officer of the Imperial Austrian army and minister of the last Austrian government before the Anschluss, was appointed German Plenipotentiary General in Zagreb. He was the type of the Austrian professional soldier who had inherited the best tradition of the old Imperial Austrian service. Von Horstenau's personal knowledge of the country and its problems was unsurpassed, and in April 1941 he submitted to Hitler certain conclusions. He suggested that as a matter of basic principle all concessions to Italy should be confined to the territory south of the Yugoslav frontier; that in Zagreb a coalition Croat Government should replace the Ustase dictatorship; and that in Serbia a Government with widest possible authority should be set up under the control of a German Military Commander.

This solution, however, was contrary to Ciano's idea of Italian interests. During the Serbian campaign he had visited Ribbentrop in Vienna and had once more used his famous method of 'blackmail from weakness'. The failures in Greece, he declared, had gravely prejudiced the prestige of the Italian Army and the Fascist Party. Germany, in her own interests, must lend strength to her ally, if she wished to avoid endangering the prospects of further success in the common cause; Fascist prestige could only be restored by the granting to Italy of large concessions by Germany. This manœuvre met with complete success—as it was frequently to do in the future. Hitler himself was quite prepared to grant Italian demands in Croatia. Ribbentrop certainly had no intention of accepting von Horstenau's proposals. Personal considerations as usual played a considerable part. From the time of the *Anschluss* sharp differences had arisen between him and von Horstenau. He was determined to push the General into the background and above all to keep from him a post which would entitle him to intervene in political affairs. A military administration in Croatia, without diplomatic representation, was unacceptable to Ribbentrop. That would have withdrawn the country from his control. He hastened to appoint an envoy to the Zagreb Government. He chose Siegfried Kasche, an old brownshirt leader from North Germany, who had hardly ever heard of the land to which he was accredited. This was to have grave consequences.

At the same time in Serbia a purely military administration was set up. A Serbian Council of Commissars was formed, but was granted neither facilities nor power. It did not merit the name of Government. It faced many difficult tasks. The stream of refugees from Croatia was unending, and the resulting economic chaos gave rise to almost insoluble problems.

I suggested as German Secret Service specialist that a properly constituted Government should be formed to work in collaboration with the German Military Commander. The Foreign Ministry should send an envoy to Belgrade, without perhaps the full status of a Minister. But that would invest the Serbian Government with some prestige abroad and at home. Ribbentrop would have been wise to accept this proposal, for a diplomatic mission in Belgrade would have given him more influence. As usual his lack of moral courage proved stronger than his vanity. For weeks he refused to submit the suggestion to Hitler, asserting that the Fuehrer was so indignant with the Serbs that to persuade him to make any concessions to them would be quite impossible.

It was only when Himmler and Heydrich approached Hitler direct that the Secret Service obtained not only approval for its plan but also acceptance of General Milan Nedic, its candidate suggested for the post of Serbian Prime Minister. Nedic, a former Minister of War, was held in high esteem and had not been known for any undue pro-German tendencies, though he always regarded a war with Germany as madness. His basic idea was to achieve a compromise with those forces which still refused to recognize the capitulation of Serbia. In these efforts he was supported by the German Secret Service, but encountered many difficulties in his dealings with the other German departments. Yet he achieved a partial success.

Meanwhile the beginnings of an organized military resistance movement began to become apparent. We had not the slightest indication of the size to which it was destined to grow. A properly organized movement was possible because of the brief manner in which the Wehrmacht had been compelled to conduct the campaign in Yugoslavia. Our High Command had been pressed for time. Hitler had decided on 15th May for the opening of the Russian campaign, but this programme was upset by the revolt in Belgrade and the military operations which followed it. He was therefore continually urging his military commanders to finish with Yugoslavia as quickly as possible. The Wehrmacht did not give itself enough time to comb the country systematically for the remnants of enemy units. It could not search thoroughly in the difficult mountain country for arms and munitions dumps. It contented itself with occupying the principal towns and the securing of its lines of communications. As a result a large number of small but determined bands were able to carry on the fight.

Apart from this, partisan warfare was something of a tradition in Serbia. The Hadjuk of the days of the Ottoman Empire abandoned his city and village life and took to the woods. His struggle against the foreign oppressor remained an inspiration for the Serbian nationalists. The Austro-Hungarian monarchy, after the occupation of Bosnia and Herzegovina, found itself committed to many years of costly fighting against the insurgents. The Serb partisans were also wedded to the old Hadjuk tradition.

The semi-military Cetniks too—the title comes from the word 'ceta', meaning a company—held to the old customs. The Cetniks were ultra-nationalist and exercised a significant influence all over the kingdom. The Chief of Staff of the Cetniks, which were organized long before the collapse of Yugoslavia, was Colonel Draza Mihailovic. He refused to recognize the capitulation and called upon the Cetniks to take to the woods and hills and continue the fight. He was promoted to General and made Minister of War by King Peter II and the Yugoslav Government in exile in London, being officially recognized by the Allies as the Commander-in-Chief of the Yugoslav Home Army.

The Cetniks attracted many adherents and within a few months their numbers had increased many times. The massacre of the Serbs by the Ustase and the forced conversion of Orthodox believers to the Catholic faith drove thousands to the woods. The disastrous policy pursued by the Gauleiters of Styria and Carinthia had a similar effect. These two provinces contained Slovenes, and in an attempt to clear their districts of racial minorities as quickly as possible, the two Gauleiters started compulsory emigration. The Slovenes, except for the intelligentsia, had never been anti-German and would have remained loyal citizens of the Third Reich as they were of the Austro-Hungarian Empire. Yet they were compelled to abandon their homes at a few hours' notice and were driven across the border into Serbia. The Cetniks found many recruits among these refugees who had been plundered of all they possessed.

This nationalist resistance sprang into being after the capitulation. On the other hand no organized Communist resistance was started until June 1941. As long as Stalin saw any chance of postponing the conflict with Hitler, he forbade his Communists in Serbia to take any part in the national resistance against the Germans. But with the outbreak of the Russo-German war, Soviet policy was reversed. In no time the emissaries of Moscow were at work in Serbia, and the Communist movement was given new orders.

The Serbian Communists had not originally intended to form their own units, but rather to obtain important posts in the Cetnik resistance movement of Mihailovic. While on the alert against the formation of a Soviet Fifth Column within his ranks, he was most anxious to do everything in his power to achieve a unified home front. His efforts however met with no success Subsequent orders from Moscow told the Communists to obtain complete command control of the resistance movement or raise their own Communist-led movement as a separate force to Mihailovic and his Cetniks.

There were during the course of 1941 a few combined actions by the Cetniks and the still small Communist group led by an old member of the Yugoslav Communist Party sent from Russia for the purpose. His name was Josip Broz. He was nicknamed 'Tito'. By the end of the year it became plainly impossible to maintain this unity of front.   Soon afterwards the first fighting between the two groups broke out. Tito, who had received his schooling as a Comintern agent, is said to have returned to Yugoslavia either at the end of 1939 or at the beginning of 1940 and to have taken a hand in the events which led up to the Simovic *putsch*. He was certainly there immediately after the capitulation, when he is known to have taken part in a Cetnik rising in the vicinity of Nis in the Kapaonik mountains. Shortly afterwards he left Serbia, accompanied by a few trusty companions, and went into the Drvar district of Bosnia. In September 1941 the first all-Communist rising took place. The Germans captured a film in Drvar in 1942 showing Tito standing on a balcony beneath a Serbian flag with the Soviet star added to it.

The obvious differences between the Cetniks and the Communists made it easier for the German Secret Service to establish contact with the former. I can testify that Mihailovic himself rejected every approach. But a number of his lieutenants, among them in particular the 'Voivode' or Cetnik leader Pecanac, were more than ready to co-operate. Pecanac enjoyed a legendary reputation. In the first war he had become famous for the guerrilla warfare which he waged in Serbia behind the Austrian lines. He was violently anti-Communist and he regarded the Germans as the lesser of two evils. When the Russo-German conflict started and a purely Communist movement began to take shape, he showed a readiness under certain conditions to cease fighting against Germany. He was by no means alone in this. A number of other Nationalist leaders were of the same opinion. They felt that Germany would undoubtedly wish to transfer as many troops as possible for the Eastern front, and would be eager to conclude an agreement with the insurgents. The fundamental basis of any such agreement would have to be an independent, sovereign Serbian State.

German policy showed itself incapable of taking advantage of the opportunity. Negotiations with the Cetniks were conducted by Germans of no official status—in the first phases by members of the Secret Service—who had no authority to conclude any binding agreement. Official circles took no interest and gave no guidance. The whole German machine in Yugoslavia was in a state of inextricable chaos. In Belgrade the Serbian Government made no secret of its allegiance to King Peter or of the fact that in all its important decisions it invariably sought the concurrence of Mihailovic. It maintained a regular courier service with him. This does not mean that there were no differences of opinion between Mihailovic and General Nedic. It is even alleged that the Belgrade Government through the Serbian National Bank paid money into Cetnik funds whether secretly or with German connivance is not known. Cheek by jowl with this Government sat a senior S.S. Police Officer, who ruthlessly sought to exterminate the Cetniks. And we of the Secret Service were doing our utmost to persuade the Cetniks to make peace and common cause against Tito!

Dr. Neubacher came as Plenipotentiary and Minister to Belgrade. That brought about a slight improvement. Neubacher, as an Austrian officer, who had commanded a Croat unit during the first war, had a profound knowledge of South Slav problems. He was also a first class business man and possessed both

imagination and moral courage—characteristics rare among the
leading men of the Third Reich. This gave him an independent
judgment and led to an independent line, which did not always
conform with that of Hitler and his Foreign Minister. Unfortunately for Germany, the efficient and positive policy of this
expert came too late to change the history of Yugoslavia. If
anyone could have reached an understanding with the Cetniks,
it was Neubacher. But in the meantime the situation had
changed. It was no longer Mihailovic's nationalist movement
which presented a problem, but the Communist movement led
by Josip Broz-Tito.

Various attempts to make peace with the Cetniks lasted a long
time. They reached a climax in 1943 with a plan to bring King
Peter back to Serbia. This idea originated with a high Cetnik
leader, who was in continual touch with the King's Court in
London. He asserted that he was acting with the knowledge and
consent of the young King. His argument was that both in
Mihailovic's movement and in Tito's the troops were mainly
Serbs. In Tito's movement only the leadership was Communist.
By returning to his country and calling all Serbs to his banner the
King would be able to put an end to the civil war between them.
He could not take up his residence in Belgrade, but must live in
the woods in the midst of his followers and direct operations
from there. A *modus vivendi* would have to be found between the
Germans and the King and his newly united Serbian people.
The Serbs would be ready to disregard Croatia, to take no action
against the German troops in occupation there and to leave
unmolested the German lines of communication through Serbia
to Greece and Bulgaria. They might even assume responsibility
for their security.

Such a plan would bring peace to the Serbian territories, and
lead to an immediate weakening of Tito. The remnants of his
forces would easily be mopped up in Serbia by the Cetniks and
in Croatia by the Germans and the Croats. The Serbs would be
prepared to prevent the Communist partisans from crossing the
Serbian border.

This plan aroused great interest in the German Secret Service.
It seemed to us to offer a good opportunity for putting an end to
the partisan war at no great cost to Germany. Kaltenbrunner,

Hitler in Austria after the *Anschluss* surrounded by (on his right) Dr.
Seyss-Inquart, the last Chancellor of Austria, (on his left) Heinrich
Himmler, head of the SS, and Reinhard Heydrich, Himmler's chief
assistant until his assassination. (Hulton Getty)

Austrian Nazi leader,
Ernst Kaltenbrunner,
head of the SS; he
became head of the
Gestapo in 1943. (right)
Kaltenbrunner being led
back to his cell at the
Nuremberg Trials.
(Hulton Getty)

Adolf Hitler, Benito Mussolini (left) and
Count Ciano in a meeting on board a train
at the Brenner Pass October 5th, 1940.
(Hulton Getty)

Admiral Canaris, served as Chief of
Military Intelligence of the high
command of the armed forces, the
Abwehr. Canaris was associated with
the 1944 bomb plot against Hitler.
(Hulton Getty)

Walther Schellenberg, combined
military and political espionage chief
in the last phase of the war.

Mussolini in front of the hotel in the Gran Sasso in the Abruzzi mountains, where he was being kept prisoner, surrounded by German paratroops who rescued him in September, 1943. (Hulton Getty)

Otto Skorzeny (right), who leapt to prominence as head of the special paratroops who rescued Mussolini from imprisonment.

The Gran Sasso Hotel in the Abruzzi mountains, from which Mussolini was liberated.

Hungarian Secret Service Chief General Uiszassi (second from left) in discussion with Admiral Canaris, head of German military Intelligence (third from left) and his chief-of-staff General Piekenbrock (far left) summer 1943.

Mueller's Foxhole in Berlin: a sketch of the subterranean escape route that Gestapo General Mueller prepared and used in April, 1945. He is believed to have found his way to the Russian lines.

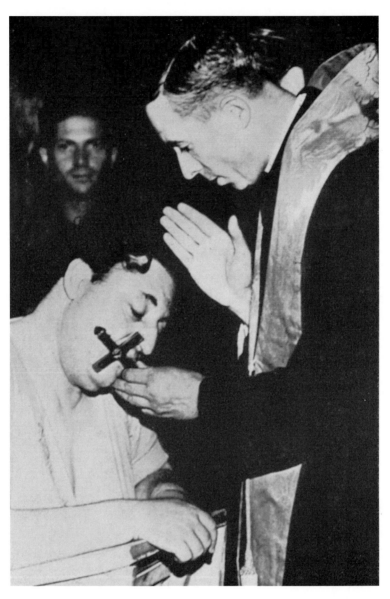

The last minutes of a Fascist: Buffarini Gridi, Minister of the Interior in Mussolini's Republican Fascist Government, was caught and executed by the partisans in 1945. This photograph was taken a few minutes before his death

Heydrich's successor, was very much taken with the idea and tried to persuade Himmler to submit it to the Fuehrer. Ribbentrop could be by-passed and was only to be informed of what was afoot after Hitler had made a decision. Himmler's reaction was not encouraging. The greatest drawback, he told me, was that the plan would have to be executed with the knowledge and connivance of the British. To bring Hitler to tolerate even a tacit co-operation with them would be quite impossible. If the plan could be modified in such a way that the British had no part in it—obviously, that would require the secret flight of the King from Britain—then Hitler might stand for it.

I gave Himmler the assurance that there had never been any question of collaboration with the British. In spite of this I could not win Himmler's active support. I discovered later that Himmler never submitted the idea to Hitler at all. He had discussed it casually and contrary to his undertaking with Ribbentrop who, of course, was wholly opposed to the plan. He too rejected it on the grounds that Hitler would never consider such a proposition. But when in the summer of 1944 Kaltenbrunner mentioned the matter to Hitler, and it was no longer realizable, he found that the Fuehrer was by no means averse to the idea. Once again it was too late.

In the nature of things it is very hard to judge to what extent the proposals had been authorized by the King, and whether the conditions would have been loyally fulfilled by the Serbs. But it has been proved beyond dispute that Mihailovic, Nedic and the majority of the Nationalist leaders regarded the plan with benevolent favour. A German wireless monitor station proved that radio telephonic conversations on the subject were in fact exchanged between the Cetnik Headquarters and a Serbian wireless station somewhere in England. In them the Cetnik leaders used the argument that the King now had nothing further to hope for from the Western Powers, who had already openly declared their support for Tito. They further suggested that some political circles in Britain would not be sorry to be faced with the *fait accompli* of the King's flight. For in that case Britain would be able to reply to any reproaches from her Soviet ally with a clear conscience. From the voluminous replies sent it was clear that the King and his advisers took all these factors

6

into consideration, and did not at least reject the plan out of hand.

Meanwhile the situation in Croatia continued to develop unfavourably for the Axis Powers. The struggle between the Cetniks and the Ustase was intensified. The massacre of the Serbs had let loose a war of endless and unspeakable horror, in which their own atrocities were matched by those of the Cetniks and indeed surpassed by those of Tito and his followers. The Mohammedan population of East Bosnia and the Sanjak suffered cruelly under the fury of the Cetniks. In the Sanjak alone, according to very conservative estimates, 70,000 Mahommedans were slaughtered. This hatred of the Serbs against the Mohammedans was a heritage from the epoch of Turkish occupation. The Bosnians had embraced the faith of the Turkish oppressors and they were therefore traitors and renegades.

The Ustase Government, out of hatred of the Serbs, tried to establish friendly relations with the Mohammedans. On the first anniversary of the foundation of the State, Pavelic himself went so far as to allow himself to be photographed wearing a fez as a symbol of his sympathies. While the Mohammedans were regarded as a religious minority but still Croats, those of the Orthodox faith were persecuted with the Serbs. Later the Ustase modified this policy and accepted the Orthodox as a religious minority and allowed them to establish their own Church under a former Russian Bishop.

We Germans favoured tolerance of the Bosnian Mahommedans hoping through them to influence the Turks to a more benevolent attitude. Between Bosnian Mohammedans and Turks the bonds of friendship were many and strong, and a large number of the most prominent men in modern Turkey, particularly in the Armed Forces, came from Bosnian Mussulman families. We did our utmost to foster and support the unification of the Mohammedan 'Church'.

But by now it was too late to take any advantage of these combinations. Turkey with a sober appreciation of relative strengths had already reached the conclusion that Germany could no longer hope to win the war.

Among other measures calculated to attract the Bosnian Mohammedans to the German side was the raising of the

Mussulman S.S. Divisions in 1943. The traditions of the old Austrian 'Bosnian Regiments' were revived. These units, almost entirely Mohammedan in composition, were among the foremost among the *corps d'élite* in the first war. They fought with success against repeated Italian assaults on the Isonzo front in 1915. The organizer of the new Mussulman S.S. Divisions was an ex-Austrian officer who had commanded a Mohammedan unit in the first war. In point of fact, the raising of these units on a religious class basis was quite contrary to the fundamental principles of the S.S. But it was nevertheless possible to obtain Himmler's consent, for he was a firm believer in the vaunted heroism of Islam. He went further and allowed the new Divisions to have their own religious teachers, a concession which the Christian Church had for years striven in vain to obtain for the S.S. units. The Grand Mufti of Jerusalem also showed great interest in these units and inspected them on more than one occasion. When later there was trouble after drafting them to France, it was the Grand Mufti who intervened and pacified them.

In 1942 the Cetniks still held a measure of superiority over Tito, but from then on firstly on account of his superior political tactics and secondly thanks to the support he was receiving from the Western Powers, Tito began rapidly to gain ground.

Mihailovic's movement was essentially Serbian in composition, and he and his subordinate leaders were incapable of adapting it to achieve a truly pan-Yugoslav unity. Indeed, Chauvinism was dominant among the Cetniks who looked down on the other nationalities of the former Yugoslav State. The Croats and the Slovenes were driven to the conclusion that the Mihailovic movement aimed at another Serbian hegemony after the war.

Tito was infinitely wiser. The basic training which he had received in the Soviet Union stood him in good stead. Continuously he emphasized the supra-national objects of his campaign. He made a strenuous endeavour to win over both Croats and Slovenes. He did all this with his tongue in his cheek, and even during his struggles with the Germans he followed an unmistakable Serbian line of policy. But that was realized only by a very few, even among his own followers. The fact that he is himself a Croat is of no significance. Many of the Croats who supported the Belgrade Government rapidly became more Serbian than the Serbs. Inhabitants of Croatia who had escaped the Ustase massacres and the Croats who had been driven from hearth and home in Styria and Carinthia found Tito apparently more tolerant than Mihailovic.

The British and Americans reversed their attitude towards the rival movements. At first Mihailovic alone had enjoyed the sympathies of the Western Powers and had received help in arms and munitions. Now, both Britain and America began to turn with much more favour to Tito. At the beginning of 1943 German operations against him had brought Tito to the brink of annihilation. Many who took part in the fighting assert that without British and American aid he would never have survived. Some of the leading Serbian politicians in exile are also convinced that there would be no Communism in Yugoslavia to-day or Albania if the British and Americans had continued to support Mihailovic. The Italian capitulation in 1943 was of great assistance to Tito. It enabled him at a single stroke to expand the territory under his rule and greatly to increase his military strength.

Fascist policy in occupied Yugoslavia was both disastrous and a direct source of increased strength to the partisans. It assumes some semblance of meaning only if one is prepared to accept that its real object was to harm the interests of the German ally. Italian Generals in Croatia parleyed with the Cetnik leaders, although Italy had no interests in Serbia. That is understandable. But General Roatta co-operated with Tito's Communist movement as well. In 1942 German Military Police captured a Communist partisan courier on his way to Roatta's Headquarters. Interrogating him brought nothing of importance to light, but it did establish the fact that the man had performed his office between Roatta and Tito many times before. In spite of this, the idea of any collaboration between the Communist guerrilla chieftain and the Italian Commander-in-Chief seemed so grotesque to the German authorities in Zagreb that they refused to attach any importance to the incident.

A little later, still in the summer of 1942, they were to learn their lesson. A large combined operation was being undertaken.

Roatta had given the German Liaison Staff the town of Sarajevo as the general direction of the Italian thrust. Suddenly and without any military necessity, he withdrew from a broad strip of territory sixty to eighty miles wide on the south side of the Italo-German line of demarcation. Tito's guerrillas immediately streamed into the vacated area. Their subsequent manoeuvres gave clear evidence of a previous understanding with the Italian High Command. Positive proof may be lacking, but these events justify the assumption that Roatta had accomplished the master-piece of conspiring with both the Cetniks and the Tito partisans against the Germans—and at the same time against the Croat State.

The longer the guerrilla warfare lasted, the more frequent became deals in arms and munitions between Italian units and the partisans. Things reached such a 'pitch that there was a fixed and recognized price for all weapons, from a rifle to a piece of field artillery, and the partisans, as can be well imagined, made handsome use of this market.

From the very beginning the German Military High Command found itself in an awkward situation. A large-scale war against partisans had not been envisaged, and immediately after the capitulation of Yugoslavia the majority of the German forces were transferred to the Eastern front. Only a few battalions remained in the country. Under the pressure of events the occupation forces had gradually to be increased to a strength of several divisions. But for action against the guerrillas even these forces were too weak, and it therefore became necessary to turn to the Italians for reinforcements. In theory the forces thus mustered should have been quite adequate for the purpose. Yet the actions always followed the same pattern. The German troops would invariably succeed in working round the flanks of the partisan forces and driving them into a position in which their complete encirclement and the subsequent capture of Tito and his entire army seemed imminent. Then at the last moment the partisans would regularly break through the Italian-held sector of the ring and escape. This could not always be due to designs or failings of the the Italian High Command. Frequently the failure was the result of a lack of the will to fight of the Italian troops. It is a mistake to condemn the Italian soldier as lacking in soldierly virtues. But he fights really well only for such causes as he understands and approves and above all in the defence of his own country. The Italian Empire, for the sake of which Fascism had led him into the field, held no place in his affections. Outside Italy, in North Africa and in the Balkans his fighting qualities and spirit left much to be desired.

Although their Italian partner consistently failed them, the German troops alone succeeded on more than one occasion in all but encircling the Tito partisans. In South Croatia, for example, a particularly successful action in 1943 by General Luethers inflicted 12,000 casualties on them. That was a high proportion of their total strength. But as long as Tito remained at liberty such successes had but a transitory value.

As the war progressed, the situation in Croatia grew worse, and the pressure of economic crises over-shadowed everything else. The Ustase had pushed aside all important leaders of the Croat Peasant Party. Numbers of Macek's adherents had been arrested and Macek himself was placed under house arrest. He owed his life to the Germans, who refused to permit him to be executed by the Ustase. General von Horstenau informed Pavelic that Germany would hold him personally responsible for Macek's safety.

In addition to this, there was the intriguing of the Ustase against such of their own party who had staunchly remained in their own country. Those too were systematically ousted and pushed into the background.

There remained at last a small clique of Pavelic's personal friends in sole authority. Even within this small clique intrigue was paramount. 'Kvaternik junior' was not dismissed for his mass murders of the Serbs and Jews, although his crimes had revolted the vast majority of the Croat people. But when he allowed himself to be drawn into a conspiracy against Pavelic, he was immediately dismissed. His father, who had been promoted to Marshal, was forced to resign.

The Ustase régime had offered the crown of Croatia to a Prince of the House of Savoy, the Duke of Spoleto. On instructions from the King and Mussolini, the Duke had accepted and had adopted the title of King Zvonimir II. Urged on by the boundless ambition of his wife Marshal Kvaternik began to form a plan to become himself the founder of a Croat dynasty. He found a number of adherents, and although his aspirations need not have been taken seriously, Pavelic feared that certain German circles might support him and that an attempted *putsch* was more than probable. He retired to his summer residence, where he remained in isolation surrounded by his personal body-guard. Actually, the Germans never had the slightest intention of supporting Kvaternik's ambitions. Kvaternik could not now save a situation which was beyond all repair. He retired from the public scene, and with his son emigrated to Slovakia. In 1946 he was handed over to the Yugoslavs by the American Forces in Austria and was executed. The same fate overtook almost all the leading Croat politicians and officers, regardless of whether they had been members of the Ustase or the oppos-sition. All who fled to Austria and Hungary and on whom the British and Americans were able to lay their hands were returned to Tito. Almost to a man they were executed. The 'Poglavnik' Pavelic himself escaped. This master of conspiracy and decep-tion lived for some months undiscovered in the American zone of Austria and then went to Italy, where he found asylum in a monastery near Rome. Thence he emigrated to the Argentine, where he still is.

Dr. Kasche, the German Minister, supported Pavelic and the Ustase régime, unreservedly against the more moderate Kvater-nik. Kasche's attitude was the greatest obstacle to me in my efforts to force Pavelic to put an end to the reign of terror and murder which the Ustase régime had started. It would probably have been possible to set up a moderate national coalition Government in Croatia. When the German Wehrmacht and the Secret Service jointly protested to Hitler against the first senseless and dangerous massacres perpetrated by the Ustase, Kasche, with the support of Ribbentrop, defeated our aruments. They replied that these were merely isolated murders, unavoidable in any revolution and transfer of power. That argument lost all force when the revolution had been completed, and the atrocities continued with unmitigated violence. But Kasche successfully found new arguments with which to support his attitude. Only once when in 1942 the Ustase had perpetrated a series of par-ticularly abhorrent murders in Slavonia, did General von

Horstenau succeed in insisting on the dismissal of a handful of Ustase leaders. Pavelic showed not the slightest inclination to punish them and supported and clandestinely kept them as advisers. In secret they planned the murder of the Croat Chief of Staff, General Prpic, and other assassinations and terrorist acts.

Efforts to educate the Ustase bands to civilized warfare were quite fruitless. Operations undertaken by the Wehrmacht were invariably marred by the excesses committed against the civilian population by the Ustase units taking part. As a result of their atrocities more new supporters threw in their lot with the partisans than had been put out of action by the operations. The Ustase troops undoubtedly showed superlative courage. They fought to the last round, and between them and the partisans quarter was neither asked nor given.

In 1943 there occurred in the course of the Croatian tragedy an incident which might well have had world-wide repercussions. During the guerrilla war in Herzegovina a squad of the Todt Labour Organization was surrounded by partisans. The squad was armed and with the certainty that execution would follow capture, they prepared to fight to the end. When their ammunition was exhausted and they were overwhelmed, the Germans were not immediately shot, as were the Croats who had fought beside them, but were despatched to the nearest Partisan Command Post. The leader of this German labour squad was an engineer named Ott. In addition to his normal duties he had been given the task of seeking a special kind of wood required for the manufacture of propellers, which could be found only in that district. In the course of his search he had come in contact with some of the partisan leaders, and this fact probably saved his life. He was quickly transferred to Tito's Headquarters and sent by him with a message to General von Horstenau in Zagreb. Tito proposed that the eleven men of the Todt Organization should be exchanged for a woman partisan leader who had been captured and was in hospital in Zagreb. Von Horstenau, attaching the greatest importance to a direct line of communication with Tito, agreed to the proposal and intimated that he would in future always be prepared in principle to consider exchanges of this nature. Thereupon Tito immediately released the eleven Germans without waiting for the woman's discharge from hospital, informing von Horstenau that his word as a German officer was sufficient.

The contact was then developed. In ensuing conversations Ott proved himself to be an ambitious and skilled negotiator. Tito fell in with the General's suggestion and proposed an exchange of prisoners on a large scale. To negotiate an agreement on the subject he sent a secret envoy, who introduced himself as Dr. Petrovic and stated that he had formerly been a barrister. Petrovic was received by the German General in a most friendly manner. He stayed ten days as the General's guest and was given permission to visit his parents in Zagreb. He was further given a written military permit to visit the territories north of the Save, where there were several contingents of Tito's partisans with whom the leader had no direct contact.

A few days later Petrovic surprised von Horstenau by disclosing that he was in fact General Ljubo Velebit and that he had been entrusted by Tito with a personal message for the German High Command. Tito declared himself ready to conclude an armistice on the following conditions. If the Germans would undertake not to attack him inside a certain reserve territory to be agreed upon, he would refrain from extending his revolt to other parts of the Croat State. As an earnest of his good faith he was prepared also to abstain for an agreed and specified period from all acts of terrorism and sabotage.

The significance of this offer and the importance of the personage who had brought it were such that General von Horstenau did not feel justified in continuing the conversations without first consulting the German Government. An armistice of this nature would have radically altered the whole military and political situation, and that the proposal had been made in earnest was proved by the choice of the individual selected to make it. General Velebit was the son of an Austrian officer, who later became a General in the Yugoslav Army; son of a Croat father and a Serb mother, he had been a Communist from his student days at Belgrade university, and since 1941 he had been one of Tito's most intimate colleagues and his principal adviser on foreign affairs. He became Ambassador of Yugoslavia in London in 1952.

6*

As Glaise von Horstenau considered quite rightly that so bold an idea as an armistice with Tito would get no support, either from his own superiors at Wehrmacht Supreme Headquarters or from the German Foreign Ministry, he first approached Branch VI of the Secret Service, hoping in this way to be able to bring the case through Himmler direct to the attention of Hitler. I was the senior officer of Branch VI South (Yugoslavia) and so it was my duty to discuss with General von Horstenau personally how this game with Tito might be made into an earnest endeavour to free our flank from the partisans.

Tito's reasons for wishing to conclude an armistice with the Germans are of considerable interest. For a very long time, in collaboration with Section Ic, the Intelligence Section of the German Army in Croatia, the Secret Service had intercepted and deciphered Tito's radio communications. The information thus obtained was primarily of importance from the point of view of military operations. On frequent occasions it had enabled the High Command to forestall actions planned by the partisans. Tito, who could not have failed to realize that the German High Command frequently knew of his intentions in advance, at first suspected treachery and carried out a series of purges. When these had no effect, he at last hit on the real solution that his wireless operators were inefficient and his codes were far too primitive. He then changed his codes with great frequency but without success. In the spring of 1943 the Germans picked up a number of messages from which it became clear that Tito's relations with his Anglo-American allies had gravely deteriorated. Tito had ordered that all personal contact between members of the Partisan Army and the British and Americans was to cease under pain of severe penalty. Officers of the Western Powers were in no circumstances to be allowed to obtain any insight into the condition and the intentions of the Partisan Army. In addition, wireless messages from partisan transmitters in the coastal area spoke of an imminent Anglo-American landing on the Adriatic coast of Yugoslavia. All this information was not taken very seriously by the German Secret Service, until suddenly the mission of General Velebit put a very different complexion on the whole affair.

The conclusions which the German Secret Service had reached were almost immediately confirmed from an independent source. In the vicinity of Pecs (Funfkirchen) in Hungary, members of Section II of the Hungarian General Staff—the extremely efficient Hungarian military espionage organization—captured a courier who made sensational disclosures. He asserted no less than that he was the bearer of the following orders from Stalin to Tito:

> The Kremlin had confidential information that Churchill had persuaded Roosevelt to undertake a landing on the Adriatic coast contrary to the agreement with Moscow. If this were attempted, Stalin formally authorized Tito to make common cause with the German troops against the Anglo-American invasion forces, and that to this end he approved of Tito's making an agreement with the German High Command.

The Hungarian officer who had conducted the interrogation of the courier was a Captain Zoltan Gat, who had already done excellent intelligence work in Yugoslavia. His information had invariably proved both accurate and reliable, so in the present case must also be treated seriously. Captain Gat deserted to Tito; and later returned to become a Major-General and Director of the Hungarian Intelligence Service, one of the most important members of the Soviet espionage group against the Western Powers. As secretary of the Kossuth Academy he was responsible for the political education and Communist upbringing of the Hungarian officer cadets.

Shortly after the capture of this courier, General Velebit received a messenger in Zagreb apparently from Tito's Headquarters. He immediately asked for an interview with General von Horstenau and asked that a representative of the German Foreign Ministry should be present. Von Horstenau invited a member of the Legation to attend. General Velebit then delivered a further important message to the effect that Tito in the event of an Anglo-American landing was prepared to co-operate with the German divisions in Croatia in common operations against the invaders. There was now no further doubt as to the genuineness of the courier's statement as reported by the Hungarians. It had already been frequently proved that Tito often received his orders from Moscow simultaneously through several different channels. The instructions which the captured courier had been bringing had apparently been received through some alternative channel as well.

Time was precious. General von Horstenau no longer felt justified in incurring the delay involved in a circuitous approach to Hitler. Equally, any decision without Hitler's approval was out of the question. He decided to approach the Fuehrer direct through Ribbentrop. Hitler's reply was immediate and laconic: 'I don't parley with rebels—I shoot them.'

That was that. But these negotiations between Tito and the Germans remain a most interesting episode.[1] They certainly proved the important fact that the Soviet Union was determined to resist any incursion into its sphere of influence, if necessary by force of arms and even with Germany's help. It is possible too that Tito learnt from the incident a lesson which he has never forgotten. The Kremlin would never have the slightest compunction in sacrificing its allies to its own interests. This may well have a direct bearing on his present attitude towards the Soviet Union.

The struggle between the Germans and Tito continued. In June 1944, the Germans decided to try and deal the partisans a decisive blow by robbing them of their leader. Paratroopers were to carry out a raid on Tito's Headquarters at Drvar in West Bosnia and capture him and the whole of his staff. The raid went according to plan, but Tito himself escaped by a hair's breadth. All that he left behind was a handsome new Marshal's uniform, which he had just had made and which subsequently graced the Military Museum in Vienna. Two British journalists attached to Tito's Headquarters were captured, whom I later saw as prisoners of war in the offices of the Secret Service in Vienna; but they were little compensation for the escape of the big prize. Lack of co-ordination between the different German branches was also partially responsible for the failure. My Secret Service branch had worked out almost identical plans

---

[1] No comment can be obtained in Yugoslav quarters as to the accuracy of the above account of negotiations between Marshal Tito and the German occupying forces in Yugoslavia. It must be remembered that intelligence with the enemy is usually capable of a double interpretation, particularly when such negotiations have not led to any concrete result.—*Editor*.

with almost exactly the same timing, but the Wehrmacht did not keep me properly informed of its own intentions. My agents were already close to Tito's Headquarters in preparation for the coup, and had my subversive plan been co-ordinated with the military plan and carried out jointly, the chances are that Tito himself would have been caught.

The withdrawal of the Germans and the advance of the Russians enabled Tito to seize Belgrade, Sarajevo and Zagreb, one after the other. The Germans retired partly into Central Austria and partly into Hungary. In the north-west of Yugo-slavia, the Germans and their Croat allies supported even by a few Serb units held out until May 1945. For the first time when it was already far too late, some sort of a united front was formed by the peoples of Yugoslavia against the advance of Communism. Cetniks and Ustase, Serbian and Croat police units, Mohamme-dans and Montenegrins, who had all been fighting each other to the death, were now joined by newly formed neo-Fascist volun-teers. The whole combined with the Germans to form a common front against the Red Army of Tito. Even those two deadly enemies, Pavelic and Mihailovic, agreed to sink all their differ-ences and to unite. Resistance was only abandoned when the general situation showed that it was utterly hopeless to fight on.

The present movement against Tito—the 'Krizari' ('Crusaders') is formed in Croatia of former Ustase, in Bosnia of 'Mladi Musilmani' (Young Mahommedans) under the banner of the Crescent, and in Serbia of royalist nationalist groups of the Cetniks. They began to unite their front in the final phases of the war. But the *émigrés* have already forgotten the lessons of 1945. Serbian and Croat exiles, attack each other for all the world to hear, an attitude which has made Tito strong and helped to keep him in power.

CHAPTER X

THE KING WHO FOOLED US

WHEN in June 1940, Russia compelled Rumania to cede Bessarabia and North Bukovina, and in August Germany imposed the Arbitration Award which gave North Transylvania to Hungary, the régime of King Carol II was severely shaken. His kingdom had shrunk. These defeats of his foreign policy strengthened the opposition which for years had sought the removal of a Government that reigned by repression and thrived on corruption.

Foremost among the opponents of the Government were a group of Army Officers and the Iron Guard. The latter movement started among university students in the 1920s. While it was similar to other Fascist movements elsewhere, it was as yet anything but a replica of any one of them. Its members were more intellectual than those of, say, the German Nazi Party, and the principal difference which characterized the movement was the strong religious feeling of the original Iron Guardists— a feeling that bordered on mysticism. The movement found strong support in the country, and the Government to remove this threat indicted, and later ordered the murder of, the Iron Guard leaders, among them Codreanu.

After the Vienna Arbitration Award, the King decided to select a new man as Prime Minister, and he chose General Jon Antonescu. Antonescu was no Iron Guard, nor can it be said that he was among the strongest characters or most striking personalities of the military group which opposed the King. He belonged to the Officers' opposition group against the King, but it was only at the time of the secession of Bessarabia and North Bukhovina that he established contact with the Iron Guard. Further, he was in very indifferent health and suffered from leucoma, and on one occasion he had been put into a Home for nervous diseases apparently not so much on medical grounds as for political reasons and at the request of the King.

King Carol probably hoped that in time he would gain sufficient influence over him to be able to use him as a pawn against the Legionaries of the Iron Guard. At that time the King had no intention of abdicating. All he wished to do was to try and bolster his tottering throne by means of a change of Government.

There is good reason to assume that at an early date the German Legation used such influence as it possessed in favour of a solution which did not leave the power entirely in the hands of the Iron Guard. The Minister Dr. Fabricius, and his Councillor, Dr. Stelzer, were both of the opinion that a Government in the hands of the Iron Guard would not serve Germany's best interests. The organization had lost the whole of its leaders, the brains behind it, as it were, were gone, and to entrust the destiny of the country to it would be a grave error. It would not be capable of governing or of maintaining that measure of law and order in the country which was essential if Germany were to be able to exploit to the full the natural resources, chiefly in mineral oils, which Rumania had to offer to her. On the other hand, a Government which was not acceptable to the Iron Guard would be equally unable to govern, and in these circumstances the best solution seemed to be a compromise— a mixed Government of Generals and Iron Guardists in which the military element would be predominant.

For the Iron Guard the appointment of General Antonescu was the signal for a general rising. Parades and stormy demonstrations were held throughout the land and the 'Legionaries' succeeded in winning supporters in every class of the people. Under this incessant and violent pressure the King admitted defeat and on 6th September, 1940 the monarch who had already spent from 1926 to 1930 in exile, once more signed a declaration of abdication. He was succeeded by his son Michael, who had already been on the throne during his father's exile. Accompanied by his amie Magda Lupescu, whom he later married, and the detested Court Marshal Jon Urdareanu, Carol slipped in most unkingly fashion through a side door of the castle and departed. But he did not go without first having collected everything of value that he could grab in his haste and stow in his special train, nor were the Rembrandts in the royal castle of Sinaia forgotten, and the pictures later found in the original frames were copies. The ex-King's train was shot at by Legionaries as it passed through Timisoara but no one was hurt.

The young King confirmed the appointment of General Antonescu as Prime Minister and accepted the Government he had formed. To emphasize the authoritarian character of his régime Antonescu took the title of 'Conductorul Statului'—the Head of the State. He appointed Horia Sima, Codreanu's successor and the new leader of the Iron Guard, as Deputy Prime Minister. Horia Sima was a much weaker character than his predecessor and he never gained either the personal authority of Codreanu or the great mass influence which he had wielded, but preferred rather to be guided by the resolutions passed by the 'Forum', the Superior Council of the Iron Guard, composed of the Commandants of the various Legions. Legionaries were also appointed to a number of Ministries and the most important of them, Prince Mihai Sturdza, the former Minister in Copenhagen, became Foreign Minister, and Vasile Jasinschi, who later became prominent, assumed the office of Minister of Health and Labour.

It soon became obvious that any attempt to unite the Iron Guardists and the former military opposition group was doomed to failure. It would have been an unnatural alliance; the two elements of the coalition fundamentally opposed in both outlook and structure could not be fused, and each faction strove to eliminate the other and to gather the entire power into its own hands. Antonescu began his campaign by dismissing some Legionaries from the high positions they occupied and sidetracking many others; and these measures, of course, drew the sharpest of protests from the Iron Guard. It seems likely that Antonescu, seeking an excuse to throw the whole Iron Guard, root and branch, out of the Government, deliberately planned to provoke the Legionaries to open rebellion, and as the situation developed, it became clear that the leaders of the Guard would be faced with the alternative either of surrendering unconditionally to the Head of the State or of seizing power by force.

The balance of power between the two parties was profoundly

affected by the arrival of the German Military Mission. The events leading to the appointment of this mission are a little-known story. It was the outcome of an agreement reached between Morosov, the Chief of the Rumanian Secret Service, and Colonel Bentivegni, the representative of Admiral Canaris, Chief of the German Military Intelligence. They agreed to co-operate in guarding the Rumanian oilfields, against which the British Secret Service was known to be planning acts of sabotage. This agreement assumed a wholly unpremeditated significance in the future. The requirements of security against sabotage were the reason given for sending German military personnel to Rumania. The idea of a German Military Mission to reorganize and train the Rumanian Army and Air Force originated with the German Air Attaché in Bucharest, Colonel of the Luftwaffe Gerstenberg. Antonescu was easily convinced that a corps of instructors would prove most useful. He invited the German Government to send the requisite personnel. The invitation was naturally accepted. In October 1940 the first units of the German Wehrmacht under the command of General Hansen arrived in Rumania. Gradually these demonstration units were reinforced to a strength of two Divisions and they constituted a potential source of strength whose intervention could be decisive in Rumanian internal affairs. (Morosov, one of the original negotiators, was also in close touch with the British Secret Service. After the abdication of King Carol he was arrested by the Legionaries who had many scores to settle with him, and later, in company with a large number of other prisoners suspected of being implicated in the death of Codreanu, he was put to death in Jilava prison by the Legionaries but without the knowledge or consent of their leaders.)

In the meanwhile the relations between the Legionaries and the Antonescu group had deteriorated to such an extent that the fateful decision—capitulation or an attempted *coup d'état*—could not be postponed much longer. The Iron Guard felt that the time had come to settle the issue with the Head of the State and it decided to appeal to force. With German troops in the country, success or failure for the Iron Guard depended on the attitude which Germany would adopt. Although no binding declaration had been given, the leaders of the Guard felt justified in believing that German sympathies would be on their side. The German Secret Service in Rumania had particularly cordial relations with the leading Legionaries and it had done its utmost to recommend the Iron Guard as the most reliable partner for Germany in her policy in South-eastern Europe. At the end of October 1940, Himmler had sent one of Heydrich's men to Rumania to organize a 'Legion Liaison Group', whose task was to be the re-moulding of the Iron Guard to conform to German pattern. The Legions, admittedly, were not enthusiastic but the mission was well received and eventually a semi-police legionary organization was formed much on the lines of the German S.S. The Overseas Section of the German Nazi Party also made contact with the Legions but this liaison was of no political significance.

Signs were not lacking of tension with Germany. The Iron Guard put obstacles in the way of German economic expansion in Rumania. They opposed the German aim to take over industrial plant and property of countries occupied during the campaign in the West—particularly the Creditul Minier, a French oil company, and the Dutch Danube Navigation Company. They resisted the passing into German control of the Malaxa heavy industry works. Malaxa was a Rumanian industrialist who as a supporter of ex-King Carol had been dispossessed by the State. The Rumanian Section of the German Ministry of Economics tried with the collusion of the Antonescu group to incorporate Malaxa's plant in the Hermann Goering Works. But the Iron Guard insisted that a company should be formed, in which at least 51 per cent of the shares should remain in Rumanian hands.

There were also difficulties over the Iron Guard's opposition to the Second Vienna Award. This displeased Ribbentrop immensely for he was very proud indeed of his arbitration. Then again the activities of the *Volksdeutsche Mittelstelle*, the Liaison Office of the German Minorities Abroad, in Rumania under S.S. General Lorenz, left an unfavourable impression on the Iron Guard. To transfer the German population from Bessarabia, which had been agreed upon by Berlin and Moscow, a numerous staff of the aforementioned office had established itself in Rumania. This staff formed a close liaison with the German minority which resulted in strenuous efforts being made to procure a special status for German minorities. The newly appointed leader of the German Minority Group, Schmid, and the Foreign Ministry official and Consul General in Kronstadt, S.S. Colonel Rodder, were particularly active in this. The Legionaries regarded such activities as a menace to the unity of the Rumanian State. Much as they desired to support friendly relations between Germany and Rumania, they had no desire to see a German State within the Rumanian State.

These resistances to German plans naturally reacted on the German attitude towards the Iron Guard. It gave rise to a feeling of disappointment which all but amounted to distrust. Frank discussions cleared the air a little. But these pinpricks and difficulties remained unknown among the rank and file of the Guard. They believed firmly in German friendship towards them and their cause.

Misunderstandings of this sort would not decide Germany's attitude towards the Legionaries. Only Hitler could do that. Therein two factors were decisive. In November General Antonescu had paid a State visit to Berlin. Horia Sima also invited had refused. Presumably he did not wish in any way to jeopardize his claim to leadership of the nation by appearing as a subordinate behind the Head of the State on so important an occasion. It was during this visit that Antonescu made that well-known 'good impression' which counted for far more with Hitler than any sober reflection. In this case reflection also seems to have weighed in Antonescu's favour. At that time Hitler had already decided to embark upon the vital conflict with Russia. Soviet expansion in Eastern Europe had convinced him that the great reckoning with Bolshevism, never struck out of the list of his intentions, must be made without delay. He thought of Rumania strategically. In view of the struggle before him he felt that General Antonescu, representing the Rumanian Armed Forces and law and order, would alone be the right and proper ally. Horia Sima with his Iron Guard would assume power only by means of revolution and civil war. That would drastically reduce Rumania's military value for a long time to come. Hitler then had no doubt as to which side Germany should support in the Rumanian internal struggle.

Like the various German services in Rumania, the leaders of
the Iron Guard had no idea that Germany had already decided
against the Legion. They assumed that in the final reckoning
between the Iron Guard and Antonescu the Germans would at
least remain neutral. What finally put the match to the powder
cask has never been clearly ascertained but the revolt burst
suddenly on 21st January, 1941, in Bucharest. In the first onslaught the Legionaries gained possession of nearly all the public
buildings in the capital. At one moment the issue hung in the
balance, and only the Prime Minister's residence in the new
Foreign Ministry building and the streets around it remained
in Antonescu's hands. His military power had been paralysed
by the fact that many of the troops sympathized with the Iron
Guard and refused to take action against them.

Then the units of the German Wehrmacht intervened. They
fired no shot but German tanks patrolled the streets and took
up positions at strategic points. It became obvious that if
necessary they would go into action on Antonescu's behalf.
During this interlude Rumanian troops true to Antonescu had,
on German demand, been successfully brought into the capital.
The Legionaries' cause was lost. Germany had forsaken the
Iron Guard, the victim of Hitler's cold and calculating reasoning, which forbade any consideration for the luckless Guardists.
That his reasoning was wrong in spite of its apparent logic
became clear only later. The disintegration of the Legion
movement meant that the Antonescu régime lost all contact
with the people. Like the royal dictatorship of King Carol
before it, it became an automaton. In its hour of need later
not a hand was raised in its defence. A little palace plot sufficed
to bring it down in ruins. Antonescu's triumph, won with
German aid, was destined to be a Pyrrhic victory.

In desperation the Legionaries had decided to continue a
struggle which was already useless, and which could have ended
only in their wholesale destruction. The Chief of the German
Secret Service in Rumania, S.S. Captain Otto Bohlschuring,
therefore undertook to arrange a capitulation. Thanks to him
the Legionaries agreed to cease fighting, provided that they were
given a complete amnesty and a safe conduct to withdraw their
forces. In the middle of the night Dr. Neubacher accompanied

by the Secret Service Chief called on Antonescu to persuade
him to accept these conditions. Antonescu agreed. But next
morning when the Legionaries began to evacuate their positions
they were arrested by the score or shot to pieces with machine-
guns. Eight hundred dead were left lying in the streets.

This breach of a solemn undertaking showed only too clearly
that the Iron Guard leaders if they were caught would certainly
be executed, regardless of whether they were brought to trial
or not. The German Legation could do no more. The new
Minister, Manfred von Killinger, had arrived a few days previously. He came with express orders from Hitler to support
Antonescu in all circumstances and at all costs. The German
Secret Service again intervened in spite of the fact that their
action would be obviously contrary to the intentions of the
Foreign Ministry, to which at the time they were subordinated.
They decided to save the Iron Guard leaders on their own
responsibility. Fourteen Legion Commanders were kept hidden
for a long time. Finally they were transferred to Germany in
military ambulances disguised as German soldiers.

Horia Sima was entrusted to the care of Schmid the leader
of the German Minority Group, a fact which was to have a
fortunate sequel. The intervention of the Secret Service was
regarded by Berlin as a serious breach of discipline and an affront
to General Antonescu, the friend of the Fuehrer and the ally of
Germany. Killinger informed the Chief of the Service that he
had received instructions to place him under arrest. In this
extremely dangerous situation the fact that Schmid by harbour-
ing the Iron Guard leader, had shown himself to be a party to
the 'plot' proved to be the saving factor. Schmid was the son-
in-law of the S.S. Headquarters Commandant, General Berger.
To justify himself he asked his father-in-law to defend the
German Secret Service in a talk with Himmler. The latter was
quite converted by Berger's arguments, and he took up the case
on behalf of the Secret Service with great energy. His strong
criticism of the policy of Ribbentrop and the Foreign Ministry
led to the first serious rift between the Political Branch of the
Secret Service and the German Foreign Ministry. For months
all communication between the two Departments ceased.
Himmler and Ribbentrop were no longer on speaking terms.

Himmler quite rightly regarded Ribbentrop, whose reports had been mainly responsible for Hitler's decision to support Antonescu, as the exponent of the anti-Iron Guard Policy. But in the end Ribbentrop once again prevailed. He persuaded Hitler to forbid the Political Branch to engage in any further intelligence work of any kind in Rumania.

Himmler acknowledged these instructions. But Heydrich had not the slightest intention of obeying them. It is true that during the decisive weeks he had not shown himself to be pro-Iron Guard, and there is good reason to believe that he considered Hitler's policy to be correct. But he would not submit to the elimination of the Secret Service from Rumanian affairs. He supported every effort made to regain a footing in that country. The Chief of the Secret Service in Rumania, who had escaped punishment thanks to the Schmidt-Berger intervention with Himmler, was later arrested on some other pretext and spent many months in the cellars of the Gestapo Headquarters in Berlin. A similar fate awaited the other members who, contrary to Hitler's orders but in accordance with the 'unofficial' instructions of their immediate superior, continued to take part in intelligence activities.

It is perhaps permissible here to forestall events and to follow the fate of the Iron Guardists to its end. Large numbers of them were transported to Germany where at the insistent demand of Ribbentrop they were incorporated into the German Labour Corps. They were given the same status as other foreign workers in Germany with this difference—that they were not allowed to communicate with their own country, and Ribbentrop further threatened, if they disobeyed this condition, to return them to Rumania and hand them over to Antonescu. In the late autumn of 1942 Horia Sima fled to Italy. He attempted to persuade Mussolini to intervene on the Legionaries' behalf. That brought about a change for the worse. Not only was he arrested, but sent back to Germany on the demand of the Foreign Ministry and put into a concentration camp. His fellow Legionaries too lost even the small measure of freedom which had been granted to them. They too were arrested by the Gestapo in June 1943 and 'quartered' in Buchenwald and Dachau. There they remained, treated with a little more con-

sideration than the ordinary prisoners, until the *coup de main*
against Antonescu and the exit of Rumania from the war in
August 1944.

After that Horia Sima was invited to form a Rumanian
Government in exile, to which he agreed. He and his companions were released forthwith. What persuaded him to accept
this invitation is not clear. It is possible that he still believed in
an ultimate German victory or he may have felt that in spite of
the hopelessness of the situation, he must fight on with the
Germans against Bolshevism to the bitter end. But any suggestion that he purchased his release and that of his comrades with
this acceptance is entirely false. Horia Sima had often proved
an upright man and a man who knew how to face adversity and
suffering. The Government in exile set up in Vienna under the
general supervision of the German Secret Service, did not accomplish much. No longer did Horia Sima as Prime Minister have
the unanimous support of his Legionaries. A split developed
in the ranks of the Iron Guard, of which for obvious reasons
nothing was made public. The opposition element which contained many of the more firmly established leaders of the Guard
categorically refused to co-operate with Germany in any way.
It was only the pressing threat of Russia, the common foe,
which restrained them from direct action against the Germans.
They tried to establish contact with the Western Powers, but
in this they met with no success.

With the Iron Guard destroyed in Rumania a new force
emerged. By the spring of 1940 Soviet Secret Service activities
in Rumania had expanded very considerably. Numbers of
agents had been distributed all over the country and the personnel of the Soviet Legation in Bucharest had been increased
in a most suspicious manner. Big sums of money were being
spent on bribery—with considerable success. The German
Secret Service knew that the Russians had bribed the Rumanian
postal authorities to install a listening-in post in the Soviet Legation to tap all important diplomatic telephone conversations.
When, after the secession of Bessarabia and North Bukovina,
the new Soviet Minister Georgi Lavrentiev arrived in Bucharest,
these secret activities increased still further. He brought with
him hundreds of agents who immediately set about preparing

the ground both by propaganda and organization for a seizure of power by the Rumanian Communist Party. Money was no object. The *Siguranza* or Rumanian Security Police alone confiscated no less than a hundred thousand dollars in January 1943 found on a few Russian agents. Most of these notes were forgeries. In reality this was the beginning of the Rumanian Communist Party, kept alive by active Russian support.

After the German withdrawal from the Caucasus and Italy's change of sides in the summer of 1943, the Rumanian Government realized that Germany could not win the war. To remain longer at her side would involve Rumania in a catastrophe. National survival demanded a drastic revision of Rumanian policy. The man who wished to see his country steer a new course was the Deputy Prime Minister and Minister for Foreign Affairs, Miha Antonescu. He was without any doubt the cleverest man in the Government with great and increasing influence over his namesake, the Marshal and Prime Minister.

Mihai Antonescu's programme was simple—peace with the Western Powers, coupled with a request for protection against the Soviet Union. But the idea had one fundamental weakness. It was based on the fatally erroneous assumption that a separate understanding with the Western Powers to the exclusion of Russia was still possible. Mihai Antonescu had completely misappreciated the realities of the political situation—or perhaps did not wish to face up to them. Britain and America had already written off South-eastern Europe. Rumania belonged to the Russian sphere of influence and the road westwards was irrevocably barred to her. Mihai Antonescu's heroic effort ended in exactly the same way as similar efforts by Horthy in Hungary and Muraviev in Bulgaria—but with this difference, that the Rumanian statesman lost his life in the attempt.

It must have struck the Germans as significant that on Mihai Antonescu's demand the Italian Minister, Bova Scoppa, who had joined Badoglio's party, was allowed without demur to remain at Bucharest. Mihai Antonescu could not have prevented the new North Italian Government from also sending its own diplomatic representative to Bucharest. But until such a time as Bova Scoppa was repudiated by him no new man could present his credentials. As a result the newly appointed Ministers of Bulgaria and Croatia could also not officially take up their appointments. For diplomatic etiquette precluded them from taking priority over Mussolini's Minister, and he had not yet been able to present himself to the King!

Maniu, the leader of the Peasant Party, with Mihai Antonescu's concurrence, tried to get in touch with the Western Allies. At the end of March 1944, after the Russian break-through near Uman, he succeeded for the first time in so doing. Captain of the Rumanian Air Force Prince Mattei Ghika-Cantacuzino fled from the airport of Pipera to Malta. With him in the plane were Max Auschnitt, the most important industrialist in Rumania, Alexander Raconta, an official of the American-Rumanian Telephone Company, and Radu Humurzescu, a Rumanian diplomat. They took with them a letter addressed to the British, as a result of which Anglo-Rumanian talks were opened. Instead of saying at once and quite clearly that Britain and the United States neither would nor could come to any decision regarding Rumania without some sort of concurrence from the Soviet Union, the British dragged on the negotiations. This raised false hope among the Rumanians that they would be able to cease hostilities with the help of the Western Powers and place themselves under their protection. There may well have been sound operational reasons for the omission of any mention of this vital factor at the first tentative meeting. But the British failed to make the point clear when a second Rumanian delegation was sent to Britain. That appears to me to be sadly irresponsible conduct.

The second delegation headed by Prince Barbu Stirbey arrived in London from Cairo just after the Normandy landings. It had the support and blessing of Mihai Antonescu, who had skilfully obtained the concurrence of the German Legation to the Prince's journey to Egypt ostensibly for urgent reasons of health. And Prince Stirbey was thus able to leave Rumania legally and in possession of his genuine passport. In Alexandria he met his son-in-law Major Boxhall of the British Intelligence Service who, until the outbreak of war, had been working in the Rumanian petroleum industry. Boxhall made the necessary arrangements for Stirbey's onward journey and ensured that he would be received in London. While in Cairo and later in

London, Prince Stirbey had direct wireless communication with Niculescu Buzesti, a senior official of the Rumanian Foreign Ministry who, among other things, had charge of the cypher section. He was perhaps the most important and certainly the most active member of the Rumanian peace party. The first reports from London were couched in most optimistic terms and there seemed to be more than a chance that Britain and the United States would conclude a preliminary separate peace with Rumania, later taking up the question of Rumanian affairs with the Soviet Union as protectors of the country.

The German Secret Service knew the broad outlines of Mihai Antonescu's real intentions, but was in no position to intervene. That some sort of liaison existed between the British and some Rumanian party was made obvious to the expert by the case of de Chastelaine, a Colonel of the British Intelligence Service dropped with two wireless operators into Rumania by parachute some months before Stirbey's departure for Egypt. Without any doubt Chastelaine had been sent to act as Liaison Officer between London and the Rumanian peace party. Thanks to some lack of co-ordination he was arrested by the Rumanian Security Police, and the incident became publicly known. The German Secret Service naturally did its best to find out all about de Chastelaine's mission, but Mihai Antonescu cleverly managed to confuse the issue. German officers took part in the interrogation of de Chastelaine, but brought nothing to light. The Rumanians had already agreed with the British officer on what he was to say. Germany demanded that he be handed over, but so strong was Marshal Antonescu's position that Rumania felt able to refuse the demand without incurring any serious risk.

At about the same time as Prince Stirbey left Rumania, King Michael independently started a movement to bring about the desired revolt by means of a military *putsch*. The idea was that the Rumanian Generals at the front should set up a rival Government and place troops at its disposal. At the same time a revolt was to be raised in the north and a 'march on the capital' was to end in the seizure of Bucharest. The Chief of the Royal Military Chancellery visited the Eastern front in May 1944 to win over the Commanders serving there but he met with little enthusiasm. In any case the Rumanian units were so integrated into larger

German formations that they did not possess the liberty of action essential to a military *putsch*. Eventually the scheme was abandoned.

In the meantime the Rumanians at last realized that their attempt to avoid the clutches of Russia by signing a separate peace with the West was doomed to failure. Prince Stirbey could negotiate no agreement of any value and the Normandy campaign would obviously engage the Anglo-American forces to a degree which precluded any operations in South-eastern Europe. At the same time Russian pressure on the South-eastern front increased until the danger became both pressing and imminent. In these circumstances the Rumanian opposition leaders instructed General Aurel Aldea to make direct contact with the Red Army. They authorized him to conclude an armistice in the name of the Rumanian people. An announcement to this effect was signed on 17th August, 1944, by the leaders of the four parties, the National Liberals, the National Zaranists, the Social Democrats and the Communists. Prince Stirbey and the Soviet Minister in Stockholm, Madame Alexandra Kollontai, were informed of the fact.

The Russians, however, did not bother their heads about the Rumanian negotiators. They had not the slightest intention of modifying their military operations on account of an offer of an armistice by Rumania. On 19th August the Red Army on the Moldau front assumed the offensive and the same day Jassy fell. Although this was a great shock for the Rumanian people to think of it in terms of a military catastrophe was still premature. The new Chief of the General Staff, General Rakovitza, nevertheless gave the order without consulting Marshal Antonescu for general withdrawal of the Rumanian Army to positions behind the line of the Sereth. A few weeks previously Rakovitza, then commanding the Third Rumanian Army, had received at Hitler's Headquarters the Oak Leaves to his Knight's Cross. Now he was passionately for peace. After the armistice he got his reward in the shape of command of the Fifth Rumanian Army, which he then led into action against the Germans in Hungary. The Sereth line consisted of a strong defensive system, well organized in depth. In the opinion of military experts it could not have been rapidly over-run

by the Russians in the face of resistance. Rakovitza's order
for the withdrawal was probably a condition which he was
compelled to fulfil before the Russians would agree to any
further negotiations.

Now the situation was desperate. If Rumania were to save
anything from a total collapse by concluding a separate peace,
immediate action was absolutely imperative. In this crisis the
young King and his advisers decided to act.

On the morning of 23rd August a Cabinet meeting was held
with Marshal Antonescu presiding and the Prime Minister was
to report the result to the King that same afternoon. Without
waiting, King Michael summoned his most trusted followers,
Niculescu-Buzesti, Mocsony-Starcia the Court Marshal, and
Generals Sanatescu and Aldea. They decided to put forward
the date previously agreed upon for action against Antonescu
from 26th August to that very day. They had to act swiftly.
If Marshal Antonescu decided himself to open negotiations with
the Russians, the King and his adherents would find themselves
out-manœuvred.

At three o'clock on the afternoon of 23rd August, when the
Head of the State, accompanied by his Deputy, Mihai Antonescu, sought audience of the King, he found that General
Sanatescu was present. Only the King and Sanatescu have
given any first-hand version of this historic meeting. For the
two Antonescus did not survive very long. Marshal Antonescu,
it is said, described the dangerous situation at the front and
pointed out that an immediate armistice was now essential.
He had, he said, already discussed the matter with Dr. Clodius,
the representative of the German Reich. This statement gravely
disturbed the King and his adviser. If a representative of the
Reich already knew about Rumania's intentions to conclude an
armistice it could be assumed with certainty that Hitler would
take immediate counter-measures, set up a new Government
and himself assume supreme command of the Rumanian armed
forces. The King therefore broke off the conversation and
retired to another room. The others of his adherents were
waiting for him. Rapidly he explained the situation, and his
friends, recognizing that the King's concern was only too well
founded, urged him to act without delay.

King Michael returned to the audience chamber. He did not resume the conversations, but curtly and in a tone which brooked no argument he stated that the policy of the Government in office was injurious to the interests of the Rumanian nation. He was therefore constrained to dismiss it forthwith. Taking no further notice of the Marshal, the King left the audience chamber and ordered a Major of the Palace Guard to arrest the Head of the State and his Deputy. Marshal Antonescu does not at first seem to have realized the seriousness of his position. While on his way out under escort, he met the Commander of the Palace Guard, to whom he cried: 'You miserable people! To-morrow you'll all be shot!'

The conspirators now proceeded without delay to seize the other leading members of Antonescu's régime. General Sanetescu summoned them to a conference at the Palace and most of them, including the Minister for War Mihai Pantazi, and the Minister of the Interior General Vasiliu, fell into the trap and were arrested on arrival. The Chief of the Rumanian Secret Service Colonel Christescu, and the Commandant of the Gendarmerie General Tobescu, were suspicious and disregarded Sanatescu's summons. Instead they went straight to the German Legation and informed the Minister Killinger that the Head of the State and his Deputy had been detained at the Palace.

Manfred von Killinger was that type of war-time soldier who had never been able to settle down again in civil life. At the end of the first war, after serving in various volunteer corps, he quickly came to the brownshirts and became one of Roehm's closest supporters. Soon afterwards he was appointed National-Socialist premier of Saxony. The purge of 30th June, 1934, all but swept him away and the execution squad of the S.S. was already in position to shoot him when the instructions which saved his life arrived. After this narrow escape he understandably had a distinct aversion to anything connected with the S.S. When Ribbentrop started to renovate the Foreign Office by giving jobs to deserving Party members, by diluting the diplomats de carrière whom he detested, he chose Killinger too. After a short interlude as Consul General in San Francisco Killinger was appointed Minister in Bratislava and at the same time

Inspector of the Foreign Ministry Political Intelligence in the
Balkans. He was shortly relieved by another Storm Trooper
leader, Ludin, and sent as Minister to Bucharest instead.
There were now five Storm Troop Ministers in South-east
Europe (Ludin in Bratislava, Kasche in Zagreb, Becherle in
Sofia and von Jagow in Budapest). Killinger in Bucharest was
the most impossible. Not that the remaining four came in any
way up to standard. They were all undoubtedly gallant officers,
bold and resourceful members of guerrilla bands and revolutionary soldiers of the Roehm type. But they were certainly not
suited to the offices to which they had been sent. While the
others did their best to appear as conventional diplomats,
Killinger did the reverse and lost no opportunity of exhibiting
his contempt for diplomatic custom and usage.

Devoid of any political sense, lacking the imagination and
sensitivity which are the essential attributes of a good diplomat,
he refused to take notice of reliable information about the activities of the peace party in Rumania. The German Secret
Service reported to him on the conference of opposition leaders
at the Royal Palace of Sinaia, and the formation of the so-called
Democratic Bloc. This made as little impression on him as did
the news that King Michael had told the Allies of his intention
to extricate Rumania from the war. Killinger allowed nothing
to disturb his bluff indifference. To the very end he had no
conception of how serious the situation was. Even when events
themselves spoke in a manner which even he could not mis-
understand, he attempted airily to explain them away. On the
night of 23rd August, when Antonescu's régime was tottering
to its fall, all efforts to persuade him of the dangers failed.
Inevitably confusion and indecision reigned in the German
legation.

Nor can it be said that the other side was distinguished by its
unity of purpose. Maniu saw more clearly than the other leaders
and had no illusions as to the real intentions of the Soviet Union.
He did his utmost to protect Rumania's national interests against
the claims of the Russians. Bratianu, too, agreed entirely with
Maniu, but had not a like courage of his convictions. Maniu
argued for hours on end with the Communist leader, Patrascanu,
to gain his point, but in vain. Through Anna Pauker, Patrascanu

had received his orders from Moscow and had no intention of deviating one inch from them. It was only when the news of the arrest of the two Antonescus and the summoning of Sanatescu to form a Government was brought to them by a King's Messenger that Maniu gave way, and an agreement between the four opposition parties was reached. Had Maniu adopted any other attitude decisions would have been taken over his head and his influence would have been gone for ever. The ministerial posts of the Sanatescu Cabinet were filled mostly by Generals while the leaders of the four parties of the Democratic *bloc* were invited to join the Government as Ministers without portfolio.

The new Foreign Minister, Nicolescu Buzesti, instructed Prince Stirbey with his colleague the future Foreign Secretary Visoianu in Cairo to proceed without delay to conclude an armistice. He was given full powers to do so. The Soviet Ambassador in Cairo expressed his willingness to act as intermediary. By 28th August all was ready for the Rumanian delegates to go to Moscow and sign the treaty.

German counter-measures were not only ineffectual, but actually made the catastrophe even worse. They could have saved something from the wreck only if they had forestalled the King's *coup de main* against Antonescu, or had at least been put into force as soon as it occurred. The German Secret Service had furnished more than enough material to justify action against the King and his entourage, the leaders of the nationalist bloc and the unstable elements in the Antonescu régime. Such action could have been taken with quite small German forces, for here was no popular movement but a comparatively small circle of individuals. Intervention immediately following the arrest of the two Antonescus would most probably have succeeded. It would have postponed the crisis and afforded a breathing space. The vacillations of the German Legation, the inefficiency of Killinger and Hitler's wrong appreciation of the Rumanian scene, led to vital hours being wasted.

The same evening, 23rd August, Dr. Stelzer, the Legation Councillor and Chargé d'Affaires, was summoned to the Palace. The new Foreign Minister officially informed him that relations with the Axis Powers were broken off. The Minister offered

safe conduct for the withdrawal of German troops, provided
that they engaged in no hostile acts. This was a concession, as
under Clause 1 of the armistice with Russia, Rumania was required to change sides and continue the war against Germany.

It was only at midnight on 23rd August that the German
Military Mission in Bucharest received Hitler's order to 'smash
the *putsch*'. The confused reports of the Minister had given
the German Government no clue to the real march of events.
Not until ten o'clock, when the King proclaimed the cessation
of hostilities against the Soviet Union, was the true situation
revealed to the Fuehrer's Headquarters. The delays could never
be made good.

In accordance with their unshakeable adherence to the
Fuehrerprinzip, nearly all important German nationals in
Bucharest, including the three Service Chiefs of the German
Military Mission, Generals Hansen and Gerstenberg and
Admiral Tillesen, assembled at the Legation to wait upon the
German Minister as senior representative of the German Reich.
There they were promptly cut off from the outside world by
Rumanian Security troops. General Gerstenberg of the Luft-
waffe, on the pretext that he wished to restrain German troops
from committing any excesses, was allowed by the Rumanian
Commandant to leave the Legation for a few hours. He did
not, however, keep his part of the bargain, but tried instead to
organize military counter-measures. In so doing he was guilty
of an error of judgment which was to bring grave consequences.
A counter-stroke should have been initiated very much earlier,
and even then it could have succeeded only if it had had the
support of at least some of the Rumanian troops. Some political
counter-stroke therefore would have been an essential before
any military action. The chances of obtaining the co-operation
of some of the Rumanian units against the new Government
would not have been bad. Such as they were, Gerstenberg
destroyed them. At the beginning the Rumanian Army was by
no means eager to accede to Russian demands and turn on their
former allies. In spite of minor irritations, which are unavoidable in any military alliance, the Rumanian front-line troops
harboured no dislike for the Germans. On the contrary, a
common purpose and a common foe had given birth to a genuine

THE KING WHO FOOLED US

sense of comradeship, and an overnight change of sides did not
come easily to the Rumanian soldiers. The whole idea was
repugnant to them and a moderately wise attitude on the
German side would undoubtedly have strengthened their hesi-
tations. But Gerstenberg's action, in view of the weakness of
the German forces, was stupid from the military point of view.
It compelled the Rumanians to take sides with the enemy. The
last tenuous bonds between the erstwhile allies were broken by
the Stuka attacks ordered by Gerstenberg against Bucharest on
24th and 25th August.

The fate of the German troops in Bucharest could not have
been improved by this senseless act. Equally unsuccessful were
the attempts made by relieving forces from the Danubian port
of Giurgiu to press into Bucharest and restore the situation.
They thrust to within a few hundred yards of the Hotel Ambassador, where the officers of the Military Mission had taken up
their position, but without reinforcements and armed as they
were with only small arms they could do no more, and the
German hold on Bucharest and Rumania was lost for good.

The German Minister, who had faced the oncoming blows
of fate with uncomprehending bewilderment, shot himself and
Fräulein Petersen his secretary on 2nd September, just before
the Rumanians burst into the Legation. All the other members
of the Legation and most of the German colony in Rumania
after a brief internment were deported by the Russians to an
unknown destination. With very few exceptions they have none
of them been heard of again.

With the success of the *coup de main* against Antonescu and
the Germans, Russian victory in Rumania was complete. The
whole country now lay open to the Red Army, and in a few
days Soviet units were able to seize the Carpathian passes and
the fate of South-eastern Europe was sealed.

And how did the Kremlin reward the men whose *putsch* of
23rd August had opened the doors to Rumania and the roads to
the Iron Gates and the Carpathian passes for the Red Army?
The young King who at the time of crisis had shown himself to
be a determined and responsible statesman, was quickly forced
by Vyshinsky to renounce his throne and depart. After a series
of mock trials at which they were condemned as 'Fascist con-

7

spirators', the other politicians of the 'peace conspiracy' disappeared for ever into the Soviet dungeons. Even the Communist leader Patrascanu, who had the temerity to make modest representations in the Rumanian national interest but within the framework of the Communist *bloc*, was deposed and replaced by that trustworthy handmaiden of Moscow, Anna Pauker. A few complacent nonentities like Petru Groza the Prime Minister were of some use as a façade to hide the purely Communist dictatorship. These were all that survived, and though the Communists have since turned on each other in Rumania, their tyranny remains.

CHAPTER XI

THE TRAGEDY OF HUNGARY

GERMANY invaded Hungary on 19th March, 1944, to the surprise of the whole world. The surprise was less great to those who were aware of the policy Hungary was pursuing behind the façade of the official friendship with Germany. On the surface relations between the two countries were smooth; but beneath it were undercurrents of sharp tensions. To appreciate the chain of events which led up to Germany's action, let us follow the development of German-Hungarian relations.

In 1934 Giula Gömbös—the Hungarian Prime Minister—was the first statesman in the world to break down the barriers of the policy of isolation which had been generally adopted towards the German National-Socialist régime. The event was not of any particular importance. Hungary's weight in world politics was not very great. But Hitler appreciated the gesture highly. It was really nothing more than a gesture by Hungary; for its foreign policy was more concerned with a *rapprochement* with Italy than anything else. The Hungarian statesmen feared that their country might become a satellite of Germany. They regarded a *rapprochement* with Italy as a wise precaution against such a menace. They desired to see their country within the Italian sphere of influence, firstly because they thought that Germany would be bound to respect Italian interests and secondly because Italian strength was, unlike that of Germany, no potential menace to Hungary. Italy still saw Hungary as an outpost, but for the Reich the country could well be the point of departure for German expansion towards the South-east. The responsible Hungarian leaders were further convinced of the soundness of this appreciation by the fact that Austria also was striving to maintain her independence with Italian help. In this way a chain of States was formed which had some chance of being able to resist the increasing pressure of Germany.

After the collapse of the Stresa front, which had safeguarded the Italo-Austro-Hungarian entente for so long, and after the absorption of Austria into the German Reich, Hungary still continued to believe that Italy could be used as a counter-poise to German pressure.

At one time, indeed, it looked as if Hungary was seriously thinking of both tightening her bonds with Italy and making them permanent. Between 1939 and 1941 the Hungarian Minister at the Quirinal held a series of talks with Mussolini and Ciano on the possibility either of providing the Kingdom of Hungary with a new monarch in the person of an Italian Prince, or of binding the two countries by means of a royal union. Admiral Nicholas Horthy, the Regent, was known to be supporting these suggestions, although this did not prevent him from laying plans for the foundation of a new Hungarian dynasty by his own family. As his first step in this direction he aspired to make the office of Regent a hereditary appointment.

At the same time Hungary proceeded outwardly to cultivate friendship with Germany, which promised and brought swift and rich reward. In the two Vienna Arbitration Awards of 1939 and 1940 Hungary received important territories, which had previously formed part of the Kingdom of St. Stephen, and was also permitted to absorb the Carpatho-Ukraine. The Hungarians also hoped that Germany would give them a free hand against the Rumanians, or that they would be permitted to participate in any action that Germany might be contemplating against these arch enemies of the Magyar world. Whenever the slightest opportunity occurred, the Hungarian General Staff always marched troops to the Rumanian frontier—generally the irregular formations known as the 'Rongyos Garda'—the 'Brigade of Tramps', so named because they possessed no uniforms, an ultra-nationalist corps of volunteers whose aim was to restore the Kingdom of St. Stephen to its pre-war size. The Brigade of Tramps had become prominent in 1920-21, when they made an inglorious attempt to reconquer Transylvania for Hungary.

Hitler agreed to the territorial gains of Hungary in 1939 and 1940, and again in 1941. This was based on purely tactical grounds. He undoubtedly had a strong leaning towards the Hungarians, in whom he saw the descendants of those brave Asiatic horsemen who had been the terror of Central Europe and had later become the foremost defenders of the West against the menace from the East. He admired equally their glorious history, their resistance to the Peace Treaty of Trianon, their overthrow of the Communist Government in 1919 and the strong anti-bolshevist policy of the 'Protectors of the Race'-movement of Prime Minister Gömbös.

In spite of this, Hitler was conscious of a feeling of profound distrust towards the Regent Horthy. He regarded him as a fossilized old Austrian Admiral, completely in the hands of his Anglophile and Jewish entourage and imbued with a strong aversion to National-Socialism and the person of its Fuehrer. When Gömbös died prematurely in 1936, Hitler could see no successor as Prime Minister, on whom he could rely, and he watched developments in Hungary with some concern. He was kept well informed by the German Secret Service of the secret diplomatic activities of the Hungarians. For all that, he refrained for a long time from any intervention in Hungarian internal affairs.

The rise within Hungary of political movements more or less similar to that of the German National-Socialist Party did not cause him to alter his attitude. The most important of these movements was that of the Arrow Cross Party of Ferenc Szalasi, a former Major of the Hungarian General Staff. This still youthful Officer—he had just passed out of the Wiener-Neustadt Officers' Academy when the First World War started —had little true Magyar blood in his veins. One of his grand-parents was of Armenian, another of Slovak and a third of German origin. A few noteworthy and able men joined his Party, but initially it made very little general appeal because Szalasi was a vague, intellectual type, devoid of any idea of organization.

Szalasi had already been dismissed from the Army on account of his political activities. When he was arrested, and Dr. Kalman Hubay, that expert in propaganda, provisionally took over the leadership, the Party at once got a surprising number of recruits. By 1939 it was the second largest Party in Hungary—a fact which is not generally known. It did not remain so for very long. Szalasi, returning from his dungeon with a newly-won martyr's halo and enhanced visions of his own infallibility, took over the leadership and in a few years succeeded in reducing the movement to a small and insignificant group. The best brains in the Party, including Hubay, left it; some of them later formed their own Hungarian National-Socialist Party, but they achieved no great success.

Towards the Arrow Cross movement the Reich observed a policy of complete neutrality. Germany was not prepared to lend its support merely on account of common ideas, at least until such a time as support promised material advantage. The National-Socialist leaders were helped in the maintenance of their aloofness by the distinct Hungarian policy which was part of the Arrow Cross programme. The fundamental principle of this party foreign policy was that Europe should be divided into spheres of influence. The German sphere of influence would be Central Europe. Italy should have Southern Europe, including the entire Mediterranean coast, and South-eastern Europe should be entrusted to Hungary. Such an idea could not be reconciled with Hitler's foreign policy. The German Government also held itself equally aloof from the newly formed party of the former Prime Minister, Bela Imredy, although his programme contained nothing of the Arrow Cross ideas. His foreign policy was based on a close and exclusive co-operation with the Reich. Germany intervened and helped the Arrow Cross to power only when to do so seemed to be advantageous to Hitler.

The first differences between Germany and Hungary came in the spring of 1941, when Hitler was making preparations for the Yugoslav campaign. A typical example is the suicide of Count Paul Teleki. A short time before, Hungary had concluded a treaty of friendship with Yugoslavia, the ratification of which had been completed on 27th February. Now Germany was inviting Hungary to attack her new friend—admittedly in return for large rewards, for she was to get back all her former territory that had been ceded to Yugoslavia in 1918. In addition Hitler had promised Horthy in a secret conference that he could also have the Serbian Banat district.

Horthy himself had scant compunction about seizing this booty, but the Prime Minister, Count Teleki, considered it both dishonourable and politically wrong to tear up a treaty which had been so recently concluded. When Horthy pressed him to sign the orders for general mobilization he found himself face to face with a problem of conscience which he could not solve. Eventually he obeyed the wishes of his Regent, but feeling that as a Hungarian nobleman he could not be guilty of breaking his bond and continue to live, he shot himself before the first Hungarian soldier crossed the Yugoslav frontier.

The Regent played a similar part when the attack on Russia was in contemplation. Eagerly as this admirer of England desired to avoid conflict with the Western Powers, he welcomed with equal ardour the thought of a preventive war against the Soviet Union. The Russo-German pact of non-aggression of 1939 came as a shock to Horthy, as it must have done to the majority of the Hungarian people. Until the outbreak of hostilities in 1941 Horthy sent Hitler warnings about Russian preparations, based on information gathered by the Hungarian Secret Service. His influence on Hitler in this connection must not be belittled, and he undoubtedly strengthened the resolve of the German Fuehrer to attack Russia. Hitler himself made this abundantly clear in the course of a number of conversations. He generally added that if Hungary came in on Germany's side, he would have no cause to fear any treachery.

Horthy also intervened by forcing the Prime Minister, Laszlo Bardossy, to countersign the declaration of war on Russia. When he was accused at Nuremberg of complicity in Hungary's attack on Yugoslavia in April 1941 and her declaration of war against Russia in June 1941, he tried to shift all the responsibility on to his Ministers and colleagues of the time. Bardossy's attitude was very different. He regarded his allegiance to his Head of State as sacred. To the very end he made no mention whatever of the tremendous pressure brought to bear on him by the Regent when he ordered the Hungarian Army into action against Russia.

It must be noted that the majority of the Hungarian people and the Hungarian Army were eagerly behind Horthy in his desire to fight Russia. But it soon became obvious that the preparations for a war of this nature had been completely inadequate. Lack of organization told on the luckless soldiers at the front. The Hungarian troops suffered, their losses were heavy, their successes few. A series of dreadful defeats over-took them. In a military catastrophe of the first magnitude the First Hungarian Army was totally annihilated on the Don. The Hungarian people, whose ardour in a first offensive is high, lack the qualities of steadiness and endurance. They became war-weary, and those leaders who began in the spring of 1943 to seek a separate peace, saw that the nation would be behind them.

Their most important points of contact with the Western Powers were the Hungarian Legations in Stockholm, Berne, Lisbon and Ankara. The driving force for a peace with the West was the Prime Minister himself, Miklos Kallai. As an adviser Count Bethlen, who had been Prime Minister for many years, played an important role. Horthy too knew of these efforts, condoned them and kept in close touch with develop-ments. In practice it was the Hungarian Secret Service which alone had the means of establishing unobtrusive contact with enemy countries. The principal confidential agent of the Regent and his Prime Minister was the Chief of the State Security Service—the counterpart of the German Gestapo. He was Major-General Ujszassi, who received much help from the Chief of Section II of the General Staff, Colonel Kadar.

It was only about the beginning of 1944 that any concrete results began to emerge. The Hungarian intermediaries had declared that Hungary wished to conclude a separate peace and desired to be informed of the terms on which an armistice would be granted. There now appeared on the scene as repre-sentative of the Western Powers an American Colonel. He did not have any powers to negotiate, being simply an Officer of the American Secret Service, the O.S.S. or Office of Strategic Services. In a wireless telephone conversation with Ujszassi this Colonel proclaimed his readiness to come to Hungary by air to discuss further details. The visit was fixed for the middle of March 1944.

I was well informed by Hungarian intelligence officers about all these negotiations and particularly about the liaison between Ujszassi and the American Colonel. I reported these happen-ings to Berlin. Now Hitler decided to act. The intention of Hungary to conclude a separate peace must be thwarted, he commanded, if the southern section of the Eastern front were not to be placed in the greatest danger. Preparations began at once. The Army Headquarters Staff, at Hitler's orders, worked out the Operation Margarete I—the securing of Hungary. Plans for another operation, Margarete II, the securing of Rumania, were also worked out, but when the time came, troops were not available.

Hitler's original intention had been to occupy Hungary with German troops, but also to allow some Rumanian and Slovak units to take part in the subsequent occupation. In general terms, but without any official commitment, he had informed Marshal Antonescu and President Tiso of his intentions. Both were enthusiastic at the prospect, though they were given no details on which they could base any military preparations. The Army plan did not envisage support by Rumanian and Slovak units, but was based on the employment of German troops alone. Hitler intended to announce that the Serbian Banat would never be allowed to fall into Hungarian hands, but would be transferred forthwith to the Serbian Government of Nedic.

Hitler's plan was automatically praised by both Ribbentrop and Himmler, though both were quite convinced that it was all wrong. As adviser on South-eastern Affairs of the German Secret Service I hastily drew up a memorandum suggesting an alternative plan. Both Ribbentrop and Himmler refused to submit it to Hitler, because different from the plan the Fuehrer himself had made. At the last moment, however, a man was found who was bold enough to do so—Walter Hewel, the Senior Liaison Officer of the Foreign Ministry at the Fuehrer's Headquarters, a man who often gave proof of far greater moral courage than most of the V.I.P.s of the Reich.

My memorandum pointed out that it would be catastrophic to use Rumanian and Slovak troops. The Hungarians would immediately abandon the war and turn with everything they possessed to defend themselves tooth and nail against the Slovaks and above all against the Rumanians. Any pacification of Hungary, and particularly of the Carpathian and Transylvanian territories, which would be of primary importance in military operations, would be quite impossible. A violent partisan war in the Transylvania frontier districts would be inevitable. The result would be exactly opposite to what Hitler had in mind, namely, the securing of the lines of communication of the South-eastern front. The memorandum added that in no circumstances should the Regent be overthrown. On the contrary every effort should be made to keep him on Germany's side. This would preserve that constitutional balance without which order could not be maintained in Hungary. Horthy should be persuaded to dismiss the Kallai Government and to replace it by a coalition, continuing the common struggle against Russia until final victory was achieved.

Hitler was convinced by these arguments, abandoned his own plan and adopted that suggested in the memorandum. As a preparation for the execution of the new plan, he invited Horthy to a conference in Berchtesgaden. At this meeting he spoke quite bluntly. He could no longer stand aside, he declared, and watch the Hungarian Government make attempt after attempt to come to terms with the Western Powers; Kallai must be dismissed and the man entrusted with the formation of a new Government must be one upon whom Germany could rely to put a stop to these efforts to withdraw Hungary from the war. He did his utmost to convince Horthy that Hungary had no choice in the matter, that the Western Powers had no intention of helping Hungary, and certainly none of protecting her against the Russians. With impressive arguments he showed how by withdrawing from the war, Hungary would be delivering herself irrevocably into the hands of the Soviet Union.

His arguments made a profound impression on the Regent. Horthy accepted his anti-bolshevist reasoning without hesitation. Hitler very quickly persuaded him that the despatch of German troops to Hungary was a vital necessity, but senior S.S. and Police Officers with German Police units were accepted by Horthy only after considerable demur. The condition which Horthy resisted most stubbornly was the nomination as new German Minister and Plenipotentiary of Dr. Veesenmeyer, who had been sent to Hungary on a secret mission by Ribbentrop in 1943 and whose recall, on the grounds that he was conspiring against the person of the Regent, Horthy had successfully demanded only a few weeks before. Hitler was equally stubborn, and in the end Horthy was compelled to swallow this humiliation.

Veesenmeyer was put forward by his protector, the Under-Secretary, Dr. Keppler. The appointment was strongly supported by Ribbentrop for personal reasons. He was determined at all costs to prevent the important post being given to his opponent, General von Horstenau, the German Consul General in Zagreb. The suggestion that von Horstenau should be appointed came from the German Secret Service. They pointed out that the General possessed the dual advantage of being not only a distinguished expert on Hungarian affairs, but also a personal friend of the Regent. His appointment would most certainly have been regarded by Horthy as a friendly gesture and would have eased the situation considerably. There is equally no doubt that if this experienced and skilful Austrian diplomat had been nominated, he would both have had great influence on the Regent and found ways of moderating the policy of Germany.

Early on the morning of 19th March, 1944, Horthy returned in his special train from Salzburg to Budapest. Dr. Veesenmeyer, the new German Minister and Plenipotentiary, was on the train with him. He must have been waiting on the platform, as it were, gloating on his triumph. Seated in his train, Horthy had no idea that Operation Margarete I, in somewhat modified form, had already started. Hitler did not altogether trust Horthy's promise that Hungary would fight on. He had directed that the operation was to be completed before the Regent arrived at the Hungarian capital. At dawn on 19th March some *élite* German battalions from Austria and Serbia reached the vicinity of Budapest. They occupied strategic points. They were followed by some very weak German units which barely sufficed for the occupation of the remaining key positions. The Hungarians offered no resistance whatever. On the contrary, the German invaders were everywhere received with such enthusiasm that the affair was regarded as 'just another German battle of flowers'. Reports that German military trains were shelled by artillery and that flak engaged the supporting German aircraft are pure invention. Had that happened, there would have been severe retaliation.

This attitude of the Hungarian population becomes more understandable when I say that the advent of German troops

was regarded by the Hungarians as proof that Germany would
defend Hungary against Russia. With the menacing Eastern
front pressing ever closer to the Carpathians that was uppermost
in all minds.

As was usual on such occasions, the German Gestapo was in
the advanced guards of the German march on Budapest and
other big towns. They had also their lists of leading Hungarian
personalities who were opposed to co-operation with Germany.
During the morning of 19th March the Gestapo carried out a
number of arrests. They had not however thought in terms of
mass arrests on racial grounds. The Commandant of the
Security Police was therefore very surprised when at midday
Himmler telephoned to inquire how many Jews had already
been taken into German custody. In his desire to satisfy his
superior, the man hit on an ingenious idea. He hastily sent for
the Budapest telephone directory, selected a couple of hundred
doctors and lawyers with particularly Jewish-sounding names
and ordered their arrest! On the evening of the same day he
proudly reported to the S.S. Reichsfuehrer that 200 leading
men of Hungarian Jewry were now safely in his hands.

The Regent was not called upon to commit any breach of the
constitution. He returned as usual to his residence in the Royal
Castle of Budapest, guarded by his own bodyguard. There he
took all the necessary steps strictly in accordance with constitutional procedure. Allegations that he returned to Hungary
virtually a prisoner are untrue.

His first task was to find a new Prime Minister. Dr. Veesenmeyer had a candidate—Bela Imredy, who had already been
Prime Minister some years before. But Veesenmeyer had a
surprise in store for him. Imredy refused on the grounds that
he did not think he would be acceptable to the Regent. The
Hungarians thereupon suggested General Dome Sztojay, the
Hungarian Minister in Berlin. He was well liked in German
Government circles, but he had not distinguished himself in any
way in the internal politics of his country. It was exactly for this
very reason that he seemed suited to form an interim Cabinet.
This he swiftly succeeded in doing, and his Government was in
no sense a Party government of the extreme right, but a collection of experienced men of the previous parties in office. One

Ministry only was offered to the Hungarian National Socialist Party. This too was occupied by a specialist. The Arrow Cross Party got nothing.

In a few days the whole affair was smoothly settled, and life in Hungary resumed its normal course. The parliamentary system functioned as before. It seemed as though nothing had changed, and that the country after a minor upheaval had once more been brought into line with its German ally. In reality, with this swift and bloodless victory Germany had gained a breathing space. But it did give her an opportunity to harness Hungary firmly to the German war effort. Could she succeed in co-ordinating the great industrial capacity of Hungary more closely to the needs of war, and in building up a new Hungarian Army? It was too late, and Veesenmeyer was no man to make up for lost time.

Veesenmeyer neither knew Hungary nor did he fill the gaps in his knowledge. He had not the sense of discrimination to choose the right type of mentors. A cunning conspirator, he failed completely when faced with a task of a constructive nature. He proved himself to be incapable of mobilizing Hungarian industry for war purposes. Even more serious was his utter failure to improve relations with the Hungarian armed forces. Yet he had a particularly promising opportunity. Large sections of the army, headed by the junior officers, were genuinely anxious to continue the fight, and many more, though not friendly towards the Germans, would have been ready to do their best in the defence of their country. Any German suggestion to defend the Danube basin along its natural escarpment, the Carpathians, would undoubtedly have been acclaimed with enthusiasm by the whole Hungarian Army.

But to Veesenmeyer any talk in the spring of 1944 of a defensive campaign on the line of the Carpathians smacked of defeatism. What he wanted to do was to send the Hungarian Army forth to battle on the steppes of Russia. Such an idea made no appeal at all. A golden opportunity was lost of making preparations, which might well have led to the repulse of the Red Army at the Carpathian mountain passes.

The course of the last phases of the war might have been radically different, had Hungarian divisions been firmly in position in the Carpathian passes. In the opinion of both German and Hungarian military experts these could have held up the Russian advance long enough to allow Germany to complete the reorganization required by the defection of Rumania. With the exception of the Swiss Alps and the Pyrenees, there is no range of mountains in Europe which offers a better natural line of defence than the Carpathian and Transylvanian Alps. Resistance on this mountain line would have made it hard for large mechanized forces to break through, and all but impossible if the Russians did not have command of the air. Had this defensive opportunity been seized, it is probable that Hungary and Austria would have been spared from occupation by the Russians. The political situation in Central and Eastern Europe would be very different to-day. All this, of course, cannot be blamed on Veesenmeyer personally. The blame rests largely too on those Hungarians in power who seemed incapable of realizing the gravity of the situation.

Horthy's previous attempts to come to an understanding with the Western Powers had not led to any concrete results. Eventually the Hungarian negotiators were told plainly that in accordance with an agreement with Moscow Hungary belonged to the Russian sphere of influence and that any proposals for an armistice must in the first place be addressed to that Power.

This answer shocked the anti-Communist Horthy so deeply that he lost his self-confidence and became confused. In the summer of 1944 he once more came to the conclusion that Hungary had no alternative but to fight on with the Germans against the Communists to the very end. He had received some information which he regarded to be of the utmost importance. Through friends he heard that certain German groups had started negotiations with the West. In actual fact only an unofficial approach had been made, but the information was deliberately passed on to Horthy in order to convince him that an agreement with the Western Powers might still be a practical possibility, even while continuing the war against Russia. It was a ruse of ours to convince Horthy that there was still hope, even if he fought on by the side of Germany.

The German Secret Service made a determined effort to exploit the disappointment of Horthy with the West. It encouraged a group of Hungarian politicians to form a front for prolonged resistance as the only way Hungary could avoid occupation by the Russians. We worked for a Hungarian War Coalition against surrender to the Communist enemy. It was made plain that this front need not be friendly towards National Socialism. The first vital task of the new Government must be the swift and effective preparation of a defensive line along the whole length of the Carpathian chain. At the request of the Hungarians participating in these talks it was agreed on the German side that in the event of an Anglo-American landing on the Adriatic coast, Hungarians would not be called upon to oppose the invasion. The Chief of the German Secret Service, Schellenberg, gave this assurance at once. He felt that with their commitments in the Normandy theatre the Allies would anyhow be in no position to undertake a second combined operation in the Adriatic. At the time it was not known in Germany that in the face of opposition from Roosevelt and Stalin, Churchill had been compelled to abandon his plans for an offensive in South-east Europe. Schellenberg also succeeded in gaining Himmler's support, and in this way at the eleventh hour there was a last opportunity for real mobilization of Hungary against the Red Army.

The difficulties did not seem very serious. Szalasi refused to accept the two posts offered in the new Government to his Arrow Cross Party. But that was received by most other politicians with satisfaction. They had only sought the co-operation of the Arrow Cross in the interests of the all-party principle. When Szalasi, like Hitler in 1933, declared that he would only consent to join a Government as head of it, and that the German Minister had already promised him the premiership, he was brushed aside. The new premier, Count Mihaly Teleki, submitted his Cabinet and policy to Horthy and won his approval. The way seemed clear.

What had not been taken into consideration was the entire lack of harmony in German policy. I had not known that Veesenmeyer as plenipotentiary had indeed promised Szalasi to make him national leader. The German envoy felt bound to honour his undertaking. We both appealed to Hitler, explaining our different way of thinking. My great argument was that the safety of South-east Europe was at stake and that all else must be ignored. Veesenmeyer retorted that the Hungarians supported by the Secret Service were open friends of the Western Powers and were known to be in contact with them. Mihaly Teleki, he pointed out, had been educated in England and was a notorious opponent of National Socialism.

This struggle for the support of Hitler was still at its height when suddenly Rumania was struck by the full crisis that took her out of the Axis camp. A new situation arose in Hungary. The Regent veered once more in favour of peace talks. After the Rumanian coup of 23rd March, 1944, he realized that for Germany the war in South-east Europe and everywhere else was irretrievably lost. He felt that Hungary had no alternative but to seek an understanding with the Russians as quickly as possible. Although he had given his word to support an all-party Government under Count Teleki, abruptly he installed a military government led by General Lakatos. It was composed of men devoted to Horthy. This done, he sought immediate contact with the Russians.

He went about it in various ways. His greatest hopes were pinned on the skill of that same General Ujszassi, as Chief of the Security Service, who had conducted the negotiations with the Western Powers when Kallai was Prime Minister. To save them from arrest by the Gestapo afterwards, Horthy had confined Ujszassi, Colonel Kadar and Major Kern in honourable arrest in the Nador barracks. Ujszassi's freedom of movement was thereby restricted but not entirely cut off. In great secrecy he was allowed to slip out of barracks. Horthy now instructed him to make contact with the Hungarian resistance movement and through it to get in touch with the Russians. This idea was grotesque. Ujszassi, as Chief of the Security Service, had always been the most bitter foe of the Hungarian Left party. His brutal methods had earned their implacable hatred. Yet in spite of this, Ujszassi succeeded—thanks less to his own personal efforts than to those of his friend Kathalin Karady.

A brunette of striking physique, full lipped and of passionate temperament, this woman wanted to be a great film star, although her talent for the drama was slight. She had besides the ambition to play in films another to play a leading role in political society. She felt that any means justified success. Her rise had been slow and arduous. Not many years before she had been a hostess in dubious Budapest night-clubs. Then she was taken up by the various Officers' Clubs, as the younger Army officers discovered her. One of her friends obtained her first film engagement for her, but no one cared to give her a second. In the meanwhile she had acquired a potent protector in high society, none other than the Chief of Hungarian Security Services, Major-General Ujszassi. Her employers could not avoid renewing her contract after that on much more favourable terms. She had the patronage of prominent members of Budapest society. It may well have been them who gave her a sudden taste for politics. Ujszassi, who even got engaged to her, became her devoted slave. Asserting that she was one of the most valuable agents in the Security Service, he managed to furnish a princely apartment for her. He asked her assistance in the difficult task of contacting the Hungarian underground movement. She was enthusiastic and her residence became the focal point of the conspiracy. Ujszassi used to slip out of his open arrest and visit her secretly. He wanted to establish touch with the man who had been entrusted by Moscow with the leadership of the Hungarian Communist Party. This was Laszlo Rajk.

The Hungarian resistance movement had been developed in a curious manner. After the overthrow of the Bela Kun Government in 1919 Communism ceased to be a factor in Hungarian politics. Its leaders fled to the Soviet Union and tried from there to organize an illegal Communist Party in Hungary. But the Hungarian Secret Police invariably succeeded in destroying such cells as were set up. The refugees had to be content with working either for the Comintern or for the Soviet Union, preparing for an eventual seizure of power in Hungary itself.

The cleverest of the Hungarian Communist immigrants in the Soviet Union was Jeno Varga. He was the son of poor Jewish parents. A baker by profession, he later became a merchant and had taken a course at the university and matriculated. He was then appointed Professor of Finance and Economics at the Budapest School of Commerce. A number of articles which he published on economics attracted attention. He took great in-

terest in politics and at first joined the Social Democrat Party.
But when Bela Kun established his Government in 1919, Varga
at once went over to the Communists and took over the People's
Commissariat for Finance. On the collapse of the Communist
dictatorship he fled to Austria, where he was interned for a while
and then went to Moscow. Persevering he gradually carved for
himself an important place in Russia. Finally he became a
member of the Soviet Supreme Economic Council, and he
played a part in working out of Five Year plans.

His position was for a long time threatened by Andrei
Zhdanov, who accused him of strong sympathy for the capitalist
economics of the West. This was partly because Varga had
warned against pinning too much hope on any general economic
crisis in the capitalist world. The main reason for Zhdanov's
hostility was probably the fact that Varga was not a Russian.
Zhdanov was an ardent nationalist who detested all foreigners.
When Zhdanov died, Varga quickly worked his way back to the
top, and although his economic theories were criticized by
official spokesmen, there is no doubt that he was one of the
most important of the men in the Soviet economy.

The other 'brain' among the Hungarian Communist emigrants
was Erno Geroe. He had lived in Moscow for more than twenty
years and returned home as a Soviet Colonel with the advance
guard of the Red Army. He became Minister for Commerce
and Communications and later Finance Minister, showing real
ability in both appointments.

When it came to appointing a Party Chief for Hungary,
Moscow's choice fell upon Matyas Rakosi, the Hungarian
Adviser on the Comintern. Rakosi—his real name was Roth,
but he changed it in order to hide his Jewish origin—had been
the leader of the Hungarian Communist Party at the time of
Bela Kun's dictatorship. He had personally ordered the execution of numerous 'reactionary' politicians. He had been condemned to death in 1924, but the sentence was later commuted
to penal servitude for life. He remained in jail for sixteen years
and then at last in 1940 he was exchanged for a few Hungarian
standards, which a Czarist Russian expeditionary force had
captured from Hungarian rebels in 1849. Rakosi went straight
to Moscow and remained there. Unlike Bela Kun who became

one of the victims of the anti-Trotsky policy, Rakosi always
managed to fit his views to those of the rulers of the Kremlin.
Although he supported him, Stalin could never quite overcome
his distrust of Rakosi. Therefore it was customary to have
close watch kept on him. This task was given to Natasha, the
woman who was said to be his wife. A daughter of a Siberian
nomad tribe, the Yakut, she was of Turkoman-Tartar origin
and enjoyed Stalin's real confidence. She became a power
behind the scenes, and Rakosi could not move a step without
her.

The remaining members of the Hungarian Section of the
Comintern were Mihaly Furkas, who became Minister for War
in 1948, and Zoltan Vas, alias Weinberger, the first Communist
Mayor of Budapest. They were of minor importance and have
since lost what little influence they ever possessed. The Moscow
group was yet fully supported by the Kremlin. These overruled
their fellow-Communists who had remained at home.

The most important of these home Communists was Laszlo
Rajk, a man of a lower middle-class family in the Szeklerland, an
isolated Magyar-speaking colony in Transylvania. A scholarship
to the Eotvos College had given him education and he obtained
a post as a schoolmaster in a grammar-school. He was dismissed
on account of his extreme left views and went to Spain, where
he fought with the Rakosi Brigade in the civil war. After
Franco's victory he went to Moscow to train for his subsequent
task in Hungary. In 1944 he was sent by the Russians to Budapest to assume leadership of the Hungarian resistance movement. Rajk had six brothers, all of whom were actively engaged
in politics. But they were all members of the Arrow Cross
Party. One of them, Andras, even became an Under-Secretary
in the Szalasi Shadow Cabinet. It was thanks primarily to him
that Laszlo quickly regained his liberty after being arrested by
the Secret Police at the end of 1944. This fact was strongly
resented by the Moscow group, who went as far as to accuse
him of being a spy in Hungarian pay. From that time he failed
to come to any working arrangement with the Moscow group.
His relations with them grew steadily more strained. After the
war he was removed from his important post as Minister for the
Interior and transferred to the Foreign Ministry, which had no

more than the task of carrying out the policy dictated from Moscow. In the spring of 1949 he fell at long last into the clutches of his enemies. Accused of 'Tito-ism' and espionage on behalf of the Western Powers, he was found guilty after a mock trial, condemned to death and executed. It is possible that his loudly expressed anti-Semitism played no small part in his downfall. He had frequently complained that the Hungarian Communist leaders who had been foisted on the country by Moscow were all Jews. Rakosi never forgave that.

Rajk was without any question the only real underground leader of the Hungarian resistance movement. He worked against us with outstanding skill and courage. Rakosi and the Moscow gang never dared to move out of the immediate protection of the Red Army, but Rajk did not hesitate to organize and expand his movement under the very noses of the Hungarian Secret Police. Few Hungarians, however, possessed the true partisan spirit. Rajk's success remained very modest. The Communist resistance movement was confined to a few groups in the poorer suburbs of Budapest and other big industrial towns.

Some men whom I noticed in secret opposition might be called moderates. They later achieved some prominence in public life. There were two Prime Ministers, Ferenc Nagy and his successor Lajos Dunnyes, of the Small Landowners' Party. Bela Kovacs, the Secretary-General of the same Party, was later arrested by the Russians. Deszo Sulyok and Istvan Barankovits, were founders of the Freedom Party and the Catholic Peoples' Party respectively. Peter Veres started the National Peasants' Party. His colleague and Secretary-General was Imre Kovacs, who later fled the country. The historian Giula Szekfu became Hungarian Minister in Moscow. Count Geza Teleki, a university professor, afterwards became a Minister.

These men, for the most part members of the intelligentsia, had played no part in Hungarian public life before the war. During it they cannot be said to have founded real resistance movements. But they organized a series of little social circles, in which they argued and violently criticized the Government and its conduct of the war without daring to try and do anything about it. This group enjoyed its hour of fame when Budapest was occupied by the Russians. The Russians for tactical reasons wished to avoid placing Communists too prominently in the foreground. They fell back therefore on intellectuals with leftish ideals and sympathies and on professional politicians. These men were appointed to the higher offices. But as soon as the Communists were firmly in the saddle, the moderates were all discarded.

CHAPTER XII

RACE FOR THE CARPATHIANS

But Communist rule in Budapest still seemed remote early in 1944, though it was such men as these that Horthy wished Ujszassi to contact. Ujszassi succeeded and on one occasion Laszlo Rajk was received secretly by the Regent in his residence. The results were negative. The various Hungarian groups and petty cliques possessed no organization strong or enterprising enough to be of any use.

Of far greater importance for the execution of Horthy's plan was the Army, the only organized force in the country. The Regent's first concern was to win over Generals Miklos-Dalnoki and Veres-Dalnoki, the General Officers Commanding the First and Second Hungarian Armies respectively. Horthy's plan envisaged a *coup-de-main* by Field Marshal Bakay the Commandant of the Budapest against the German garrison, and he counted on the German forces re-forming and attempting to recapture the city. Miklos-Dalnoki and Veres-Dalnoki were then to advance rapidly, and simultaneously from the north-east and south-east, attack the Germans from two sides and relieve the city.

Bakay and Miklos-Dalnoki were prepared to act, but Veres-Dalnoki had grave doubts about the operation. He had no illusions as to Russian intentions to destroy the old Hungary, he was convinced that a Rumanian collapse was imminent. In that event the plan he favoured was re-occupation of the territory inside the Carpathian mountains, ceded by Hungary to Rumania under the second Vienna Arbitration Award. He wanted to defend the mountain passes against the advancing Russians. His motives were partly strategic and partly nationalist. Be that as it may, the plan was sound in conception— and it would have served German interests well.

Sheer fear of an accusation of defeatism prevented the Germans from taking a possible Rumanian collapse into their strategic considerations. When confused and disturbing reports began to arrive from the Rumanian capital, the fatal weakness of the 'Fuehrerprinzip' manifested itself in disastrous fashion. Instead of immediately giving the Hungarians permission to march into the Rumanian portions of the Transylvania, and supporting them with every German available, the German mission hesitated, referred to Fuehrer Headquarters and begged for instructions from Hitler. As usual, the first reports on the Rumanian situation to reach Fuehrer Headquarters were tinted with rosy optimism which gave no clue to the real gravity of the position. Several valuable days were wasted before the truth was realized. When Hitler eventually gave sanction for the occupation of Transylvania, it was already too late. By forced marches the Russians had already reached the Iron Gates, the entrance to the Hungarian plain, and without opposition had burst asunder the Carpathian girdle of mountains which barred the way to Central Europe. General Veres-Dalnoki's troops poorly armed but fighting gallantly had reached Timisoaru and Arad in their thrust to gain the mountain passes, but they could get no further, and in the face of greatly superior forces they withdrew in stubborn and bloody battle. They had lost the race to the Carpathians.

This catastrophe removed Horthy's last hesitations. He decided to capitulate to the Russians. As delegate he chose the Commandant of the Gendarmerie, Field Marshal Laszlo Farago. These preparations for a surrender, and above all the preliminary negotiations had to be kept closely hidden from the Germans. The *coup-de-main* against the German garrison of Budapest was to follow later. From this point of view his choice of delegate was a cunning move on Horthy's part, for Farago was well known as a great Germanophile and a bitter opponent of Communism. He was the last person to be suspected of having any truck with the Russians. From 1936 to 1940 he had been Military Attaché in Moscow and on his return had written a scathing criticism of Stalin personally and of the whole of the Soviet system. Horthy directed him to go via Ankara to Moscow and negotiate a surrender. He hoped that his delegate's personal acquaintance with senior members of the Soviet Government would facilitate his task. What results were achieved by Farago

on this mission are not really known. When Horthy proclaimed
the capitulation without having first consulted the Russians,
they condemned his action as a breach of the treaty and declared
that they no longer considered themselves bound by the agreement reached with the Farago mission. But it is in any case
more than probable that Farago achieved nothing more or less
than unconditional surrender.

The German Secret Service, aware of Horthy's intentions to
the last detail, was undoubtedly in a position to take the necessary counter-measures. The conspiracy involved no great mass
of the people. All that was required was the check-mating of a
small circle every one of whom was known. But once again a
dispute arose as to the best means to be employed.

The Secret Service regarded it as the height of folly in the
midst of so serious a military situation to bring about the complete overthrow of the existing régime, which could not but
result in widespread unrest and a wholesale disruption of law
and order throughout the country. They suggested instead that
the ring-leaders—Bakay, Hardy, Miklos-Dalnoki and Veres-
Dalnoki—should be unobtrusively but swiftly arrested, while
Horthy should be deprived of his liberty of action but not of his
personal freedom.

Throughout this period a variety of factors were at work.
Horthy, as was well known, was doing his utmost to obtain the
appointment of Regent as a family heritage. His eldest son
Istvan, who at Horthy's insistence had been appointed Deputy
Regent, crashed in his aircraft after a champagne breakfast
behind the front line. (Officially he was killed in action, and a
heroic legend was woven round the manner of his death.) At
first Horthy thought of having his small grandson, Istvan's son,
proclaimed as his successor, but in view of the many years which
must elapse before the little boy attained his majority, he
abandoned the idea in favour of the appointment of his own
second son, Miklos.

No one could have been less suited for the dignity of Head of
the State than this young man, physically a slight, somewhat
degenerate type. An accumulation of most unsavoury incidents
had already compelled him to leave the country for some time,
and except among the proprietors of night clubs where he was a

regular and royally open-handed visitor, he had neither friends nor supporters among the Hungarian people. But with all his irresponsibility and lack of talent the young Horthy combined strong political ambitions. He thought the break with Germany, coupled with the known aspirations of his father, offered him a great chance of succession. He had even been in touch with the resistance movement and had had a number of talks with Rajk, but his upbringing, his outlook and his personal attitude and behaviour found no favour in the eyes of the opposition and he made no headway.

He decided to act independently and sent an emissary to the Headquarters of the Soviet Field Marshal Tolbukhin. In actual fact his courier never got there. Having preferred to take the opposite direction towards the west he had fled with a great hoard of foreign currency via Austria to Switzerland. Shortly after this Horthy was told by Ujszassi that the Hungarian Secret Service had an agent named Marty who lived in Gyekenyes and was in touch with Tito. This seemed to young Horthy to be a most promising avenue. If he could come to a formal agreement with Tito regarding the future relations between Hungary and Yugoslavia, then Tito might well be persuaded to use his good offices with Stalin on his, Horthy's, behalf. Through his friend and colleague, Felix Bornemisza the Director of the Hungarian Danube Port Company, he got into touch with Tito and suggested a treaty whereby Hungary would solemnly renounce all claim not only to the Serbian Banat, but also to the island of Mur and the Baschka. Unfortunately for him young Horthy did not know that Ujszassi's confidential man Marty, was in fact working for the Germans and faithfully reporting all he knew to them. The Secret Service decided to plant two of its own men on young Horthy as 'representatives of Tito' and suggested to Hitler that the young man should be arrested in the act of negotiating with the bogus Yugoslav delegates.

The Regent should then be confronted with the following ultimatum: either he must at once nominate a General selected by Germany and give him full powers to act, in the name of the Regent, as Head of the State and the Government; or the German Government would make public, through radio and press, the full story of his and his son's intrigues with Tito—and the House of Horthy could then abandon all hope of retaining its dominant position in Hungarian affairs. There is little doubt that Horthy would have accepted.

But Hitler decided on a compromise. He agreed to the hood-winking of young Horthy and the arrest of the ring-leaders but rejected the most important suggestion, the avoidance of a complete overthrow of the existing régime. In its place he accepted Veesenmeyer's proposal that the Regent should be deposed and that plenipotentiary powers should be given to the leader of the Arrow Cross Party. Anticipating that these drastic changes would cause trouble, he appointed to the military command of the operation the famous S.S. Colonel Otto Skorzeny, the liberator of Mussolini. And as neither he nor Ribbentrop had much faith in Veesenmeyer's ability after his recent failures, he decided to entrust the political side to the Ambassador Dr. Rahn, who had given marked proof of his diplomatic skill as representative of the Reich with Mussolini's neo-fascist Government in Salo. At the decisive moment in October 1944 Rahn arrived in Budapest with instructions 'to support and assist Veesenmeyer'.

The first part of the modified plan went quite smoothly. In the early morning of 10th October Bakay, young Horthy's friend, was arrested by the Gestapo as he stepped from his car into the Ritz Hotel. There was a thick fog at the time and the incident passed completely unnoticed. Bakay simply disappeared and his fellow conspirators did not know what had happened to him. This arrest of the key man who was to carry out the *coup-de-main* against the German garrison jeopardized the success of the whole plan, and Horthy decided to postpone action and the proclamation of the surrender which had been fixed for the next day until 20th October, and he informed the Russians accordingly.

A little later General Hardy, the Commander-in-Chief of the Danube Flotilla, was hauled out of bed and arrested without any trouble. General Miklos-Dalnoki, on the other hand, secure in the protection of his troops, escaped arrest. He refused to recognize his dismissal from the post of Army Commander, but on 15th October, when he saw that with the arrest of Bakay and Hardy the plot was bound to fail, he deserted with the whole of his Staff to the Russians. Veres-Dalnoki, who failed to follow

suit, was arrested without any difficulty at his Army Headquarters.

Action against young Horthy had been fixed for 13th October,
but an incident, not without its comic side, caused a postponement. At the meeting between young Horthy and Bornemisza
on one side and the two German agents posing as Tito delegates
on the other, without any warning the Regent himself suddenly
appeared! The two S.S. officers playing the parts of the Tito-ites
were now in a quandary. In the end they decided to cancel that
part of the play in which their fellow negotiators should have been
arrested. The whole act flowed smoothly and without dramatic
tension to its end—to be followed by a gentle epilogue, in which
the Regent begged the 'Yugoslav' delegates to explain to Tito
that he had never been a Nazi and that in his ripe old age no one
could now expect him to become a Communist! At this confession, delivered in the soft and pleasing Austrian dialect which
Horthy preferred to use, the 'Tito-ites' completely lost their
composure. They later confessed that they had been very
worried about their outburst of merriment which seemed quite
out of keeping with their role of dour and beetling partisans on
official business. But the Regent was much heartened by this
display of good spirits and left the meeting in a very contented
frame of mind.

Not so Horthy, the younger. When he accompanied the
'Yugoslavs' to the door he found a grim-looking man waiting
about in a most suspicious manner. It was the Criminal Commissar of the Gestapo Otto Klages, who was in charge of
'Operation Mouse'—the name given to the arrest of young
Horthy from his nickname, Mickey. This unfortunate meeting
all but ruined 'Operation Mouse'. At the next meeting which
had been fixed for 15th October at Bornemisza's office in the
vicinity of the Danube Quay, young Horthy arrived, this time
accompanied by a powerful security squad from his father's
bodyguard—selected men, whom he proceeded to post in all
the adjoining rooms and on the roofs of neighbouring houses.
Two could play at that game, and the Germans called up a
section of Skorzeny's men to support Klages's small squad. The
arrest was accomplished without much resistance, and it was
only when the car with its prisoners moved off that any shooting

took place. Then Klages was killed as well as two Hungarian soldiers.

After this events moved fast. The German Minister and Plenipotentiary, instead of calling on the Regent and confronting him with the alternative of resignation or scandal, decided to await his reaction to his son's arrest. The Regent completely lost his head. Contrary to the message which he had sent to the Russians that the capitulation would be announced on 20th October, to which he had as yet received no reply, he suddenly announced on 15th October over the Hungarian radio that an immediate armistice had been concluded.

The next sixteen hours were packed with one dramatic incident after another. One of the most important of the conspirators backed out, General Voros, Chief of the Hungarian General Staff. Assuming that the attempted coup had failed he tried hastily to get in with the Germans, proclaiming to the Hungarian Army that the armistice announced by the Regent did not exist. Pending further orders, the fight was to be carried on beside the German allies. As later became known, the majority of the Hungarian Army had in any case no intention of obeying the Regent's orders and laying down their arms; but the counter-proclamation of General Voros was nevertheless of great importance. It caused much confusion among those who were aware of the plot.

Meanwhile during the evening and night of 15th October, the Ambassador Dr. Rahn was in negotiation with the Regent and extracted from him a promise that he would take no further steps in the direction of a formal capitulation.

Horthy thus wasted many precious hours. About this time the position of the German Legation became very awkward. Its building was in the Herrengasse on the Burgberg and as the Hungarians had occupied the whole district surrounding the Castle, the Legation was completely isolated, and the greatest difficulty was experienced in maintaining touch with the remaining German departments outside. Horthy or any determined General could certainly have overcome the weak German forces, but the Hungarians wasted the short time at their disposal and their resistance was finally broken by a chance incident which proved decisive.

On 15th October some new Tiger tanks on their way to the Eastern Front were in a goods yard of one of the Budapest suburbs. In the afternoon of the 15th they were hastily unloaded by S.S. General Pfeffer-Wildenbruck, Commander of the S.S. in Hungary. He filled them with such petrol as could be found and had them driven round Budapest to show the flag. The demonstration made a tremendous impression. Horthy could now see no alternative and at five o'clock on the morning of 16th October he gave up the struggle and placed himself under German protection. At the same time he declared that he was ready to entrust Szalasi, the leader of the Arrow Cross Party, with the formation of a new Government and would lay down his office of Regent. This declaration, transmitted officially to the German Plenipotentiary by the Regent's Prime Minister General Lakatos, was accompanied by a request that asylum should be granted in Germany for the Regent and his family. On the same day he bade farewell to the Hungarian people and the Army. He confirmed that General Voros had been right in issuing his counter-proclamation, and he called upon the Army to fight on and show themselves worthy of the great traditions of their forbears. This appeal was followed by an order from General Lakatos to all Hungarian army and police units to desist from acts against the Germans. In passing, it may be mentioned that throughout all the negotiations of 16th October, General Lakatos displayed prominently his Knight's Cross of the Iron Cross with which Hitler had decorated him for his services on the Eastern Front.

Szalasi took power with all the outward signs of constitutional legality. Horthy sent a hand-written letter to each of the Houses of Parliament in which he announced his resignation. This enabled Szalasi to appoint a Regency Council of three. In a combined session of both Houses on 20th November Szalasi was vested with the general powers of the Head of the State. Election of a Regent was postponed on the grounds that the country was a theatre of military operations. He was also appointed Nemzetveszeto—'Leader of the Nation'.

Thus Szalasi achieved his great ambition. Like Hitler before him, he succeeded in uniting the offices of Head of the State and Chief of the Government in his own person.

As a result of this last-minute favourable turn of events, 'Operation Panzerfaust'—intervention by Skorzeny and his men—became superfluous. In a few hours the Arrow Cross Party in co-operation with German Police occupied all the strategic positions in Budapest and the other principal cities of the country. There was no serious opposition but because Horthy in his confused state of mind had forgotten to give the order to cease resistance to his own bodyguard, the Commander of the guard ordered his troops to open fire on Skorzeny's men as they advanced to occupy the Castle. Very few of his troops obeyed and the action quickly degenerated into a mere skirmish and petered out. A German anti-tank gun fired a few rounds at the immense Baroque castle, or rather palace, which dominates the Danube. This was a superfluous demonstration designed to impress the Hungarians.

Events in Hungary after 15th October justified the arguments of those German and Hungarian groups which had issued warnings against the overthrow of the régime in power. The morale of the Hungarian Army deteriorated rather than improved, and many of its most distinguished officers could not bring themselves to fight on under the command of the new Head of the State. In Budapest and throughout the country, the Arrow Cross Party, in the frenzied flush of victory, committed many atrocities. As usual the riff-raff joined enthusiastically in exploiting the opportunities offered for lawlessness and looting, and their excesses too, were debited to the account of the Arrow Cross Party. Through lack of suitable Party members, many of the administrative posts at all levels were left vacant, and the Arrow Cross Party was eventually compelled to fill them with any unsuitable men who possessed the wit and plausibility to prove their enthusiasm for the cause. As a result the administrative machine all but ceased to function. Far from there being any question of an orderly mobilization of the industrial and other resources of that part of the country which still remained unoccupied, the confusion and chaos increased and efficiency diminished to vanishing point. The net result of the change of Government was the acceleration of the final collapse.

With his country on the point of being submerged in a flood of Bolshevism, Szalasi exhibited the inefficiency which those who knew him had foretold. This man who while in prison had seen 'visions', and who declared that he received his instructions as the future Head of the State direct from the Mother of God, was totally incapable of any practical and constructive leadership. He withdrew to a castle in the neighbourhood of the Austrian frontier where far from the disturbing influences of the outside world he settled down to write the history of his life, very much on the lines of Hitler's *Mein Kampf*. In March 1945 he had completed the first part. By that time but a few square miles of Hungarian territory remained unoccupied. No printing presses were in operation, and so he asked that the volume should be printed with German help in Vienna. Such was the power of the illusions with which his make-believe world was filled that he ordered, as Hitler had done, that every newly-wedded couple should be given a copy as a wedding present and that no officer or Government official should be promoted who had not passed an examination on its contents. He was completely useless to his country and his régime gradually crumbled and fell to pieces.

Szalasi's rule was a disaster for his supporters. Tens of thousands of Hungarians who as members of the Arrow Cross Party had lived for years as outlaws and who a few weeks before the Russian invasion appeared on the scene as the masters of the country, now had to pay with their lives for the brief success of their leader. The Soviet troops and the Hungarian communist detachments killed instantly everyone who was denounced as a member of the Arrow Cross. Only an immediate profession of Communist faith offered a possible chance of survival, and in this way not a few ex-members saved their lives.

The rest of the story is a tragic epilogue. From the end of 1944 onwards the military situation deteriorated with increasing speed. On Christmas Eve Budapest was surrounded by Marshal Tolbukhin's forces. In an attempt to bolster the prestige and authority of the Arrow Cross régime, Hitler ordered that the city be relieved. The Commanders of the German and Hungarian forces within the city were told that the siege would soon be raised and that all they had to do was to hold on until the relieving force reached them, and with this prospect in view they elected to remain and hold the city till the promised help arrived.

A bitter disappointment awaited them. These hastily impro-vised and poorly trained units fought most gallantly. The whole capital was defended as a single fortress. The fight raged from street to street and from house to house. Lack of munitions and food added to the difficulties of the hard-pressed garrison and attempts to supply them by parachute and aircraft crash-landing on air-strips, hastily prepared in the heart of the city, brought only partial alleviation. But the defenders fought on stubbornly. The Budapest-East railway station was defended to the last by small detachments of Germans and Hungarians in which even young lads of fifteen fought like men. In a few days Marshal Malinovski had had to sacrifice the equivalent of four full divisions.

The attempted relief on 26th January, 1945, was a singularly painful and tragic interlude. From Gran in the north-west units of the much lauded German Viking Armoured Division had advanced parallel to the Danube through the Pilis mountains, and with a few Tiger tanks had appeared suddenly on the very threshold of the capital. Taken completely by surprise, the besieging Soviet forces offered no resistance and were driven from all important positions. Advancing in support behind the Viking Division came that superlative fighting machine, the German Armoured Division *Das Reich*. Success was there for the taking. The Viking Division had but to press on and exploit surprise. As far as anything can be certain in the hazards of battle, nothing could have prevented it from raising the siege of the city and covering the orderly withdrawal of its hard-pressed garrison. But once again that fatal weakness of the 'Fuehrer-prinzip', the reluctance of subordinates to assume any responsi-bility, paralysed us. The attempt to relieve the city from the north-west had not been ordered by the German High Com-mand. Hitler's special permission, it was argued, must therefore first be obtained before continuing the action. But communica-tions between Army Group and Fuehrer-Headquarters was not functioning. Hitler was known to be planning the relief from the south-west and so no one dared to seize the chance and on his own responsibility clinch an action which had opened so auspiciously. The advanced guards of the Viking Division were withdrawn. Budapest and its gallant defenders were doomed and abandoned.

The hard-pressed city was on the verge of utter chaos. Soviet agents wrought havoc both as artillery observers and as saboteurs. Among them were many Jews and Hungarian retaliation took the form of ugly pogroms against the Jewish population. At the beginning the Budapest garrison had been confident that it would be relieved and this optimism prevailed even after the withdrawal of the Viking Division. But the great relieving offensive planned by Hitler from Lake Bulaton in the south-west failed. The sudden Russian offensive on the Silesian front robbed it of the reserves without which it could not have hoped to succeed. It started, faltered and finally stopped. The defence of Budapest undertaken more for political and propaganda purposes than for military reasons, had not only failed but had cost the lives of tens of thousands of soldiers. The garrison finally made many and desperate attempts to break out. In the last dash towards the north-west a bare seven hundred of the twenty-five thousand who started, staggered in a deplorable condition into the German lines. The remainder were killed or taken prisoner.

When the positions in the eastern sector of the city had become untenable, the garrison had withdrawn across the Danube to the Ofen district where they held no more than the fortress itself. The fight was as futile as it was heroic. The men had practically no food or ammunition but they surrendered only when the last round had been fired. With a total disregard for every tenet of civilized warfare the Soviet troops committed the most hideous atrocities in each quarter of the city as they occupied it. In the famous Gellert Hotel there were several thousand wounded. As there was no food for them and as the front line was steadily approaching nearer and nearer, the hospital was handed over to the Russians in all good faith. They barred all entrances and exits, drenched the building in petrol and set fire to it. The wretched casualties were all horribly burned to death. Nor did the final capitulation on 12th February stem the fury of the Russians. Prisoners were shot wholesale and Red Army tanks

8

drove mercilessly through the tightly-packed columns of captured and disarmed troops, leaving a long trail of mangled
corpses in their wake.

With the fall of Budapest the old Hungary came to an end.
The ruling class which had governed the country for centuries
and which had hoped to save something by capitulation, was
itself stricken down and annihilated. Only a few succeeded in
making good their escape. The majority were either gruesomely
murdered by Soviet troops and Communist gangs of terrorists,
or disappeared for ever into Hungarian dungeons and Siberian
camps. Not Budapest alone but the whole country was subjected
to an agony of occupation by the Soviet forces. Moscow had
never forgiven Hungary for failing to play her part, at the time
indicated in the series of revolts against the Germans which the
Soviet Government had organized. In Rumania, Bulgaria and
Slovakia the Russian troops behaved with some semblance of
civilized discipline. In Hungary they raged like wild beasts.
Far from making any attempt to curb the atrocities of their men,
the Russian High Command encouraged and applauded every
fresh outburst.

So the Hungarian people paid bitterly for its rulers making
common cause with the Germans. The mistakes of its leaders
were taken as reason enough to punish all.

CHAPTER XIII

SPYING ON ITALY

Up to 1943 there was no German Secret Service in Italy. Hitler had forbidden any sort of intelligence activity against the country of his 'most faithful friend and ally, the Duce'. Only when it was too late were the foundations of a modest Intelligence Service laid—even then it was done without Hitler's knowledge. Up to that time the German Secret Service had to rely on the co-operation of the appropriate German and Italian Departments, principally the Attachés of the three Wehrmacht Services, the Police Attaché at the German Embassy in Rome and the Military Security Service which, however, was also not allowed to operate any secret branch against Italy.

Close co-operation between the liaison officers of the Wehrmacht and the Italian High Command did not exist. Mutual confidence was entirely lacking. The senior German Attaché, General von Rintelen, was for the most part occupied with the thankless task—which he performed with great skill—of forwarding an endless stream of complaints, easing the tension in moments of crisis and smoothing the ruffled feelings of the touchy Italians whenever they felt that they had been slighted.

Between the police representatives of the two countries, in theory at least, relations were quite different. Himmler and his Italian counterpart Arturo Bocchini felt themselves bound to follow the example of Hitler and Mussolini, and were zealous in maintaining the closest and most friendly relations. Co-operation between the two Police forces by the Police Attachés in Rome and Berlin was detailed and far-reaching. Liaison officers were attached to the various Police technical branches. Stress was laid on the exchange of views and experiences. From 1941 onwards a German section was attached to the Italian Colonial Police to be trained for their work in the future German colonies in North Africa.

These ideal relations did not deter the Italians from setting up a most efficient Secret Service in Germany, with particular emphasis on Berlin. Obviously they did not have absolute confidence in their allies, and they felt the need of a secret organization of their own to confirm or to amplify the information given to them officially.

The German Secret Service on the contrary adhered strictly to Hitler's orders. As the German Government was badly served by its diplomatic reports from Rome, this lack of reliable information on Italian affairs was to have grave consequences. Up to the great re-shuffle of 1938 Ulrich von Hassell had been Ambassador to the Quirinal. He had a deep and comprehensive knowledge of Italian politics, and his reports had always been blunt, objective and to the point. His successor, von Mackensen, had not that insight which is essential to a correct appreciation of events and, what was far worse, he was a most zealous exponent of the current habit so common among German officials of reporting to his superiors only what he thought they would be pleased to hear. Von Mackensen's shortcomings were fully realized in Berlin, but out of deference for his father, the illustrious old Field-Marshal, the Foreign Ministry was reluctant to order his re-call. Instead he was given a Deputy, Prince Otto von Bismarck. Thanks to his connections with the highest circles of Roman society, Prince Otto was regarded as an appropriate man for the appointment. He took charge of the Chancellery of the Embassy but he also proved to be a disappointment. Admittedly he gave the most sumptuous receptions, but his haul contained nothing beyond the usual society gossip. Apart from this his wife was an ardent opponent of National-Socialism, and she missed no opportunity of criticizing the German system of Government.

Von Bergen, who was Ambassador to the Holy See until 1943, could not make up for the inadequacies of the Ambassador to the Quirinal. He was an old man in poor health who had no political ambitions and all he desired was to be relieved as quickly as possible of his thankless task. Himmler's delegate to Italy, S.S. Colonel Dollmann, was equally unsuccessful in gaining any insight into the secret machinations of Italian politics. His talent was more for conspiracy than for serious politics, and he owed his appointment to the fact that Himmler

regarded Kappler the Police Attaché as a mere creature of
Heydrich and was most anxious to have in Rome his own man
whom he could trust.

In these circumstances it is easy to understand why the
Government of the Reich remained for so long without any
authoritative information on the true situation in Italy. But in
the spring of 1943 personnel changes in Rome led to a marked
improvement. In April of that year the former Secretary of
State at the Foreign Ministry von Weizsaecker relieved von
Bergen, and then for the first time Hitler began to receive
detailed reports which made no attempt to tone down the
seriousness of the severe internal crisis in Italy. Weizsaecker's
exceptional talent as a diplomatist enabled him swiftly to form
a detailed and accurate judgment on the situation. I became
the Chief of the advisory section for Italy of the German Secret
Service in February 1943. I agreed with von Weizsaecker that
we should do our utmost to give Hitler the true facts of the
crisis which faced the Fascist régime. We agreed too on another
and even more important point: that the German Government
must be persuaded to alter its policy towards the Church and
should then in return invite the Vatican to act as an intermediary
with the object of concluding a peace with the Western Powers.

In order to prepare the ground for the acceptance of such a
suggestion we both emphasized in all our reports which eventually reached Hitler via Ribbentrop and Himmler respectively,
that the total destruction of Germany and Italy was completely
contrary to the vital interests of the Vatican and that the latter
realized only too well such a catastrophe would benefit Soviet
Russia alone. It would not therefore be difficult to persuade
the Vatican to invite the attention of the Western Powers to
this possibility. But a prerequisite to any Papal co-operation
would be a drastic modification of the hostile policy towards the
Church which had been so marked a feature of German domestic
policy.

In April 1943 the Secret Service submitted a particularly
important report which exposed the weakness of the Fascist
régime in its entirety and expressed the opinion that it would
be incapable of coping either with the threatened loss of North
Africa or the subsequent invasion of the Italian mainland which

would follow inevitably. The war-weariness of the Italian
people, the sabotaging of the war effort by some of the more
important war departments, the growing personal opposition of
some of the most powerful of the Fascist leaders to Mussolini
himself—among them Ciano, Grandi and Bottai—the physical
and mental degeneration of the Duce, were all mercilessly
described with a wealth of impressive and substantiating
examples. The report concluded that it had become obvious
Mussolini no longer possessed the energy to intervene and put
a stop to the welter of corruption which was undermining the
moral fibre of the nation and bringing the State to the verge of
complete disintegration.

Hitler did no more than acknowledge receipt of this report.
He had not the slightest intention of modifying his policy
against the Church and he further refused to sanction the setting-
up of a regular branch of the Intelligence Service in Italy. But
even he could not deny the gravity of the situation although his
faith in the person of Mussolini remained unshaken and he
was convinced that the Duce would win through in spite of
everything.

This was a conviction which the Secret Service could not
share. Its Chief Schellenberg decided to ignore Hitler's orders
and to set about organizing a proper service. Of course it was
impossible to make up for lost time but by the spring of 1943
the Service was sufficiently organized to have discovered beyond
question that a rising against Mussolini was about to take place.
In this tense situation the local authorities of the Secret Service
took the risk of installing a secret wireless station in Rome in
order to ensure direct communication with Germany, come
what might. The first reports transmitted told of the summoning
of the Fascist Grand Council, warned that a most unwelcome
surprise might result from this session and suggested that
Germany would do well to be ready with counter-measures to
meet the situation. During the night of 24th–25th July, 1943,
Rome and Berlin were in incessant wireless communication but
in spite of the most strenuous efforts failed to bring home to the
German Government the real seriousness of the situation.

The man primarily responsible for the false impressions in
Berlin was von Mackensen. He bombarded the Foreign Ministry

with a series of soothing telegrams. To prevent the transmission of any dissenting reports he went so far as to ban all telephonic communication with Germany, with the exception of his own private line which was connected directly with von Steengracht, Under-Secretary of State in the Foreign Ministry. He did not know that the Secret Service had a wireless station of its own in Rome. The culminating result of this stupid and illusory policy of appeasement was the grotesque telephone order which Mackensen received from Ribbentrop when the latter heard on 25th July of the arrest of Mussolini. 'In the name of the Fuehrer,' ran Ribbentrop's message,

'I order you forthwith to place Badoglio and his fellow-conspirators under close arrest and to bring Mussolini on a State visit to Germany.'

It seemed hardly possible that the man should have been so misinformed. How did he expect his orders to be carried out? The whole Fascist system had collapsed like a pack of cards; within a few hours every Party badge and emblem had disappeared and the staunchest and oldest Party members were declaring that they had become Fascists only under compulsion. The Fascist Militia had tamely allowed itself to be disarmed without even a gesture of opposition. Mussolini's own bodyguard, a Division armed to the teeth with the most modern weapons from Germany, had remained motionless on the outskirts of Rome with not a thought of trying to rescue their leader, and in a short time Rome and every other important city in Italy was in the administrative power of the new Government.

Badoglio had been entrusted by the King with the formation of a new Government and he held the power firmly in his hands. There were no German troops in Rome for they had all been withdrawn when, by agreement, it was declared an open city, and the Germans had no clue as to Mussolini's whereabouts. In these circumstances Ribbentrop's orders were simply nonsensical.

It was some time before the German organization was in any position to take counter measures. But at the end of July the German Secret Service in Ankara was able to report that the

Italian Ambassador to Turkey (Guariglia, who later became
Foreign Minister) had approached the Turkish Foreign Minister
and asked him to act as intermediary with the Western Powers.
Guariglia had always been suspected as being the liaison between
the anti-Mussolini group and the Allies and for a long while he
had been kept under close observation by the Secret Service.
Reports of similar attempts to conclude a separate peace also
came in from Madrid and Lisbon and from a German agent in
the Vatican.

An interesting interlude occurred at this point. Towards
the middle of August 1943 a senior Italian officer who claimed
to be—and in fact was—a colleague of Marshal Badoglio, approached the German Secret Service with a suggestion which
he asserted conformed to the Marshal's intentions. Italy, he
said, was bound to bow to the will of the Italian people and
sooner or later withdraw from the war. Germany, however,
could profitably forestall events by evacuating Italy and taking
up a defensive position on the line of the Alps. If Germany
were to do so, the Italian Government would be prepared to
guarantee Italy's future neutrality. Details of the German withdrawal could be agreed upon later, but in Badoglio's opinion it
should be carried out in successive, pre-arranged stages.

The weak point in Badoglio's plan was immediately apparent.
How could an Italy, defeated, conquered and militarily im-
poverished, possibly defend, maintain and 'guarantee' her
neutrality? It could not be assumed that the new Government
would be able to deny to the Allies the use of Italian soil as a
theatre of war and later as a strategic base for future operations.
The suggestion was not worth considering, but what interested
the German Secret Service was Badoglio's motive in making the
suggestion. Was this Italian officer merely an *agent provocateur*,
or was he a responsible officer, who had persuaded Badoglio
that the suggested plan was the only possible solution to Italy's
dilemma between breach of alliance or total defeat?

An agreement with Germany which released Italy, tacitly at
least, from her treaty obligations and at the same time protected
the country from becoming a theatre of war might well commend
itself to the new Government. Badoglio's repeated assurances
that there was no question of an Italian withdrawal from the

war might well be a subterfuge. The second visit of this officer shed a little more light on Badoglio's real intentions. The Marshal, who was a very vain man, was resentful, the emissary complained of the slow progress and constant interruptions to which his negotiations with the Western Powers were being subjected. He was now more than ever in favour of the suggested neutrality agreement with Germany.

What were Badoglio's real motives? It was not possible to divine them. He may have been perfectly sincere in his proposals—and we German officers who negotiated with his delegate held this view. But it is equally possible that Badoglio had approached the Germans with the sole object of bringing pressure to bear on the Allies and thus to urge them to a speedy conclusion of the armistice negotiations. In the latter case Badoglio's game should have been to see to it that his proposals to Germany for evacuation and neutrality became known to the Allies. Whether he did so or not remains so far unknown.

The proposals of Badoglio were submitted to Hitler, with a minute prepared by the German Secret Service in collaboration with a senior officer of the German High Command in Italy. In this memorandum we claimed that apart from Badoglio's offer, the best military solution for Germany was undoubtedly a withdrawal from Italy, and a new defensive position from the Swiss frontier along the line of the River Po to the Adriatic. Such a line could be held by comparatively small forces. The plan offered the additional advantage that between 300,000 and 400,000 troops would be released for duty on the Eastern Front at the cost of releasing an already beaten and war-weary partner, and losing North Italian industry, in any case not indispensible to Germany's war potential. The possibility of Italy maintaining her neutrality was not even mentioned in this appreciation of the situation.

Hitler's reaction to this memorandum came as a shock even to those well acquainted with his temperamental instability. Disregarding completely the reasoned arguments in the document, he screamed that it was the work of 'a frivolous and irresponsible defeatist'. He would not be talked into leaving his friend Mussolini in the lurch. Such was his rage that he ordered the immediate and exemplary punishment of the authors of

8*

the report.   Only Kaltenbrunner's intervention saved us from
punishment.   When it was too late Hitler admitted that the
suggestions made at the time were sound and right.   In March
1945 he told Kaltenbrunner that he bitterly regretted not having
followed the advice of the German Secret Service as regards
Italy, which he complained had been the cause of nothing but
difficulty and loss.   The situation on the Eastern front would not
have developed so disastrously had the German Army Group
in Italy been available for operations in the East.   For once his
opinion coincided with that of the outstanding German military
experts.

In the end nothing was done either to evacuate Italy or to
prevent a change of sides by the new Italian Government.
Instead Hitler ordered Himmler to prepare a plan for the
rescue of Mussolini and the arrest of all those who had taken
part in the *coup d'état* against him, and in particular of the
King and Queen, the Crown Prince and his consort, Badoglio
and the leaders of the Fascist Party who had voted against
Mussolini in the Grand Council.   Under the title of Operation
'Alaric', plans for the above were indeed worked out to the
last detail in Berlin, but on the spot in Rome, through lack of
any German police personnel, preparations had to be restricted
to reconnaissance of the houses in which lived the forty people
who were earmarked for arrest.

One of the German Police Attaché's Italian agents who was
engaged in spying out the land was arrested by the Italian
police.   It appears that at his interrogation he told the Italians
an attempt on Badoglio's life was in preparation.   Badoglio
thereupon sent his Foreign Minister Guariglia to the German
Embassy to say that he was aware of the plot against him.   In
point of fact, not only had no such thing ever been contemplated,
but by that time (September 1943) Operation 'Alaric' had
already been abandoned on the recommendation of the Secret
Service.   Its implementation would inevitably have involved
regular battles with the Italian Army and German troops for
such operations were not available.   But the liberation of Mussolini and his family was to be undertaken.

The special Commando for this task was organized by the
Secret Service in Berlin and was composed entirely of seasoned

men of the Waffen-S.S. On arrival in Italy it was reinforced by a group of specially selected paratroopers. The total strength amounted to less than a battalion, and it was commanded by Skorzeny. When the Commando arrived on the scene the abandonment of Operation 'Alaric' had not yet been announced, and training and preparation for the whole operation went on for some time regardless of the fact that the force was far too weak to undertake it. The Commando was quartered at Pratica di Mare near Rome, and the individual sections had to be brought one by one into the city to acquaint themselves with the whereabouts and lay-out of the houses of the men they were to seize. At that time there were no S.S. units in Italy and as S.S. uniforms would therefore be conspicuous in Rome the whole party was put into paratroopers' uniforms. The camouflage proved successful, and the Chief of Police Senise, one of the most efficient men in the new Government, failed entirely to discover the base of operations. He thought that something was being organized from the office of the Police Attaché and he had a close watch kept on everyone who went there. Senise was further misled by the statements made by the German Police Attaché's captured Italian agent, for they too pointed to Kappler but not to Pratica di Mare and Frascati, where Commando Headquarters had been established.

On the recommendation of Himmler, Hitler had entrusted the command of the enterprise to the S.S. Colonel Skorzeny. He was of middle-class Viennese stock and had been educated at the Vienna Technical High School. Then he entered the engineering business of his father-in-law. His interest in motor transport led him to join a civilian S.S. motor unit. During the war he was transferred to the Waffen-S.S., in which he attained the rank of First Lieutenant of Reserve, and on account of his technical qualifications he was employed for the most part as an instructor of tank drivers.

Kaltenbrunner, who knew Skorzeny from his student days, came across him in the Waffen-S.S. and put him in command of a newly raised section of the Secret Service which dealt primarily with technical matters. When a commander who combined soldierly qualities with sound technical knowledge was being sought for Operation 'Alaric', Himmler produced

Captain Skorzeny. The Gran Sasso raid naturally transformed this unknown Captain into the hero of the hour. But he has to thank Dr. Goebbels for the fact that his fame has spread so far and survived so long. For propaganda purposes the latter was greatly in need of some German success which he could 'put over in a big way'. Hitler too had an affection for this courageous officer who made an imposing impression with his six foot four of brawn and muscle and his face scarred with the duels of his student days. He was the ideal man to lead any raid or foray, but when in the last phases of the war Hitler entrusted him with the command of larger formations he was not so successful. He was a lone fighter and a Storm-Trooper *par excellence*, but no divisional commander.

The rescue of Mussolini was no easy task. First and foremost the Germans had no idea where he was, as the section of Carabinieri who had escorted him from the Villa Savoia after his arrest on 25th July had done their job so well that no trace of his subsequent movements could be found. It was, admittedly, later established that he had been put in the school barracks of the Carabinieri, but the knowledge was of passing interest for he was only there for a short while, and by the time the information had been obtained he had long since been removed to an unknown destination. The problem seemed all but insoluble. The German Secret Service so recently set up and served by so meagre a network of agents did not know where or how to begin.

It was by a stroke of good fortune that we succeeded. In the establishment of the Fascist Militia was included a section known as the Harbour Militia, composed of men of proven reliability. I had succeeded in enlisting and keeping, after the events of 25th July, a small caucus of former members at the disposal of the German Secret Service. The new Government had apparently first come to the conclusion that an island would be the safest place to keep Mussolini and his movement thus came within the observation of the ex-Harbour Militiamen. They reported that he had been put aboard the corvette *Persefone* at Gaeta harbour on 28th July, bound for the island of Ventotene. In this way the trail was picked up. It was followed without check until it led to the Gran Sasso in the Abruzzi mountains.

At first one slight complication occurred for the *Persefone*, after a brief stay off Ventotene, went on to the island of Ponza. While Skorzeny was on a preliminary air reconnaissance of the island his aircraft crashed into the sea, but the intrepid Skorzeny managed to free himself and his companions from the sinking plane and the whole party swam safely to some nearby rocks. By means of a signal pistol Skorzeny attracted the attention of a passing Italian anti-aircraft cutter, which rescued the stranded party and took them to Olbia in Sardinia. A little later this happy soldier of fortune, with a broken rib or two but otherwise in fine fettle, was in Corsica celebrating his escape in a circle of German sailors at Bonefacio.

The report that Mussolini's trail had been picked up was received at Fuehrer Headquarters with a caution which all but amounted to disbelief. Since he had had our memorandum advocating withdrawal from Italy, Hitler had regarded every report which emanated from the Italian section of the German Secret Service with deep mistrust. On this occasion too his only comment was, 'I'll believe it when I hear something from Mussolini direct.'

Himmler's behaviour was even more curious. His firm belief in the occult arts had urged him to seek Mussolini's whereabouts with the aid of black magic, but this was not easy to do. Hitler had roundly blamed the occult sciences and their practitioners for the discreditable and damaging flight of his Deputy to England, for Hess had laid great store by these pseudo scientists and had constituted himself their patron and protector. After the Hess affair a nation-wide witch hunt had been carried out on Hitler's orders and most of the soothsayers, clairvoyants and fortune tellers in the country had been incarcerated in concentration camps. Himmler therefore had to comb his own camps before he could gather together his team of astrologers and magicians. He housed these pre-eminent exponents of their science in a villa on the Wannsee near Berlin and set them the task of divining Mussolini's whereabouts. I have an account of this episode from S.S. General Karl Wolff, Chief of the S.S. in Italy. It would probably have been a long time before they obtained any results, for the poor devils, who had starved for years on the diet of the concentration camps, joyfully and whole-heartedly gave themselves up to the delights of the flesh-pots, the bottle and the fragrant cigarette. But somehow or other a Master of the Siderian group worked out—or by cunning good fortune guessed—that Mussolini was 'on an island to the west of Naples'. There is no doubt that Himmler's long delay in giving orders for the enterprise was due to his desire to achieve certainty by means of the opinions of the occult powers—such were the grotesque imponderabilia upon which the weighty decisions in the Third Reich sometimes depended! And it is a depressing thought that the man in Germany most important after Hitler himself, the man in whose hands the fate of millions of his fellow-men rested, should be a disciple of the fortune tellers.

Thanks to the ex-Harbour Militia we of the Secret Service knew that Mussolini had been transferred from the island of Ponza to the island of Maddalena, thence to the Gran Sasso d'Italia on the mainland. His liberation was above all a tremendous feat of airmanship. The landing of gliders at a height of nearly 10,000 feet in the midst of a rugged and broken mountain range was an exceptionally difficult manœuvre. The take-off in a little Fiesler Storch, a desperate and dangerous hazard! The small plane overloaded with Mussolini, the bulky Skorzeny and the pilot cleared the escarpment of the precipitous cliffs opposite by the barest margin. The weather was appalling, and the direct flight to Germany originally planned was out of the question. But skill and good fortune prevailed and Mussolini was unexpectedly landed in Vienna on the evening of 12th September.

On the same day his wife Donna Rachele with her two youngest children, Romano and Anna Maria, were rescued by a Commando of the German Secret Service and taken safely to Munich by air. They had been taken from Rome to Rocca delle Caminate, an ancient fortress which had for many years been the country seat of the Duce and his family. There they were kept completely cut off from the outside world and guarded by Carabinieri. Mussolini's eldest son Vittorio had already fled to Germany. So the whole family was now safely out of the grasp of the new Italian Government.

During Mussolini's journey to Germany, Skorzeny rummaged

in the Duce's luggage and found a slender note-book. This attracted the attention of the German Secret Service. It was an ordinary exercise book such as is in common use among Italian school-children and it was filled with notes in Mussolini's handwriting. He had apparently procured it during his stay on Ponza. A cursory glance showed that it was a sort of diary which he had kept during his captivity on Ponza and Maddalena islands. The pages were photographed, translated and submitted to Hitler. This human and historically valuable document was preserved in spite of Hitler's strict orders that all files were to be destroyed. I reproduce it as the next chapter as an exposé of the thoughts of the Italian dictator during the difficult days of his imprisonment.

On principle, Hitler required all translations from foreign documents to be as literal as possible—probably because he was afraid that otherwise the translator might seize the opportunity of surreptitiously inserting ideas which he would not dare to express in the ordinary way. Thus, this diary of Mussolini was translated almost word for word into German. Although the original Italian version is not available, the translation has not, I think, lost any of its original vividness.

CHAPTER XIV

MUSINGS OF A DICTATOR

THESE are notes made by Mussolini during his imprisonment on the islands of Ponza and Maddalena, August 1943, which Skorzeny discovered in the baggage of the Duce.

The 25th of July, 1943

On the conclusion of the meeting of the Grand Council, at about 2.30, I went back to my office, followed by Scorza, Buffarini, Tringali, Biggini and Galbiati. We discussed the legality of the things which had been agreed upon, but this was not a question which interested me very much. Scorza who, as the last speaker at the meeting, had delivered a somewhat colourless and unconvincing speech, asked permission to accompany me home which I granted. When I look back on Scorza's attitude on various occasions in the past, I begin to have grave misgivings. The peroration of his speech in Adriano, when he discussed the possibility of 'falling'—albeit with honour—left a most sinister impression in many circles.

He had adopted an attitude which was openly hostile to the State and had taken steps which gravely disturbed the tenor of his administration. Some of his proposals, which I rejected, betrayed to my mind a lack of feeling and equipoise. After Gentile, he wanted to allow Croce to speak (the eternal riddle). He suggested to me that the Party which he represented should officially approach the Pope and ask for a million for the reconstruction of San Lorenzo. At the end of the agenda Scorza included a motion of respectful greeting to the Pope. To this the Grand Council did not agree, as in the opinion of Count Ciano and others such a greeting would not be acceptable to the Vatican.

One day Scorza suddenly said to me: 'Now I'm going to say something "yellow"—extremely "yellow" (unpalatable) to you!

Are you sure of the people who surround you?' I replied that it was a question I had never asked myself. Later—a few days before the meeting—he repeated the question and added: 'What would happen if one night someone broke into the Villa Torlonia?' I replied: 'Nothing, probably.' I contented myself with mentioning this to Cesare, without however making any particular point of it.

Did Scorza know what was in store and had he already been informed of the wording of the Order of the Day? He certainly did, at least as far as the first version is concerned, for he showed it to me and told me how he had come by it. But the version submitted to the vote was shorter.

When I said good-bye to Scorza at the Villa Torlonia, I went to my wife, who was anxiously awaiting my return. With the sensitivity and the subtle instinct of a woman she had a premonition that something of the highest importance was afoot. Poor Rachele! How little happiness I have given her—and how much pain!

During the whole of thirty years not one single week of peace! She deserves perhaps a different and better fate than to be bound to my stormy existence. We exchanged a few words, and then I fell asleep. It was one of those short but eternal slumbers which have always been the prelude to the decisive moments of my life.

At seven o'clock I got up. At eight o'clock I was in the Palazzo Venezia. As I had regularly done for the last twenty-one years I settled down to my working day—the last! There was nothing of any importance in the post, except a petition for the reprieve of two 'Dalmatian partisans' who had been condemned to death. I telegraphed in the affirmative to the Governor, Giunta. To-day I am glad that my last official act saved two lives, two young lives! Shortly after this, Scorza telephoned to say that many who had voted in favour of Grandi's Order of the Day were now regretting having done so. I replied that it was now too late. At the same moment a letter from the Minister Cianetti was delivered to me, in which he wrote that he had withdrawn his vote. The fact did not seem to be of the slightest importance to me. I sent for Grandi. I simply wanted to ask him why, when he came on Thursday to bring me the protocol of the London Committee, he had asked, nay beseeched, me not to convene a meeting of the Grand Council. Alibi? Manœuvre? I had replied that it was now too late, that the invitations had already been sent out and that any postponement would not be possible. On the morning of 25th Grandi was nowhere to be found. He had gone off somewhere in a car without saying where he was going. In the meanwhile I had sent word to General Puntoni asking him whether the King could receive me at 17.00 hours either at the Villa Savoia or elsewhere. I received an affirmative answer. At twelve o'clock, in the presence of Bastianini, I received the Japanese Ambassador, who came in the name of his Government to ask my opinion of the situation. I replied that the whole situation depended on how the battle on the Eastern Front developed and that every endeavour must be made to get Russia out of the war, even if this meant giving up the territories already conquered. He agreed with this and we parted. If Bastianini has left any notes of the interview, the details will be found in them.

Shortly afterwards I received Galbiati, who told me among other things that the departure of 'M' Division had not taken place, because of the bombing of the Rome railway system. He suggested that I should visit the bombed areas. I remarked that my visit would seem to come a little late, but he said that he wished me to see how the work was progressing. Accordingly we went to San Lorenzo. The work in reality was not progressing at all—or hardly at all. In any case the whole area was practically wiped out. A few groups of the local inhabitants surrounded me, described various episodes and made many complaints. I made arrangements for relief measures. Near the church of San Lorenzo a group of naval cadets improvised a demonstration. It was three o'clock. An oppressive and sultry heat burdened the souls of men and pressed down from a motionless sky on the city of Rome. I returned to the Villa Torlonia. I had my usual breakfast and spent an hour chatting with Rachele in the little music room. My wife was more than depressed, and her fears that something was going to happen were very great.

At 4.30 I changed into plain clothes and accompanied by Cesare went to the Villa Savoia, where His Majesty was awaiting me on the threshold of the Palazzina. Our conversation lasted half an hour, and when we parted the King shook me warmly by the hand. My car was waiting for me on the right hand side of the Palazzina, and as I was making my way towards it a Captain of Carabinieri stopped me, saying: 'His Majesty has ordered me to take your person into my protection.' As I was about to enter my car, he stopped me and led me to an ambulance which was waiting. Cesare, naturally, got in with me! Strictly guarded by two plain clothes policemen armed with machine pistols, we drove a long and uncomfortable way with such bumps that the car all but overturned. After a short halt in some barracks of the R.R.C.C., the name of which I forget, we arrived at the barracks of the Allievi Carabinieri. I was taken into the Colonel's office. Sentries with fixed bayonets were posted in the corridor. I was treated with great friendliness by the officers. On the 26th General Ferone, whom I had met in Albania, brought me a letter at one o'clock from Marshal Badoglio, which I reproduce below.

'To His Excellency the Cav. etc.—The undersigned Head of the Government desires to inform Your Excellency that what has happened to Your Excellency has happened in Your Excellency's own personal interest, as exact details of a serious conspiracy against Your Excellency's person have come to hand. While the undersigned deplores the necessity, he desires to inform you that he is prepared to give orders for your safe conduct, with appropriate ceremony, to any place which Your Excellency cares to name.'

Signed ———

I dictated a reply and said that I should like to go to Rocca delle Caminate. Colonel Tabollini told me that the General who had been sent to La Rocca to see whether all was in readiness, had reported all in order. Monday passed.

Colonel Chirico, Major Bonitatibus and Colonel Tabollini often used to come and talk to me (and I shall never forget the kindness of Tabollini's wife, who used to bring me ices and tea); General Delfini the doctor, also used to come, and Lieutenant-Colonel Santillo of Caserta who of course was very worried over the loss of the province of Caserta—which was silly!

I was now quite convinced that I should be taken to La Rocca. But about ten o'clock on Tuesday evening they brought me downstairs and handed me over to General Polito of the Military Police, in whom I recognized my old friend, the Commissar of Police Polito, who had worked with me for seventeen years and to whom I had entrusted many a successful police enterprise.

During our journey we talked of this and that, and then I was able to see which direction we were taking. We were neither on the Flaminian road nor the Appian way, but were heading for Gaeta, Molo Ciano, and the corvette *Persefone* with an Admiral Maugeri from Gela, very spruce and decorative. During the crossing, I met the son-in-law of Professor Frugoni. Short halt in Ventotene, a long stay not possible. On towards Ponza, where I arrived about eleven o'clock. It is not the place of residence that I chose—or ever would have chosen. Treated cordially. On this first day Colonel Pelaghi and then Colonel Meoli and Lieutenant-Colonel di Lorenzo were at great pains to ensure my safety, though now that the conspirators have attained their object and secured my person, I could not see that my safety was threatened any more than that of any ordinary individual.

Mussolini.

Ponza. 2nd August, 1943.

1. P.S. This is a confidential report which I am entrusting to the discretion of Colonel Meoli, who is not authorized to impart it to anyone without my permission.

2. It is possible that some of the opinions expressed above do not conform with the facts, because since the 25th of July I have been morally completely isolated and do not know what has happened since that date. M.

26*th July*, 1943.

I. I am anxious to thank Marshal Badoglio for his concern about my person.

II. The only place of residence at my disposal is Rocca delle Caminate, and I am ready to go there at any time.

III. I assure Marshal Badoglio that in recognition of our collaboration of previous days that for my part I will not only refrain from making any difficulties, but shall be ready at all times to continue our collaboration.

IV. I agree with the decisions taken, that the war against the Allies must be continued, as is demanded by the honour and the interests of our country, and I hope that the task which Marshal Badoglio has been entrusted by His Majesty the King, whose loyal servant I have been for twenty-one years and still am, will be successfully accomplished. Long live Italy!

Signed Mussolini.

I

Everything that happens is predestined to happen, for if it were not meant to happen, it would not happen.

2

As far as gratitude is concerned, animals are superior to human beings perhaps because they have instincts and not reason.

3

Dictators, it would appear, have no choice. They cannot fade away, they must fall; nevertheless their fall evokes no happiness. Even when they are no longer feared, they are either hated or loved.

4

The thing we call life is nothing more than an almost invisible dot between two eternities—the past and the future. A comforting thought.

5

Two books have greatly interested me of late—*The Life of Jesus* by G. Riciotti and *Giacomo Leopardi* by Saponero. Leopardi, too, was crucified to a certain degree.

6

According to del Croix, my life was destined to be divided into seven-year periods of decisive events: 1908–09 ejection from

Austria; 1914–15 Intervention; 1922 March on Rome; 1929 Reconciliation of State and Church; 1936 Foundation of the Empire; 1943 Overthrow; 1950 . . . death . . . at last!

7

The Pontine musings are ended, for at one o'clock this morning I was awakened with the words: 'Danger approaches! We must go away!' I dressed in all haste, packed up my papers and effects and went on board a cruiser which was waiting for me. Here I met Admiral Manzoni, who told me that our destination was the island of Maddalena, near Sardinia. To-day my thoughts turn to Bruno. It is the second anniversary of his death. Under present circumstances, I feel the loss more deeply than ever. Dear Bruno! His photo is in front of me, as I write these words in the new house of banishment on the second anniversary of his death.

The journey lasted twelve hours through a rough sea. The villa to which I have been brought, belonged to an Englishman named Webber and is magnificently situated. A large park of pines surrounds it; it faces the sea, and beyond it are the rugged mountains of Sardinia.

A year ago I visited Maddalena amid the great enthusiasm of the population. To-day I arrive secretly. Who knows whether any one ever thinks of my son and all he accomplished in his short, wonderful life!

Twenty years' work has been brought to nothing in a few hours. I refuse to believe that there are no longer any Fascists in Italy. There are probably more than ever. But how bitter it is to have to confess that this has been caused by Fascists and carried out by people who wore the emblem of the Party. Fascism was a pioneer movement which interested the whole world and broke new ground. It is not possible that everything is in ruins. When I look back on all the work, the tasks, the accomplishments and the hopes of these last twenty years, I ask myself: Have I been dreaming? Was it all an illusion? Was it all superficial? And without root?

8

At the end of the first day of banishment on Maddalena I am

stricken with a feeling of deep melancholy. Now I really do feel that my son Bruno is dead!

9

In a few years memories of me and my fate will become dim and will finally fade away.

10

Since mid-day on 28th July I have read no newspaper. It is astonishing that I feel no sense of deprivation, for I was a voracious reader of a dozen newspapers every day.

11

A trick of fate: From the pinnacle of power to complete impotence, from the plaudits of the masses to complete solitude.

12

From October 1942 I had an increasingly strong premonition of the fate which was destined to overtake me. My illness had a lot to do with it.

13

Latterly requests for my photograph had become much less frequent, and my reluctance to autograph them had grown in a like degree—if not even greater. (This I used to do every Sunday.) I felt that one day these photos would either be torn up or hidden; and that must have occurred in a truly 'totalitarian' manner these days both in public and private. Those with little courage have torn them up, the more bold have stuck them in some cupboard, so that in case of a surprise, they can say they had forgotten all about them. *Sic transit gloria effigiei.*

14

All of us in the Villa Torlonia saw the film *The Small Island of St. Helena* with great interest. That was the end of a great man. So why shouldn't a much smaller man suffer the same or a similar fate.

15

After a fortnight I still do not know what I 'am' or rather, what I have become.

16

According to Admiral Manzoni there are only twenty windless days a year on Maddalena. To-day, 10th August is one of them. The sea is like a table and the trees are motionless.

17

Thales thanked the Gods for allowing him to be born a human and not an animal, a man and not a woman, a Greek and not a barbarian.

18

When a political or social pyramid crashes in ruins the effects are felt in its very foundations. A small problem arises also for the children who carried tennis rackets.

19

This morning the sun is striving to pierce a grey bank of cloud which is coming up from the east. The sea is like lead. It is the first foretaste of winter. (My sentry indeed said—'August, the beginning of winter'.)

20

His name is Felice da Nunzio and he comes from the province of Rome. The sentries on Ponza are: Torella (Frosinone), Tizzoni (Rieti). I am thinking too of the two officials who watched over me. on the day of my arrival in Ponza—Picazio from Caserta and Gentile from Syracuse. I remember too Bruni from Teramo and Vizzini from Palermo, who wanted my autograph.

Dictatorship is a typically Roman (republican) system. What is called a dictatorship in the modern world is in reality a form of indirect or collective dictatorship, which apparently cannot last for more than twenty years. There is, however, one exception—the dictatorship of Bolshevism over the proletariat.

21

To-night the guards opened fire on 'suspicious noises'. This morning, 8th August, at eight o'clock, there was an air alarm and the A.A. battery opened fire. I only saw two fighters flying towards the island. The whole thing lasted three or four minutes.

22

More surprised than anyone else at recent events must be the Japanese Ambassador: I received him at one o'clock on 25th July!

23

Gnats were the loud speakers of the night. Here we have far too many of them.

24

The individuals of my guard—Carabinieri and officials—must have many questions running through their heads. What sort of a man is this?

25

After the outbreak of war in June 1940 the first air-raid shelters in the Villa Torlonia consisted of some of the grottoes. The cellar lies in the vicinity of the theatre. It was regarded as a fairly safe place, until the competent experts inspected it and declared it to be a death trap. The cellars of the Villa itself were to have been strengthened. But after the air raids on Turin, Milan and Genoa it was decided that a proper bomb-proof shelter must be constructed—What kind of shelter is capable of withstanding the heaviest of bombs? Construction was entrusted to Major Prisella. Cost 240,000 lire, time of construction three months, work commenced December 1942. It was found, as always happens in Rome, that the site selected in the vicinity of the villa was hollow and that the excavations would have to be twice as deep as had been envisaged. The whole plan had to be enlarged and more time allowed for construction. It is curious that my antipathy to the shelter increased as the work proceeded and approached completion (end of July), and

not on account of the extra cost, which was about double the
original estimate, but because of a feeling of dark foreboding.
I had a feeling that when this shelter was completed it would
prove quite useless and that we should never go in it. In truth,
one must sometimes listen to voice of the subconscious!

26

For the first time since 1940 the Italian Headquarters communiqué speaks of the land activities of the enemy, without
mentioning our own. This may be assumed to be preparation
for the announcement that our last hour in Sicily has struck.

27

A disbanded—that is to say a forbidden—Party has a fascination
for many Italians. They find satisfaction in being Fascists, as
long as this stamps them also as 'subversive'. A strange but
contemptible frame of mind.

28

For the second time I have received a letter from Rachele with
no mention of Vittorio. Lieutenant Faiola, who has known him
since he was a child, says he is sure no harm can have come to
him.

29

The *élite* of the fighting soldiers on all fronts were incorporated
in the Party, and now all are automatically transformed into
enemies of the State.

30

The news this morning was of the departure of Colonel Meoli,
Lieutenant di Lorenzo and thirty Carabinieri.

31

It is a curious thing that towards the end I found that working
in the great hall of the Palazzo Venezia became burdensome. I
had already decided to move into the Ministry of Marine or
somewhere, which was smaller than the Palazzo Venezia. I had

chosen the latter on account of its position, opposite the national memorial. Another sign of my illness.

32

The first days of a new existence—in my case as a prisoner—are endless. Then they become filled with petty affairs and seem to hasten past.

33

To-day, 13th August, a strange restlessness has seized me which I cannot shake off; and sure enough at five o'clock the Head-quarters communiqué brought news, in addition to air raids on Milan and Turin, of the second raid on Rome. So much for the myth of the 'Papal Town' which was to be spared! And so much also for the myth that Rome had only been bombed because it was the headquarters of the Fascists.

34

Is everything really going as well as people try to make one believe? How is it possible that an Air Force Captain like Vittorio, after twenty-one days since the 'relief of the watch', still gives no news of himself.

35

Conversation between myself and my very rare visitors quickly flags and very soon the Trappist rule will prevail: Silence.

36

I have never taken any interest in cross words and such like puzzles. But to-day, having nothing to read, I killed time with one, in order as the saying goes, to prevent time from killing me. Everything here depends on one's ability to take a long view and accustom oneself to it.

37

This morning, 14th August Police Inspector Polito, now Chief of the Military Police and ranking therefore as a Brigadier General, arrived in the course of a tour of inspection, and I asked him to visit me. He came and he brought Admiral Brivonesi with him. Polito said: 'I accompanied Donna Rachele to La Rocca. The journey by car was without incident. With her at La Rocca are Romano and Anna Maria. Of Vittorio I have heard nothing. He is under Casero's orders, and he went on leave on 26th July. As regards Badoglio's promise, it was found impossible to keep it in your case; telegrams from the Prefect, the Quaestor and the Commandant of the Military Area were unanimous in anticipating grave disorders if you had been taken to La Rocca. We confirmed all this on the spot. You must remember that the change of government is a drastically complete one. Not only do you see no Fascist emblems anywhere in Italy now, but the Fascists themselves have scattered and vanished into thin air. The demonstrations of hatred against you are innumerable; I have myself seen a bust of you in a lavatory in Ancona. In Milan the mob stormed the offices of the *Popolo d'Italia*. The staff barricaded themselves in, and Vito defended himself—that is all I have heard so far.

'There have been a large number of arrests, but the leaders of the Fascist Party are nearly all still at liberty, including the much hated Starace. Count Ciano was seen on 26th July in uniform. I think he has gone to Leghorn. Grandi, Bottai and the rest have disappeared from view.

'As regards the war, the people are simply longing for it to end, even though they realize that they have put themselves into a cul-de-sac. They are quite reconciled to the idea of defeat, and they regard it as a victory that they have been liberated from Fascism.

'Your whole edifice has collapsed. It will suffice for you to know that to-day Bruno Buozzi is the leader of the workers. The Prefects have nearly all been relieved by retired men.

'The recent air raids were very severe. Milan suffered particularly heavily, and the whole of the centre of the town, with the exception of the cathedral has been completely destroyed. The attacks on Rome were equally heavy, and were directed against the same targets as the earlier raids. The Pope has once more left the Vatican.

'The attacks on German towns have been equally devastating, and casualties are reckoned in tens of thousands.

'After the conquest of Sicily, the British will land in south Italy. All the ports of Sicily are full of ships and landing gear. A further landing is in preparation for Syria, with the Dodecanese as its objective. There are no indications of any operations against Sardinia or Greece.

'Things are going badly for the Germans on the land front as well. The air supremacy of the Anglo-Americans is depressingly complete. We can only oppose a ridiculously small number of machines against the hundreds of attacking planes.

'It looks as though the British are aiming, with their terror tactics, to bring about the complete moral and material collapse of the nation and to compel an unconditional surrender.

'This war is a greater burden on the civil population than on the Armed Forces. It strikes the aged, the women and the children, and that is the explanation for the general war-weariness and for the hatred against the men responsible for the war.'

During this long speech of Polito, Admiral Brivonesi occasionally intervened, to emphasize the fact that the speed with which Fascism had disappeared would have been regarded as impossible a few days earlier, even though it was known to be in poor shape.

General Polito advised me to remain quiet; he asked me how things had been and now were with me, and added that when passions had died down a little it would be possible to arrive at a more just verdict, for 'no one can deny that your aim was to make the country rich and great'. And—'Has nobody told you? What then was your entourage doing?'

As regards letters, the Admiral said that in present circumstances they were bound to be irregular. He then said he would come and see me whenever I wished him to do so. The conversation lasted for about an hour and a half.

Bearing in mind the 'colouring' with which the P.S. officials are wont to present their reports, I was able to arrive at two conclusions:

1. That my system had collapsed
2. That my own overthrow was final.

I should indeed be a simpleton if I were astonished at the behaviour of the masses. Apart from our opponents, who have waited in the shadows for twenty years, apart from those who have been hard hit or disappointed and so on, the masses are always ready to cast down the Gods of yesterday, even though they rue it to-morrow.

But for me there is no return. My blood, the infallible voice of the blood, tells me that my star has set for ever.

38

A peaceful August day, the sea is motionless, unstirred by any breeze, and all seems settled under the sun—including my own fate.

39

This afternoon I had a visit from the Chief Medical Officer of the Military Hospital, Dr. Mendini, a doctor from Cesea (Verona). A charming and cultured man, a Venetian in the best sense of the word; one of those Venetians from the Province of Venice whom I have always regarded as the best stock in all Italy. He prescribed various medicines for me, among other things injections, vitamin C, drops and carbonate. I asked him: 'Do you think it's still worth while?' He answered: 'As a doctor and a human being I think so.'

40

When a man and his organization collapse, then the fall is irretrievable particularly if the man is over sixty.

41

God is my witness to the despairing and anxious—I repeat, despairing and anxious—efforts I made in the fateful days of August 1939 to preserve the peace. My efforts failed, and the British and the Germans are almost equally responsible for my failure. The British, because they guaranteed Poland, the Germans because they had a mighty military machine standing ready and could not resist the temptation to put it into motion.

42

To-day, 16th August, I received for the first time the *Radio-Navi* of 14th August, with news from Berlin, Tangiers, Lisbon, Madrid, Istanbul and Stockholm.

43

The collapse of my régime is the logical consequence of the cause and effect of military events. It is clear that I should not now be on this island, if the British had suffered a real Dieppe in the grand manner on 10th July in the bay of Gela.

44

As always, so in my case too, there will be those who say *cherchez la femme*. But women have never had the slightest influence on my politics. That perhaps was a pity. Women with their sensitivity are often more far-seeing than men.

45

Crispi and that quite astonishing phenomenon called 'Crispismus' fell after the defeat at Adua, and Felice Cavalotti became extremely popular. At that time, too, the people suddenly changed its mind, and there followed four dramatic years, which ended in the Park of Monza at the turn of the century.

46

One goes from the zenith of adoration to the apotheosis of degradation. Of Plato's three souls, the masses possess the first two—the vegetative and the sensitive, but they lack the higher, the intellectual. I do not find it difficult to believe that millions of Italians who glorified me yesterday abhor me to-day and curse the day that I was born, the place that gave me birth and the whole of my clan—certainly the living do and probably those who have passed as well.

47

On one occasion the Pope, the representative of God on earth, called me 'The man of Providence'. That was a happy time!

48

If mankind remained for ever close to the altar, we should come to regard ourselves as super-men or divine beings. A tumble into the dust brings us back to our human state—what is called the primitive man.

49

The more depressing the atmosphere became, the greater were the number of suggestions made to me for the reform of our internal administration. The most radical reform occurred in January, when I changed all the Ministers but two. The result was a less united and therefore a weaker Government than before. In it, defeatism was represented by Cini, who could not see how Italy could hold out longer than June. The effect of this shuffle did not last long. Other internal measures, such as the appointment of new Ministers to the Ministries which I myself had held and the handing over of a whole complex of questions to new organizations and so on, were to be put into effect immediately after some military success—a day which I called 'the day of sunshine', a day that never came. The people were looking forward to it, and even relegated to secondary importance the eternally difficult problem of food.

The people, who had counted on at least a halt of the enemy advance, was no longer satisfied with the 'points' which Scorza made again and again. Even in Fascist circles there arose a slight suspicion that Scorza was not on the right lines, and I myself began to have doubts as to his loyalty. One single day of victory —on land, at sea, or in the air—would have restored the situation. That is clear from the enthusiasm with which the rumours that the attempted landings had failed were greeted on 10th and 11th July. Rumours which were repeated in the notorious and disgraceful Headquarters communiqué of the 12th, and which were denied in the communiqué of the 13th in the most brutal and authoritative way by the announcement of the fall of Syracuse and Augusta.

On that day Act Five of the drama began. Accusations and counter-accusations poisoned the atmosphere. People talked of treachery on the part of the Admirals, first at Pantelleria and then at Augusta. The 'Twelve' who were to have spoken in the capitals of the régime, were themselves thrown from the saddle by the defeat. Scorza summoned them to a Party meeting to consider what was to be done. Then, almost without exception they came to me, and there followed an exchange of views, which could have had no other logical and practical result than my decision to convene the Grand Council. Friday and Saturday were spent in drawing up the agenda, obtaining the necessary signatures and in preparing for the attack—or should I say, the manœuvre. Three or four knew what they wanted and what they would achieve. The others had no idea of what was afoot, and they never dreamed that at this meeting the existence of the régime would stand in the balance.

50

Of all the so-called 'totalitarian' States which have been founded since 1918, the Turkish State seems to be the most solidly established. In Turkey, there is only one Party, the People's Party, the leader of which is the President of the Republic.

51

It may be that some of the foreign commentators have over emphasized the inconstancy of the Italian people in their political convictions.

52

A new morning. 16th August—a feeling of great unrest. My blood boils.

53

To-day I am thinking of three men who, it is true, came from the Nationalists, but who brought to Fascism much of the light of learning, the devoutness of faith and acceptance of the law—they are Alfredo Rocco, Enrico Corradini, Davanzati.

54

Will the consecrated apartments of the Fascio-Houses be respected? I wonder if the men who died for Fascism—men like

9

Constantino, Narina Oscar Telleni, Walter Vannini, Bor-Pisani and so many more—will still be remembered?

Was there a 'conspiracy' against me? Yes, there was—otherwise there can be no explanation for the letter which Marshal Badoglio sent me on the night of 25th-26th, in which he wrote of a 'serious plot' against my person.

Since 23rd October, 1942, Fortune has turned her back on me. The twentieth anniversary celebrations were ruined by enemy air-raids and by the enemy offensive in Libya. I therefore postponed a speech on which I had spent much time and trouble and which I was to deliver in Adriano. My speech to the Chamber on 2nd December was followed by the unhappy events in Libya. On 5th May, on the occasion of the last demonstration outside the Palazzo Venezia, I declared that we should return to North Africa, and at the same moment we lost Tunisia, the last piece of that land. On 10th July I took the salute at the march past of the 'M' Division, and on the same day the enemy landed in Sicily. The first air-raid on Rome took place while I was meeting the Fuehrer in Feltre. I will spare myself the recollection of other, perhaps less typical, blows of fate. Even so, I thought it would be cowardly to resign. I hoped to the very last to put on my head, as the saying is, the hat that luck wears, but I did not succeed. On 10th, 11th, 12th, 13th July I still had some hope, but after that I knew it was all in vain.

On both occasions when I met Hitler in Venice, ill-fortune followed.

55

12th August. Sea like a lake. A horrible sameness oppresses everything.

The past really does belong to us. Good and evil, joy and sorrow—the past belongs to us, and according to Christian theology not even God can undo that which has been done.

I cannot believe that 160 lbs. of gold were found in Farinacci's house. Latterly I had pushed Farinacci a little into the background on account of his posturing as the noble father of Fascism and his ostentatious adoption of the role of Cato.

In June two speeches were delivered—one by Del Croix on 5th and one by Gentile on 24th. Both were excellent, but of no avail in face of the flood of military disasters which came tumbling over us; and yet any Headquarters communiqué which was a little less unpalatable than usual was enough to make spirits rise again. But such communiqués became steadily rarer.

The Commandant of my Guard is Lieutenant Faiola, a Latin from Segni, with a brilliant military record. When he was severely wounded at Tobruk he witnessed the inhuman treatment meted out to our wounded and prisoners by the British, and now he hates everything that is British. In Eritrea in 1935 he met Bruno and Vittorio, who at that time were very young volunteers in the Air Force. 24th August is the eighth anniversary of their departure for Africa. Marshal Badoglio praised and promoted them. 1935 and 1936 were the 'Years of Sunshine' for Italy and for the régime. It is worth while having lived to see them, even if now we are surrounded by rack and ruin, and even if all the officials in Rome put together are still unable to give me any news of my son and nephew.

56

As I said in my book, Bruno's death was a happy stroke of fortune. How he would have suffered in these days!

57

A voice says to me: If you were now dead, would you not have left the Palazzo Venezia, and the Villa Torlonia and the Rocca delle Caminata, the friends and relatives, and everything that was dear to you? But the voice forgets that I have lost all these things—and still live. And yet, I feel as though I were dead. The eternal philosophy of the ego. Will the dead of Fascism—and there are many of them—be revered?

58

To-day, 17th August at 17.00 hours, the priest from La Maddalena came to see me at my request. Don Capula is a Sardinian and has been living here for ten years; as a priest and an Italian he enjoys the undivided respect and affection of everyone. He told me that he had been thinking about me and that he had the day before waved a greeting to me, when he saw me on the terrace. I told him briefly of the conditions under which I lived, and said that his visits would help me to overcome the severe moral crisis which I was facing and which had been brought on primarily by my solitude. He replied that he was always at my service and that I could rely on his discretion. 'Let me speak frankly with you; you have not always shown yourself to be a great man when fortune smiled. Show your greatness now, in adversity. The world will judge you by what you become from now on, rather than by what you were yesterday. God, Who sees everything, watches you, and I am sure you would do nothing contrary to the tenets of the Catholic faith, not even if ill fortune deals you yet more bitter blows.' I gave him my promise. He is coming again on Thursday afternoon. Another thing he said was: 'Many to whom you did a good deed have forgotten you. But there are others who feel towards you that respect which we pay to those that fall in battle, together, perhaps with a tinge of regret.'

59

Lieutenant Faiola told me that X . . . (some English name) had said in Rome that Eden in a speech in the House of Commons had declared that Libya would not be returned to Italy. The British radio also complained that Badoglio was 'following in Mussolini's footsteps', it then announced the capture of Messina. With this painful news, 17th August came to its end.

60

A month ago I saw Romano, Anna, Guido and Adria for the last time in Riccione. I arrived at 19.00 hours, and we all listened to Scorza's speech. On the whole it was a good speech, but monotonously delivered—and on a tragic note at that.

61

In the following pages I wish to record the behaviour of Dino Grandi, the Count of Mordano, from the beginning of 1943 to

July. It may well be of interest. Up to February his attitude
seemed quite clear; but after the ministerial crisis it began to
be somewhat equivocal. In some circles he was regarded as an
'attendiste'; in others he was bluntly put down as an Anglophile.
This last charge is unjust. At that time Grandi was very frequently absent from Rome and spent a long time in Bologna,
where he had bought the newspaper 'Resto del Carlino'. In
addition he owned the plant which went with the place
and which was worth many millions. At the beginning of
March he asked for an interview, at which he asked me to put
forward his name for the Order of the Annunziata. In justification of his request, he pointed out that he had for many years
been Ambassador to Great Britain and President of the Chamber.
I promised to speak to the King about it, and did so at one of the
audiences which the King granted me every Monday and
Thursday. The King said that Grandi's first reason carried no
weight, but the second did. As regards the time of the award,
the King said he would confer it on the Day of the Annuncia-
tion, which fell on 25th March. This duly happened, and the
newspapers reported the fact without comment. The President
of the Senate, who is not eligible for this Order, thus suffered
a loss of prestige. At the beginning of April—the exact date
can be ascertained from the facsimiles of the audiences, which I
kept most zealously—I saw Grandi again and he thanked me
with the utmost effusiveness. 'Before I met you, I was a columnist
of the *Carlino* and a modest journalist. It is you who have
created me. I owe everything that has come to me in this life to
you. My devotion to you is boundless, because—let me say
it—because I love you.' Was he being sincere? At the moment
I believed he was. I mentioned his services as Ambassador, as
Foreign Minister and as a Fascist. He then went back to Bologna.
The next time I saw him was on 5th May in the Palazzo Venezia
after Scorza's speech in Adriano. He was beaming all over his
face. 'Duce,' he cried, 'what a magnificent speech! We have all
found ourselves once again! We are back in the old atmosphere.
We have found the right path' . . . and more in the same style.
Then he again returned to Bologna. Complaints against his
'attendiste' attitude increased. At the end of July he was present
at the memorial service held by Scorza for Balbo. When he

returned, Scorza told me that Grandi had been unwilling to mount the speaker's platform and that throughout the day he had adopted a very reserved and aloof attitude. (During his sojourn in London Grandi had venomously maligned Balbo, and even his personal courage.)

We now come to July. During the week 11th–18th Scorza chose twelve outstanding members of the régime, who were to deliver speeches in various principal cities of the country. Among others he chose Grandi, who, however, telegraphed to the Party and begged to be released from this task. Scorza repeated his request through the provincial Governor, but the latter wired back that Grandi categorically refused to speak. Scorza wanted to take disciplinary action against him, but I advised him not to do so and not to raise a 'Grandi case' at this juncture. As Grandi in one of his letters to Scorza had written about the necessity of 'Sacred Union', I sent for him and asked him which 'sacred union' he referred to, and whether he was thinking of reviving the old Parties, each with its leader, which I had suppressed? He replied that he meant the sacred union of all Italians, which alone could remove the Party aspect of the war. 'It is time,' he said, 'that people stopped talking about it as "Mussolini's war". This is the war of all of us. The time has come for the Crown to emerge from its obscurity. Our national territory has been invaded, and the Crown remains silent. The King evades his duty. He must assume his rightful responsibilities for this war is also and above all the war of King Victor Emanuel III. The people want to see the Crown abandon its cautious attitude and by so doing to give the war a truly national character.' My retort was that in every war two parties form—those who want the war and those who do not. The 1915–18 war was called the war of the interventionists; the present war is called the Fascists' war. Sacred unions between parties in opposition are impossible; that has been proved by the attempts made to achieve them in France. At one moment Clemenceau stood forth as the champion of the sacred union. The conversations were on a high note and went with a swing; but I still had the impression that the man was really in the other camp and that he was already on the other side of the barricades. Scorza spoke on the evening of 18th July. The next morning Grandi telegraphed to him from Bologna: 'Your speech was wonderful. Thus spoke the great men of the Risorgimento' . . . and so on.

In a later conversation early in the week 18th–25th July Grandi told me that 'even Scorza had disappointed him, and he no longer thought very much of him'. On the Thursday and the Friday he came and beseeched me not to convene the Grand Council, while all the time the 'plan' was complete in all details. With the last part of the Order of the Day Grandi hoped to force the King to decisive action. The Crown must either accept the Order and so assume responsibility for the war, or it must refuse and hence expose its weakness. In this dilemma the King chose the first alternative, with all its attendant repercussions, on which at the moment I shall make no comment. At the meeting of the Grand Council Grandi declared that this decision could be kept secret. But the next morning all Rome knew about it, and everyone felt that something of great importance was imminent.

62

As I am writing about the past of the men who formed my immediate entourage, I will say something about Bottai, who is a brave soldier and a bold writer. His whole life's work remains incomplete. As a politician he is restless, but also enterprising. They say that he is a half-caste, and his face certainly resembles a mask; his glance is often wavering, and he is not as scrupulously clean as he might be. Has he made his pile? They say he has. He is not at all popular. At the last Old Fascists' rally in Rome on 21st April, he was all but howled down. When he left the Ministry from which he had issued the 'Carta della Scuola', he banged the door behind him. A month later he came to me and said: 'I can't remain idle any longer, and I have the following suggestion to make. Will you give me either Bevione's job in the National Institute of Security, or Giordani's job in the I.R.I., or, for the time being make me an Ambassador?' I replied: 'It is not fitting that you should take over from Bevione, who has a right to his post up to 15th June. People would say that you had slipped into a nice, quiet little corner, with two hundred thousand lire a year attached to it. As a former Minister of Guilds and Corporation, you are more suited for the I.R.I., but apart from the fact that Giordani has not voiced any intention of retiring, here, too, there are many milliards involved. I would rather try and find you an Embassy—perhaps Berlin, where Alfieri appears to have had enough of it.' He agreed to this, but a few minutes later he returned with a new solution. As the legislative session was about to end, could he not be appointed President of the Chamber? I told him that this solution would be the most acceptable to me, provided that Grandi concurred. A little later Bottai came to me again, this time with a letter from Grandi, in which the latter expressed his satisfaction at the choice of Bottai as his successor. The rest of the story is well known.

63

In all my life I have never had any 'friends', and I have often asked myself whether this is an advantage or a handicap? Now I am sure that it is a 'good thing', for now there is no one called upon to suffer with me.

64

Who knows whether the memorials erected to Bruno are still in their place in the War Museum in Milan, and whether they are still respected?

65

On Sunday, 25th July, Bastianini rang me up to tell me that Goering wanted to come to Italy on the occasion of my sixtieth birthday. I replied that I would be pleased. On the 30th Goering sent me a telegram, which a Major of Carabinieri brought over to Ponza. Here it is, as a record: 'Duce! As circumstances have prevented me from carrying out my original intention of personally conveying to you my good wishes, I send you instead my birthday greetings, coupled with the expression of my profound esteem. Animated by a feeling of sincere friendship and absolute loyalty, I want to express my thanks to you for the hospitality which you so often and so cordially extended to me in the past, and for the many proofs of your steadfast friendship which you have afforded me. For the coming year, my wife and I send you our best wishes for your personal well-being. May the strength and the personality of Your Excellency still work in the future for the good of those Europeans in the forefront of the battle, in spite of the hard trials and unhappy events of the present. As an expression of my respect I send you a bust of Frederick the Great. In steady comradeship and with the esteem and unwavering loyalty of my whole heart I remain Your Excellency's most devoted—Goering, Reichs Marshal of the Greater German Reich.'

This telegram convinced me more than ever that Goering was a true friend of Italy. I was given permission to reply, but I did not do so, because I did not wish to answer in words which would inevitably have had to be banal, so moving and so brotherly a greeting.

66

Albini: A mistake and a disappointment. Hateful in body and soul! He knew all, and told me nothing.

67

Is this what my legal position is supposed to be? Ex-Head of the Government in protective custody against the rage of the people.

68

18th August (1937 or '38?) flight from Rome to Pantelleria and back.

69

It is difficult to assess the full weight of the moral suffering that the events of 25th July must have brought to the Youth Organizations of the G.I.L. They must have been particularly painful for the men students of the Farnesina Academy and for the women of Orvieto, as well as for those in the Academies of the three Armed Forces, in Brindisi, Venice, Forli and Bolzano, whose organization, discipline and success were perfect. These were the Youth Organizations which were admired throughout the world; which gave such memorable gymnastic and sporting displays; which gave proof of their heroism in the Young

Fascist Division from Bir el Gobi to Maretta. Surely these
noble youths deserved a better treatment than this! These
youths who have suffered this bitter blow, whither will they go
to-morrow? Will they swing to the extremist views of the Left,
or will they be completely disillusioned and have neither faith
nor belief in anything again?

70

A certain Sergeant-Major Daini has just returned from the
mainland, and I have had a talk with him. He is a frank and
honest man, whose intellectual limitations give a certain solid
value to his thoughts. A strengthening of the forces of revolution, he said, was becoming apparent. The people are completely discouraged and have but one desire—to see the end of
the war at all costs. The villages of Latium are filled with
refugees from Rome.

71

Of the modest folk who have served me, there are two whom I
hope I shall always remember—Rodolfi and Navarro. The
former rode at my side every day for nearly twenty years; he
was my riding and fencing instructor, conscientious, not in the
least calculating and faithful in the best sense of the word. Will
he, I wonder, have got into trouble? Navarro was my head
servant for twenty years; well educated, respectful, discreet,
he too had no thought of self.

I should like to say a word of praise also about my chauffeur,
Boratto, who risked his own life in the two attempts made to
assassinate me. With the exception of running over a dog in
Monte Fresione, he never had an accident of any kind, although
he drove very fast.

72

And after the human beings, why should I not remember the
animals? For they, too, have had a place in my life. The names
of my horses are: Rusovich, Ziburoff, Ned, Thiene, Eron (a
present from Dollfuss). And the dogs: Carlot (a horrible little
beast, but very intelligent), and Bar, Bruno's dog. For days he

crouched on the threshold of the room in which Bruno's things lay. That is the fidelity of an animal!

73

19th August. My week of suffering, if I may so call it, began exactly one month before my meeting with the Fuehrer in Feltre. This meeting was to have lasted four days, like the previous meeting at Salzburg, and Feltre had been chosen for security reasons and on account of its proximity to the frontier. The exact date had not been fixed, and as a result of the events in Sicily, 19th July was chosen and the meeting restricted to a single day. Much too short for a detailed examination of the situation. The bureaucrats insisted on Feltre as the meeting place, whereas we could just as easily have met in the Prefecture in Treviso and thereby saved four hours; but red tape is incapable of mental gymnastics of this nature. At seven o'clock on the morning of 19th I left Riccione by air and arrived punctually at 8.30 at the aerodrome of Treviso. There I found the usual gathering of Air Force officers and men, all looking pretty glum. A little later some German machines landed bringing members of Hitler's staff, among them Field Marshal Keitel. Punctually at nine o'clock the Fuehrer arrived. He inspected the guard of honour and then we went to the station. An hour later we left the train at the station before Feltre, and from there drove by car to the villa selected for the conference, which belonged to Senator Goggia, and consisted of a labyrinth of halls, big and little, and reminded me of an Alpine range. The journey by car took us about an hour, in glorious sunshine, during which I merely exchanged trivialities with the Fuehrer.

The conference began at mid-day. Present were Keitel, General Warlimont and other German officers and the Ambassador, Mackensen. On the Italian side General Ambrosio with his interpreter, Bastianini and Alfieri. The Fuehrer opened the proceedings and spoke for two hours. His speech was taken down in shorthand, and the full text will be found in the archives of the Ministry for Foreign Affairs. Hardly had he begun to speak, when my secretary brought me a message from Rome, which said: 'Rome being heavily bombed since eleven o'clock.' I passed the information on to the Fuehrer and the others.

Gloom and despondency hung over us all, and it was deepened by the subsequent messages which told of the long duration of the attack, the large number of aircraft engaged and the very heavy damage caused to the University and the Church of San Lorenzo.

After the Fuehrer's speech, we had our first discussion in private. He gave me two most important pieces of information. 1. That submarine warfare was about to be resumed with new means. 2. That at the end of August the Reprisals Air Fleet would commence operations against London, which would be razed to the ground in a few weeks.

Among other things, I told him that, in anticipation of reprisals, the air defences of Italy would have to be strengthened. I was again called away to the telephone, and in the meanwhile the time of departure had arrived. It was only in the train on the way back that I was able to make quite clear the following points: Italy, I said, was at the moment being called upon to bear the full burden of the onslaught of two empires, the British Empire and the United States. She was in danger of being over-whelmed; the air attacks were not only undermining the morale of the people, but were also causing grave damage to war pro-duction and to the whole social fabric of the nation's life. I repeated that the African campaign would have taken a very different turn, if we had had superiority, or at least parity, in the air. Finally I told him that the moral tension in the country was very great. He replied that the crisis in Italy was a crisis of faith, and that he would send further reinforcements to strengthen the air and land defences of the peninsula. The defence of Italy, he declared, was of the utmost importance to Germany. The tone of our conversation was very friendly, and we parted on the best of terms. The Fuehrer's plane took off, and then I turned to Keitel, whom I was accompanying to his aircraft, and said: 'Send everything we require just as quickly as you can, and remember, we are both in the same boat.'

At 18.00 hours I flew directly back to Rome. As we passed over the Soratte, I ordered speed to be decreased, and on the horizon I saw a thick cloud of smoke. It was the smoke from the fire at the Littorio station, over which we passed a few minutes later. Hundreds of trucks were blazing, the workshops were destroyed and the aerodrome unusable. The locomotive sheds and the San Lorenzo district presented the same appearance, and the damage seemed to be terrific. The Prefect and a few other prominent people met me when I landed, and I went straight to the Villa Torlonia. On the way I met a great mass of people making their way into the country on foot and by every possible sort of transport. The wells were surrounded by dense crowds, for the water system had been put out of action. In the evening from the Villa Torlonia I could see the sky still lit up by the conflagration. Rome had experienced a terrible day of fire and steel, which had shattered every illusion.

During the next days I visited the most heavily bombed districts, and particularly the railway station and the aerodrome of Littorio, the Campino airport and the University; but I gave orders that no details were to be published in the newspapers.

In the meanwhile the opponents of the régime had spread the rumour that the meeting in Feltre had been completely fruitless; that Germany was leaving us in the lurch, and that after the conquest of Sicily the British would land almost unopposed in Rome. All this increased the tension which was already near to breaking point. The same tension reigned at the Royal Court. I realized this at the penultimate audience which I had with the King. Our last audience was the one at the Villa Savoia on Sunday the 25th.

74

The eagerly awaited Admiral Brivonesi returned from Rome this morning and broke my solitude. He brought me a letter from my wife, dated 13th August, in which she says that she is almost entirely cut off, that she has no telephone, and that life is a perpetual state of alarm. I don't know whether she means air raid alarms or other kinds. The Admiral also brought me a complete set of the works of Nietzsche, beautifully bound— twenty-four volumes, which the Fuehrer had sent through Kesselring, for my sixtieth birthday. He further told me that Vittorio had left the country and had been declared a deserter, which hurt me deeply; that Vito was in La Rocca and could not go to Mercato Saraceno, which may well mean that the authority of the new Government was not very strong in the

Romagna; and that in Milan the *Popolo d'Italia* was no longer appearing or had been destroyed. Some personal papers and books from the Palazzo Venezia were handed over to me. As regards my own future there is nothing new.

75

Here ends the first volume of the *Pontine and Sardinian Musings*. 19th August, 1943, at 3 p.m.

CHAPTER XV

THE END OF THE FASCISTS

THE liberation of Mussolini has received a great deal of publicity during the last few years but the enterprise which led to the rescue of Ciano and his family has remained wrapped in obscurity. Consequently the completely false story that Ciano was removed to Germany against his will and then handed over to the neo-Fascist Government for trial has gained much credence.

I was myself so closely connected with the rescue of Ciano that I can give the fullest details about it. Here is an authentic account of what happened. Towards the middle of August 1943 a friend of the Ciano family approached Dollmann, Himmler's agent in Rome, with the request that the Ciano family should be conducted to Germany as in Rome they went in fear of their lives. At that time Ciano was confined on Badoglio's orders to his Rome residence and forbidden to leave it. Now, he said, it had come to his knowledge that Badoglio intended to remove him and his family to an island in the Mediterranean in order to prevent any possible attempt at escape.

Himmler submitted Ciano's request to Hitler. The latter was prepared to agree to it and the German Secret Service was ordered to plan the rescue of Edda Ciano and her children. Hitler's orders were emphatic that 'whatever happened, Mussolini's blood in the veins of his grandchildren must at all costs be preserved for the future'. His sole real interest was in these grandchildren whom he regarded as the only important members of the family, although he had a great affection for Edda who was in his opinion the only child of Mussolini worthy of the father.

Ciano was not mentioned in Hitler's instructions. When asked he said that Ciano could come too, if he wanted, and particularly if his wife set any store by his coming. These orders were not considered precise enough, for what would be the position if Ciano said he wished to come and his wife were indifferent or even against it? Hitler had obviously been influenced by the rumours current in Germany that relations between husband and wife were as bad as they could be. He thought that Edda would be pleased at an opportunity to get rid of her husband. When the Secret Service officers entrusted with the mission asked for more precise instructions, Hitler was gracious enough to say that Ciano was also to be invited to come to Germany as his personal guest.

A rescue by force was out of the question. At the time Rome was firmly in the hands of the new Government. Hitler had explicitly refused to make available the German forces which would have been required had it come to a fight with the Italian Police and Army units in the city. The rescue could only be accomplished by stealth and guile. I laid plans accordingly and these were accepted unreservedly by both Hitler and Edda and Galeazzo Ciano, to whom they were submitted.

The removal of Edda Ciano and her children was a comparatively simple affair. The Countess had been permitted to take a daily walk with the children, followed at a discreet distance by a member of the Secret Police. On the day arranged it was agreed that they should walk along a certain street at a definite time. An American car would draw up beside them and the driver would lean out as though to make some ordinary inquiry. The children were to be bundled into the back while the Countess herself got in beside the driver, and the high-powered car would then make off at full speed. The accompanying agent would have little chance of intervention. His usual means of transport was a bicycle, and that would not make pursuit dangerous.

It was a much more difficult task to rescue Ciano himself. The main factor in favour of success was the vagueness of the orders issued to his guards. They had been told he was not to be permitted to leave the house but they had not been told what means they could permissibly use to prevent his flight or, most important of all, whether or not they should use their fire-arms in the event of an attempted escape. It was around this piece of knowledge that the plan was formulated—for we assumed that the sentries on the house doors would not open fire on a personage whose position was still the subject of controversy. No one was sure, for instance, whether Badoglio regarded him as a prisoner or whether he was protecting him from possible Fascist assassination.

At precisely the agreed time Ciano was to step out of the house and get immediately into a car which would approach at that moment, halting only long enough to enable him to get in. The plan could only succeed if the timing on both sides was observed to the second. Ciano's suggestion that he should first look out of the window to make sure that the car was approaching was not practicable. It would inevitably have aroused suspicion and so was rejected. All that was really required was for both parties to synchronize their watches to the split second. But even this simple task took two days to accomplish. On 27th August all was ready.

Both enterprises succeeded without any unexpected incident. The policeman accompanying the Countess had no suspicions at all. He was about twenty yards behind the party when the car drew up and before he could run to the spot the car was already drawing away. Count Ciano stepped swiftly out of the house at exactly the right moment, leapt into the slowly-moving car the door of which was already open to receive him. Everything happened so rapidly that the Police had no chance of taking any counter-measures, and even if one of them had opened fire the shots would most probably have gone astray. Apparently the guard did not report the whole truth of the affair to higher authority, for the most varied accounts were going round, even in official circles, both as to the time and the manner of the escape.

The rest was easy. The two cars had been ordered to make for the courtyard of a house in Rome where a closed lorry of the German Wehrmacht would be waiting to take them to the airport. The Frascati airport was too far away and to get there the lorry would have had to run the gauntlet of a number of street barriers and control posts, at any one of which its passengers might have been discovered. A landing ground nearer the city was chosen. But here too there would be Italian units who could be allowed no idea of what was happening. A Junkers transport plane was therefore ordered to be ready with its

loading-doors open. The lorry backed hard on to the plane
and the passengers were able to pass from one vehicle to the
other completely unobserved. It was as well that these meticulous precautions had been taken for when the lorry arrived a
group of Italian workmen were standing immediately beside
the plane, and one of them would certainly have recognized
Ciano.

On the way to the landing ground there was one critical
moment. The lorry had to come to a complete halt at each of
the street barriers. The Italian sentries made no difficulty for
beside the driver sat a German Air Force officer who had all
the necessary documents. But a German military policeman
nearly ruined the whole scheme. He declared that he had heard
children's laughter coming from within the lorry and was about
to investigate under the very noses of his Italian colleagues. I
sat quietly inside the lorry. The German Staff Officer in front
took charge and his angry rebuke to the sentry prevented a
painful discovery.

Even before the plane had left the ground, Ciano began to
pull gold cigarette cases, bracelets and rings out of all his pockets
and to make a first inventory. His little daughter too had a
small satchel crammed with jewellery. Before he was rescued
Ciano had already sent his valet ahead to Germany with a
small leather sack full of the most valuable trinkets. Even at
the most hazardous moment, his keen business instincts had
obviously not deserted him!

The flight to Germany was accomplished without incident,
except that to avoid any suspicion the passengers had to wear
their light summer clothes—the children were in rompers—and
as bad weather forced the aircraft to fly at a height of something
like 18,000 feet over the Alps, they were chilled to the bone.
Thanks to the forethought of Skorzeny there were two bottles
of brandy that helped to keep out the cold. Countess Edda and
the children swigged the brandy, but Ciano himself hardly
touched a drop. At Munich the party and its rescuer were
officially welcomed in Hitler's name and driven to a villa on
the Starnberger Lake.

There I had many long conversations with the Cianos. At
first Ciano tried to disguise the actions which had led to the

downfall of Mussolini, but Countess Edda made not the slightest attempt to hide the truth. Her forthright character which knew no half measures in love or hate would not tolerate any such evasion. With irrefutable logic she showed exactly where and how her father's policy had been wrong, though her affection for him was still deep. Ciano gradually came to agree more and more with her opinion, particularly when he saw that his German audience showed considerable understanding of many of his actions.

They both declared Italian misfortune had begun with Italy's entry into the war in June 1940. Mussolini had been under no illusions about the weakness of his country but he had been convinced that a final German victory was imminent, and that Italy would be losing a unique opportunity if she failed to intervene on the side of her Axis partner in the final phases of the war. Indeed, according to Ciano, Mussolini had more than once expressed the fear that when victory had been won Germany might well turn on Italy and transform her into a complete vassal State. The entry of Italy into the war against France had been Mussolini's own decision, and both the Cianos reiterated that they had opposed this step and tried to dissuade Mussolini from taking it.

But the greatest misfortune for Italy, they claimed, was Germany's attack on Soviet Russia. The Duce, the Fascist leaders and indeed the whole Italian people had regarded the Russo-German non-aggression pact of August 1939 with revulsion in their hearts. On the other hand, all had clearly recognized that a war with Russia before the campaign in the West was ended would inevitably lead to catastrophe. Neither Mussolini nor Ciano had any chance of influencing Hitler for they had been kept in the dark as to his intentions until the very last moment. The Duce had also complained often and bitterly at this German habit of delay in informing their Italian ally of most important and vital decisions until a few hours before the decisive moment. Again and again the Italian Government had found itself confronted with a *fait accompli*.

Mussolini and Ciano do not appear to have seen eye to eye on the question of the desirability of a separate peace on one front or the other. Ciano was of the opinion that every effort should be made to conclude a peace by negotiation with the Western Powers and that the war in the East should be pursued until Bolshevism was utterly destroyed. Mussolini was inclined to take the reverse view. Ciano, a shrewd calculator and superior to Mussolini in appreciating foreign affairs, wished to see Germany's urge for expansion directed eastwards where it would be occupied for a very long time and would therefore be no menace to Italian domination in the Mediterranean basin. Apart from this he was essentially a man of the west. Mussolini on the other hand was, according to Ciano, full of complexes against Britain and America. The dream of his life was to see those two powers driven to unconditional surrender and he regarded the defeat of Britain as the essential preliminary to the expansion of the Italian empire in Africa.

However, it was not the divergence of their views on foreign policy alone that was responsible for the estrangement between the two men. Ciano and his wife repeatedly asserted that with the increasing deterioration of the war situation, Mussolini's rabid Socialist views became more and more apparent. The Duce had often raved in the most violent and uncouth manner against the bourgeoisie and the aristocracy, expressing his utter contempt for them and threatening to destroy them in the future. Ciano and his group were therefore really concerned lest Mussolini should set up in Italy after the war a system which was but little different from that in Russia.

Ciano had very little love for a National-Socialist Germany and made no attempt to hide it in the conversations at the Starnberger Lake. He regarded Ribbentrop as a disaster. When he found that his German audience was in agreement with him he spoke more and more frankly.

Ciano's description of the relations between Hitler and Mussolini has already been published in detail. At first Mussolini thought little of Hitler and the knowledge that he was an Austrian and not a Prussian was repugnant to him. It was not a personal sympathy for Hitler as the leader of a political movement after his own heart which had finally driven Mussolini to Germany's side, but rather the array of nations in the political field, and in particular the sanctions imposed by the League of Nations at the time of the Abyssinian war. The impression left on Mussolini by his visits to Germany was strong. Grandiose military parades and massive popular demonstrations superbly organized in Berlin left Mussolini convinced of the might of National Socialist Germany. Later he repeatedly told his son-in-law that Italy had no alternative but to march at the side of the most mighty Power in the world. His attitude at the time of the invasion of Austria in March 1938 is perhaps proof that he realized military action by Italy against her powerful neighbour would be most dangerous.

Though siding with Germany, Mussolini had moments of doubt and crisis, said Ciano. Germany's invariable lack of tact infuriated him and caused him to rave for hours on end and utter the wildest threats. But when Ciano and those who thought like him tried to take advantage of the occasion to strengthen Mussolini's own independence, he would immediately swing to the other extreme and declare that nothing on earth could shake his absolute loyalty to his German partner.

Ciano, at least while he was in the Starnberger villa, was in complete agreement with Mussolini in his contempt for the Italian people. The situation in which he found himself may well have been partly responsible. He felt that he had been betrayed, overthrown and driven into exile. In his bitterness he cordially endorsed Hitler's assertion that Mussolini was 'the only Roman among a whole bunch of Italians'. His antipathy towards his own people sprang, however, from different sources to that of Mussolini. The Duce despised the Italians—or professed to do so—firstly because they were too weak, too docile and too peace-loving; and secondly because they remained indifferent to his dreams of a vast empire and failed to share their Dictator's conception of real greatness. It was for these reasons that he used to wish Italy had a more severe winter, which would harden his soft people. He regarded Prussian military discipline and organization as his ideal. He even went so far as to imitate the Prussian ceremonial parade step under the guise of the *Passo Romano*.

Ciano's ideals took a different line from the military imperialism of his father-in-law. He had hoped rather to see his country as the centre of a spiritual and cultural hegemony in Europe. His antipathy was more instinctive and was directed against other elements of the Italian people than those which evoked Mussolini's scorn. But the disillusionment of both sprang from the failure of the nation to rise to the different roles which each in his own mind had assigned to it. Ciano felt so strongly on the subject that he said his children were not to be brought up as Italians and were never to return to Italy. As far as he was concerned, he declared, he would rather see them become Cubans.

Ciano's account of the events which led up to the fall of Mussolini proved, on later investigation, to be substantially correct. He emphasized that the action of the Grand Council had nothing whatever to do with the conspiracy of the King and Badoglio, and that there had been practically no point of contact between the two groups. A number of eminent Fascist officials headed by Grandi and Bottai had long ago realized that Mussolini's policy was leading Italy to ruin. They regarded the Duce as physically and mentally exhausted and incapable of mastering the great problems with which the desperate situation confronted him. They also felt that the Fascist movement had lost so much of its original driving force. It was no longer an instrument worthy to wield the supreme power in a totalitarian State. They had accordingly formed a plan whereby Mussolini was to retain his position as a figurehead, but was to be relieved in a large measure of his dictatorial executive authority. The real power was to be vested in the King, who would be in a favourable position to make peace proposals to the Western Powers with every hope that they would receive quick and full consideration. These negotiations were to be started immediately by Grandi, who had already made many promising contacts via Lisbon and Madrid with London. The plan met with the full and unanimous approval of all the Fascist leaders, including Mussolini's oldest supporters like de Bono, de Vecchi and Federzoni. Ciano declared that he had repeatedly urged Mussolini to face the realities of the situation and to extricate Italy from the war. Had he done so, the *coup d'état* of the Fascist Grand Council would have been unnecessary. Mussolini had admitted the force and the justice of Ciano's arguments, but had asserted that it was incompatible with Italy's honour to leave her ally in the lurch. There had remained, then, no alternative but to table a motion of no confidence at the Grand Council.

The activities of the Royal Household against Mussolini were quite separate. There the mainspring was the Crown Princess Maria José, who had told Ciano as long ago as 1942 that she would do everything she could to get Italy out of the war. In Ciano's opinion, the royal plot had been maturing for a long time; but it had begun to take concrete form only after the Allies had landed in Sicily and the hopelessness of the situation had become apparent. The threads of the conspiracy were held in the hands of the Court Minister, Count Pietro Acquarone, whose principal colleagues were the Chief of the General Staff, General Ambrosio, and the Chief of Police, Carmine Senise. Marshal Badoglio, in whom none of the original conspirators had much faith, was drawn in much later and then only on account of the prestige of his name with the armed forces.

Such tenuous links as existed between the Fascist opposition group and the King's party were furnished by Ciano himself. The King had a high opinion of his statesmanlike qualities and had instructed Acquarone in 1942 to sound him, to see how far his co-operation could be counted upon. Ciano asserted to me that he gave no more than a non-committal answer. After his dismissal he ceased to be of any interest to the Royal party, for once out of office, he had little influence in the country. A long illness during the most important period of the conspiracy had further kept him from any active part. He had, it is true, a few talks with Badoglio, but no definite agreement for a future co-operation had been reached.

The action of the Fascists in the Grand Council was carried out, according to Ciano, 'with a clumsiness and stupidity which only German Generals could have equalled'. Not one of those responsible had any clear conception of what was to happen after the motion of no confidence had been passed. Each may possibly have had some sort of a programme of his own, but any unity of thought and purpose was wholly lacking. The King was quick to take advantage of this confusion and in-decision, which gave him the chance to carry out his coup against Mussolini earlier than he had planned. The latter fell into the trap like a child. Had he been in full possession of his health and senses he would undoubtedly have rejected with the utmost suspicion the King's invitation to a conference at the Villa Savoia.

In spite of a measure of natural personal prejudice, Ciano's appreciation of the situation was on the whole both just and correct. There were, of course, many details of which he had no knowledge, for he was not in the confidence of the inner ring of the Royalist conspirators. The opposition group in the Grand Council was divided by a multitude of various special interests and aims, many of them of a purely personal nature, and could present no united front. The majority was averse to co-opting Ciano, and it was only the consideration that the name of Mussolini's son-in-law would be of great value which finally led them to invite him to co-operate. He was, however, unable to assume any leading role in their councils, and probably for this reason: his logical summing-up of the situation carried no weight.

Ciano's opinion that the King seized an opportunity offered by the situation created by the Grand Council and made good use of it, is probably quite accurate. There is certainly no evidence to show that the two plots were in any way co-ordinated, and Mussolini is justified when he speaks of 'traitors betrayed'. The Fascist opposition group and the Grand Council were robbed of the fruits of their labours by the skilful opportunism of the King.

After his rescue, Ciano's one desire was to leave Europe as quickly as possible. He had no intention of returning to Italy, even in the event of victory, and an indefinite stay in Germany did not appeal to him at all. His intention was to go first to Spain and then on to South America. As a means of ensuring his departure he made me a good business proposition. He offered to part with his diaries in exchange for facilities for his voyage.

In the course of the talks by the Starnberger Lake, Ciano had told me so much about his diaries that there was no doubt of their political and historical value.

He had allowed it to be understood that Ribbentrop would be so compromised that he would be unable to continue any longer as Foreign Minister. This fact impressed Kaltenbrunner greatly, for if there was one thing above all others that he desired to see, it was the dismissal of Ribbentrop. Ciano had discovered this little weakness at his first meeting, and he made masterly use of his discovery. Kaltenbrunner's approval of the deal was won.

I made all the necessary arrangements through the German Secret Service. Ciano and his wife had already received their false South American passports, when the whole plan was spoilt by a bad mistake on the part of the Countess. Against my advice, she insisted on asking Hitler's permission and support when she visited him at Fuehrer Headquarters. The result was the very reverse of what she had hoped. Hitler forbade the German Secret Service to allow Ciano to depart. He wished Ciano to return to Italy, and he was sure that he would be given an important post in the new Government, for at Castle Hirschberg, where Mussolini had resided since his liberation, a complete and formal reconciliation had in the meanwhile been effected between the Duce and his son-in-law. Goebbels and Ribbentrop supported Hitler's views. Ribbentrop, who had a shrewd idea of the compromising material that Ciano could produce against him, was most anxious to see him remain within the frontiers of the German dominated territories. He confessed to Kaltenbrunner that Ciano, if allowed to go abroad, might start 'a regular stink' (*eine Schweinerei*) against him.

Therefore when Mussolini, strongly influenced by Buffarini, also demanded the return of Ciano to Italy, Hitler agreed. Ciano, though unwilling to go, feared no harm to himself. On the contrary, he consoled himself with the thought that it would probably be easier for him to get to South America from Italy than from hermetically sealed Germany. He was indeed greatly surprised when on landing at Verona he was arrested by the Italian Police and flung into prison.

In spite of this set-back, I did not abandon the scheme of furthering the departure of Ciano. I was soon in contact with him. I got my Roman secretary Hildegard Beetz smuggled in to him as a woman interpreter. She suggested to him that he should not go to Spain, but to Hungary. By keeping him in this way more or less within the confines of Germany's empire, Kaltenbrunner hoped to allay Hitler's misgivings.

Ciano agreed to this, and a Hungarian nobleman was found who was ready to receive him on his estate in Transylvania. A formal and written agreement was even drawn up and signed by Ciano and Kaltenbrunner, whereby the former promised to hand over his diaries to the German Secret Service in return for his liberation from prison. To show his appreciation, Ciano was anxious to do more and to hand over in advance a certain portion of his documents. He disclosed the hiding-place of these papers in Rome to the 'interpreter' who had won his confidence, and asked her to bring them to him at once. The documents were found in the place indicated, and this sample afforded ample proof of the immense value which the complete collection would be.

The plan of rescue was delightfully simple. On the ground that information had been received that Ciano, with the connivance of the Italian prison staff, was to be allowed to escape, the Commandant of the German Security Police in Verona was to occupy the prison with his own men. Later the Germans would simply declare that their intervention had come too late and that Ciano had already fled. As soon as his safe arrival in Hungary had been signalled and confirmed, his wife would hand over the rest of the diaries. Himmler and Kaltenbrunner had agreed thus to act on their own responsibility on the grounds that Hitler's orders had specifically only forbidden the removal of Ciano to any place outside the area of German domination. They hoped that the importance and interest of the Ciano papers would persuade the Fuehrer to give his retrospective sanction to this independent action on the part of the supreme Head of his Secret Services.

But at the last minute their courage failed them. They had heard that Goebbels and Ribbentrop were both urging Hitler to show no favour to Ciano. Fearing that this counsel might prevail, Himmler and Kaltenbrunner decided that after all they must obtain Hitler's specific permission before proceeding any further. As was only to be expected, Hitler's reply was uncompromising; he forbade any attempt to help Ciano and threatened severe punishment of anyone who disobeyed him. It was then objected that by his refusal he was practically condemning Ciano to death. But Hitler retorted: 'Mussolini will never permit the father of his beloved grandchildren to be put to death.'

Hitler, without doubt, sincerely believed that the arrest of Ciano and the case against him need not be taken seriously, that it was just a 'bit of thundering Italian bluff', and that no harm would come to the ex-Foreign Minister. He is now known to have told Goebbels that he had been sorry that Mussolini had not punished Ciano and the other renegade Fascists, but he was quite sure that he would shield his son-in-law from the extreme penalty.

As far as Mussolini was concerned, Hitler was right; but he forgot that Mussolini was no longer the Duce of yore, and that beside and against him were working forces in the neo-Fascist Government which he was not able to control. Buffarini and Farinacci were the prime movers in the campaign against Ciano. These neo-Fascist leaders apparently feared that they would be gravely compromised by Ciano's disclosures, and consequently they never ceased to demand his head. Mussolini allowed himself to be intimidated by them to such an extent that during the trial at Verona he did nothing to help his son-in-law, though it may be assumed that it was always his intention to reprieve him later. The events leading up to the execution of the sentence are still not known to the last detail, but it is clear that up to 10th January, 1944, the night before the execution, Mussolini had not received the expected petition for reprieve, and the news that Ciano had been shot came as a profound shock to him.

Ciano died next day with the bitter feeling that the Germans in their negotiations had deceived and betrayed him in the most contemptible manner. He refused to believe that his rescue had been seriously planned and had been prevented only by the cowardice of Himmler. But he retained his poise to the last, and he spent the whole night before his execution reading Seneca with Hildegard Beetz.

This efficient member of the German Secret Service not only delivered Ciano's letters to his wife and thereby gave the Countess the chance to send the diaries to Switzerland in good time, but she also played no small part in arranging the flight of the Countess herself and in ensuring, through my authority, that those who had helped her were not punished. In this way, although he had actually had nothing to do with the rescue plot, Edda's friend the Marquis Emilio Pucci was saved from certain execution.

As is known, Ciano's diaries were sold in Switzerland by the Countess to the Americans. The portions which had already been given to the German Secret Service had a romantic history. At the end of April 1945, in accordance with a general instruction from Hitler, the originals and the translation were destroyed, together with all the secret files of the State Security Service Headquarters in Berlin. (Micro-photos had been taken, but what became of them is not known.) These valuable papers seemed therefore apparently lost for ever. Suddenly, however, a copy of them made its appearance. Hildegard Beetz, who had retrieved them from their hiding-place in Rome had, strictly against orders, kept a carbon copy of the translation with which she herself had been entrusted. As the Russian armies pressed forward during the last phases, she buried them in her garden. In the summer of 1945, with the assistance of the American Secret Service, she managed to retrieve them. They were finally handed over to the American State Department. So the whole of the Ciano diaries came to be preserved, memorials of the short-lived Fascist empire.

Fifteen months after the death of Ciano, his doom was swiftly overtaking Mussolini. I was keeping a close watch on the Fascist leaders in the last months of the war, and so am able to add something to the general knowledge of the last days of Mussolini. It is a strange story of treachery that is not yet fully explained. Much has already been written about those last days and hours of the Duce, but there are still some facts without which the story would be incomplete.

Of particular interest is the part played by the flabby Buffarini, Minister of the Interior. On 23rd April, through some middlemen who were on my staff, he approached the German Security Police in Italy with the proposal that this awkward man, Mussolini, should be got rid of by luring him into the hands of the partisans. The Security Police, Buffarini suggested, should issue false passports to Mussolini and his party, and he himself would then persuade him to flee to Switzerland, taking the route via

Como and Menaggio to the frontier. But at the frontier, the partisans would be lying in wait for him. . . .

At almost the same moment Dr. Marcello Petacci, brother of the beautiful Clara Petacci, approached a German Police official in Meran with an almost identical proposal. He did not, it is true, lay any particular emphasis on the handing over of Mussolini to the partisans but—and this was much more in keeping with Petacci's character—he promised to ensure that the Duce took the treasure of the Salo Government with him. This was to be the bait for the securing of German co-operation, and Petacci contented himself with claiming only a most modest fraction of the loot for his pains. It so happened that a senior officer of the German Secret Service was in Meran at the time, and the two proposals were submitted to him. He rejected them at once and forbade any further communication with either Buffarini or Petacci. Then, feeling that perhaps he had exceeded his authority, he sent a wireless message to Kaltenbrunner giving all the details and asking for instructions. Later it was found this message never reached its destination.

Can it really be a coincidence, a pure though surprising 'Concatenation of circumstances', that Mussolini later took exactly the route which Buffarini had suggested to the German Police—and that his murderers were waiting in exactly the right place and at exactly the right time? Or had Buffarini . . .

As far as is known, Mussolini received Buffarini in Como on 26th April. The former Minister of the Interior, whom Mussolini three months earlier had said he never wished to see again, certainly suggested that Mussolini should flee to Switzerland. From his villa on the banks of Lake Como, he told the Duce he had had admirable opportunities of studying the routes used by smugglers, and he offered his services as a guide. It is, however, very curious since he knew the ropes so well that he had himself not already taken the road to safety instead of incurring the risk of waiting to assist a man whom he had hated so fiercely since his dismissal.

Mussolini's last letter to his wife which he entrusted to a policeman likewise fell into the hands of Buffarini, as is known from the memoirs of Donna Rachele, the widow of Mussolini. All these facts have some connection and they all point to dark treachery concerning the death of Mussolini. Buffarini is dead—captured in flight by the partisans at the spot which he had recommended to Mussolini and, like Dr. Petacci, murdered by them in a manner which suggests that they were anxious to be rid of their partners in crime.

Whatever may be the verdict on Mussolini, however disastrous for Italy his policy may have been, his undeniable place in history demands that the mystery enshrouding his death should be resolved, while there are still men alive to tell the truth about his end.

CHAPTER XVI

THE MYTH OF THE REDOUBT

WE now come to the last phase of the war, in which a strange myth played a remarkable part—the myth of Hitler's Alpine redoubt. But first there was the defection of our ally Italy.

Badoglio knew that Germany was contemplating counter-measures in Italy. This, of course, might have been disastrous for the new régime, which forthwith did everything possible to allay the suspicions of Germany and blunt the watchfulness of her agents. The Chief of the Italian Military Intelligence, General Cesare Amé, was ordered to take action to throw dust in the Germans' eyes. This he was well placed to do, for he was a close friend of Admiral Canaris, his German counterpart.

Canaris had been warned emphatically by his own sources of Italy's intention to give up the fight and probably to join the other side. These conclusions agreed entirely with those arrived at by the German Secret Service. In spite of this, the German Military Intelligence Service, and particularly the Admiral himself in his reports to the High Command and to Hitler, expressed the view that there was little or no danger of such a development. Hitler's mistrust was not to be allayed, and Keitel therefore suggested to Hitler that the Chief of the Military Intelligence Service should himself go to Italy in order to clarify the position on the spot with his own colleagues and with his friend, Amé. It is more than likely that it was Canaris himself who put the idea into Keitel's head.

The two Chiefs met in Venice. Amé took Canaris aside and with complete frankness told his friend the details of Italy's negotiations for an armistice with the Western Allies, adding that the Badoglio Government were gravely concerned at the possibility of some counter-stroke by Hitler. He begged Canaris to do his utmost to ensure that Italy's withdrawal from the war was not forestalled through some action by Hitler. Canaris promised to do this, and he kept his word.

Immediately after this private conversation, about which Canaris later told only his closest colleagues, the official conference took place. It all went according to programme. In the presence of witnesses Canaris posed the questions which Keitel had instructed him to ask. Amé, with a great show of injured indignation, declared emphatically that there was not a word of truth in the suspicions that Hitler harboured against the new Italian Government, and that Badoglio was determined to continue the struggle side by side with Germany, until final victory had been won. The conference ended with an inspired and enthusiastic description by Amé of the solidarity of the Axis. A report of the conference, prepared by one of Canaris' men, was submitted to Hitler. Keitel, although he had some misgivings about Canaris, at the same time relied fully on his Chief of Military Intelligence. He told Hitler with great emphasis that he was convinced that no danger threatened from the Italian side. Hitler was by no means so sure, but his intention to intervene weakened, and he hesitated. To this degree Amé's deception must be counted a success, although the difficulty of finding German troops necessary for a successful military action against Italy was undoubtedly a factor too. It may well be that the hesitation to which the ruse led was in reality the decisive reason for Germany failing to forestall the defection of Italy.

Independent of the efforts made in the autumn of 1943 to negotiate on behalf of Italy a truce with the Western Allies, other efforts had been made through the Vatican to establish contact with the Western Powers. The German Secret Service played a leading part in this too. The activities of the German Secret Service differed radically from those of the German military opposition, in that a plot against Hitler's person was never for a moment contemplated. The aim rather was to bring about a change within the framework of the existing system of Government, which would open the way for the speedy conclusion of peace with the West. As early as 1940 my group in the German Secret Service had made its first attempts to persuade the German Government to make concessions in favour of the Catholic Church in Germany, and thereby to enlist the sympathetic co-operation of the Vatican as an intermediary with the

Allies. These attempts sponsored by Glaise-Horstenau continued throughout until the end.

One of the best informed and most capable advocates of this move was the General of the Jesuit Order, Count Wlodzimierz Halke von Ledochowsky. Thanks to the information with which the widespread ramifications of his Order could supply him, he was in a position to obtain a far better comprehensive picture of the whole political and military situation than most of the other high dignitaries of the Church. He had a lively appreciation of the world-wide dangers of Bolshevism, and he knew that if total catastrophe overtook Germany, the Soviet Union would become a pressing and direct menace to the whole of Western Europe. For these reasons he was prepared on a common policy of anti-Communism, to agree to a measure of co-operation between the Jesuit Order and the German Secret Service. In the first instance, this should confine itself to an exchange of information, but this was to be the preliminary to the larger conception of an understanding between the Western Allies and the Axis Powers and the formation of a great, combined American and European coalition against Communism and against the imperialism of the Soviet Union.

This ultimate object was quickly and plainly made clear in the very early stages of the discussions. Ledochowsky already recognized the inevitability of an early military conflict between Germany and Russia, and he was at great pains to ensure that the operations of the German Wehrmacht would not be hindered by the activities of the priests of the Collegium Russicum in those territories which the German Army planned to occupy. (The Collegium Russicum has for years been engaged in training missionaries for work among the orthodox population of the Soviet Union.)

The German Government, however, refused to make any concessions to the Church, and the efforts of both the Political Secret Service and the Security Service failed to achieve anything. The attempts all but ended in disaster for the German negotiators. The Jesuit General corresponded with them through the medium of the Papal Nunciature in Berlin and the ubiquitous Gestapo had succeeded unfortunately in planting its agent in the midst of the papal mission in Berlin. Heydrich, who must have feared that the negotiations initiated without permission would come to the ears of Hitler, stepped in and took action against me. Happily the whole range and scope of the negotiations were not apparent from such of Ledochowsky's letters as had been submitted to him, and thus the direct consequences were avoided. I was reduced to the ranks in the Field, where I served with the Life Guard regiment of the S.S. On the death of Heydrich I returned to my old post in February 1943 and immediately became more active than ever in peace reconnaissance.

Throughout 1943 and 1944 I participated in the German Secret Service efforts to reach an agreement with the West. Marshal Petain, General Franco and the Portuguese Prime Minister Dr. Salazar were among the leading neutral statesmen who expressed their willingness to pass on to London and Washington information on the intentions of the German peace party. They were ready to act as intermediaries. Results were most discouraging, and for this the British and the American Governments were as much to blame as the Germans. Hitler himself was by no means averse to negotiation but he was anxious to await a favourable turn in the military situation which would strengthen his bargaining power. Then when such an occasion arose, as it not infrequently did up to 1943, he would become elated and assert that negotiations were no longer necessary. The attitude of the Western leaders was disconcertingly firm from the very beginning. Roosevelt never gave the slightest sign that he might possibly depart from his formally declared policy of unconditional surrender.

In spite of these repeated failures, the German Secret Service persevered in its endeavours. As the success of the Allied military operations against Germany progressed and the prospects of a peace by negotiation receded, the framework and scope of any possible agreement shrank until they were reduced to local surrender agreements in North Italy and the Alpine regions.

In the autumn of 1944 the Headquarters of the Secret Service in Berlin received its first intimation that an American office existed in Switzerland, the duties of which appeared to be more than those of a normal Information Bureau. The head of it was a lawyer named Alan Welsh Dulles who had become pro-

minent at the end of the first war as a member of the American
diplomatic service in the Versailles peace treaty negotiations, and
particularly in the Austro-Yugoslav disputes. The fact that he
had been installed in the American Legation in Berne, gave some
indication of his real activities. And from his wireless messages
to Washington which were picked up and for the most part deciphered and passed to the Germans by the Hungarian monitor
service, the German Secret Service was able to obtain accurate
knowledge of his views on the great problems of world politics.
Unlike the American Minister in Berne, who forwarded to
Washington as established facts the wildest and stupidest
rumours which emanated from Germany, Dulles showed himself to be not only a man of high intelligence, but also an implacable enemy of Bolshevism, whose opposition was based on
knowledge, reasoned argument and clear-sighted vision. This
unequivocal attitude seemed to their group, which had for years
sought contact with an authoritative American organ, to offer
the very chance they had been seeking so long. They set about
trying to get in touch with Dulles. Through the intermediary
of an Austrian industrial magnate and the German Deputy Air
Attaché in Berne they quickly succeeded in doing so.

Our German group fully realized that by this time, the end
of 1944, any agreement by negotiation on the basis of equal
partnership was no longer possible—and a preliminary exchange
of views gave them no concrete clue as to what could be achieved.
Their first consideration was to persuade the Americans to
abstain from delivering any great portions of Germany and
Austria into the hands of the Russians, and for this they felt
they must produce concrete proof of the duplicity of Soviet
intentions *vis-à-vis* their Western associates.

But the actual basis of negotiations turned out to be something
quite different. The German Secret Service had known for a
long time that the British and American General Staffs were
concerned at the possibility of a prolongation of German resistance in a fortified Alpine region. According to Allied information, this redoubt was said to consist of large tracts of the North
Italian-Austrian Alpine massif with an appropriate field of fire
in its foreground, and Allied military experts were of the
opinion that such a defensive locality could be successfully held

for a very long time. Where the Allied General Staffs went
wrong was in supposing that German preparations for an Alpine
resistance were far advanced.

In reality these preparations had barely entered the preliminary stage. In November 1944 the Gauleiter of the Tyrol,
Franz Hofer, sent Bormann for transmission to Hitler a complete and detailed plan for the construction of an Alpine defensive
redoubt. But Bormann considered that in view of the current
military situation it smacked far too much of defeatism to submit
to Hitler plans for a last desperate stand and so he held up the
memorandum. But later, when he learned that Hitler had
already been informed by the Secret Service of the strong Allied
apprehensions of such a possibility, and realized that the subject
was already of concern to Hitler he showed Hofer's plans to
the Fuehrer with the result that Hofer was ordered to get on
with the construction as quickly as possible.

The idea became fashionable. Rainer, the Gauleiter of
Carinthia and as such the man responsible for the defence of
that portion of the Alpine redoubt in the vicinity of the Croatian
coastal area which would probably be attacked by Tito, also
started work, though here preparations never got beyond the
planning stage. The German Army Group in North Italy
started an Alpine Defence Study Section, and Himmler had no
intention of lagging behind. He sent a group of S.S. geologists
to study in conjunction with the Waffen-S.S. Mountain Warfare
School 'the possibility of the construction of mountain defensive
positions by means of large-scale blasting and detonation'. But
the preparations further north, in the vicinity of Berchtesgaden,
had not got beyond the stage of preliminary discussion. Nor
was anything done to move industrial plant from Austria into
the mountains, though many excellent facilities existed.

The concern of the Allied High Command may not have
been justified by facts. It had arisen partly as the result of
German propaganda and partly as the result of false information
fabricated by the German Secret Service and played into Allied
hands. But it nevertheless existed and the Secret Service set
about using it as a means to obtain better terms, if not for the
whole of Germany then at least for that part of Austria which
was affected.

For the elimination of the presumed mountain stronghold, which in Allied military expert opinion might require years of guerrilla warfare to subjugate, the Allies would probably be prepared to make very solid concessions. As the fate of Austria the common homeland hung on the issue, the German Secret Service found themselves joined in their efforts to prevent senseless destruction by a host of true patriots of the Austrian liberation movement, who volunteered not from any personal motive, but impelled by pure love of their country.

From the very first talks with Dulles it became clear that the Alpine redoubt was to be and would remain the main subject of discussion. From the German point of view the object was to try and exchange the peaceful handing over of this mythical Austrian defensive locality, so formidable in Allied eyes, for some solid concessions, such as a merely symbolic occupation régime. The Secret Service had succeeded in winning to the support of their bargain scheme all the principal military Commanders who would be responsible for the defence of the redoubt, if it ever came to be defended, and the Generals entrusted with the defence of East Austria were themselves Austrians who readily agreed to support a plan which promised some hope of saving the larger part of their country.

Support was promised in this by General Loehr who had just withdrawn his army from Greece with masterly skill and was now in position on the Austro-Yugoslav frontier, and by General Rendulic the recently appointed Commander-in-Chief of the Army Group on the Austro-Hungarian frontier. Field-Marshal Kesselring, C.-in-C. Army Group South, signified his general agreement. The Liaison Officers at the Headquarters of Field-Marshal Schoerner in Czechoslovakia and Field-Marshal von Rundstedt in the West both reported that the co-operation of these two Commanders could be counted on, provided that the negotiations confined themselves exclusively to the Western Powers.

The one thing that was still lacking was the man who could emerge as the supreme authority with the power to negotiate from within this mountain fastness. If chaos were to be avoided, he must be one of the principals of the existing régime, legally and constitutionally empowered to act on his own authority.

In the last phases of the war Hitler relegated more and more power into the hands of the Gauleiters and particularly since the regional defence system had been introduced these Gauleiters had become almost independent despots. With the exception of Hitler, Himmler was the only man who could give them orders by virtue of his positions as Minister of the Interior, S.S. Reichsfuehrer, and Commander-in-Chief of the *Ersatzheer*—the Home Army. But in March 1945, in the face of the threat that Germany would be split from west to east by the probing columns of the Russian and the Anglo-American forces, he nominated Kaltenbrunner as his Deputy, with plenipotentiary powers for South Germany. Later when he heard of the part Kaltenbrunner had played in the attempted negotiations with the Western Powers, he began to mistrust him and he appointed S.S. General Berger, Chief of Staff at S.S. Headquarters, Berlin, to be Commander of Bavaria with equal plenipotentiary powers. He, however, had no jurisdiction over any Austrian territory.

Kaltenbrunner was thus given the necessary power of authority over the Gauleiters and was in an ideal position to support the proposed plan, if he were prepared to exercise the authority vested in him. From 1943 onwards he had been kept more or less constantly informed of the efforts made by his Secret Service to secure peace in the west, though he had never committed himself either way and his attitude remained confused up to this moment. But now when Germany's position was so obviously hopeless, he was easily persuaded to lend his support.

The stage was completely set and the actors were now all prepared to prevent any last minute stand in the Alpine redoubt. By the end of March 1945 the German negotiators were in a position to offer the Western Allies all the guarantees required that their undertakings could and would be honoured. One last conference remained at which an assurance was to be sought from the Western Powers that the Russians would not be allowed to participate in the occupation of Austria, or if previous treaty obligations precluded the giving of such an assurance, that Austria would not be divided into zones but would be subjected to a mixed inter-allied and associated occupation as symbolic in nature as the exigencies of the situation permitted.

This happy solution was unfortunately never realized. Other activities which had in the meanwhile been in progress, while they aimed at the same general object completely spoiled the Secret Service plan as regards Austria. The German Ambassador to the new Italian Government, Dr. Rahn, who had shown outstanding diplomatic skill in his difficult task, had himself all the time been trying to get into touch with Dulles. For this purpose he had employed a man who thanks to his contact with Himmler was able to undertake missions which would have been hazardous in the extreme for any officer of the Wehrmacht. This was S.S. General Wolff, the senior S.S. and Police Officer in Italy and for many years Himmler's Chief of Staff and closest friend and collaborator.

Wolff was not in any way the power-drunk brutal type. He had realized the hopelessness of Germany's position and he had readily agreed with Rahn that negotiation with the West was the only hope of avoiding the full horror of a catastrophe now almost inevitable. Contact with Dulles was established through the Italian industrialist Luigi Parilli who had already worked for the German Secret Service. Parilli was a friend of the Swiss Director of the Zuger Berg Educational Institute, Professor Hussmann, who was a friend of a Major Waibel, a Swiss Secret Service Officer and Liaison Officer between his own Chief and Alan Dulles of the American Office of Strategic Services.

Dulles was an Intelligence Officer of experience, and his natural suspicions, aroused by the fact that neither Wolff nor his colleagues had any diplomatic or official standing, had led to many difficulties. But through these most devious lines of communication, a first meeting had finally been arranged and had taken place between Dulles and Wolff at the American Consulate General in Zurich at the beginning of March. As a proof that Wolff's promises were backed by the authority to fulfil them, Dulles had demanded that he should release and bring to Switzerland with him Ferruccio Parri, the partisan leader who had been captured and who later became Italian Prime Minister. Wolff had complied with this demand.

If General Wolff had any illusions about the possible scope of his undertaking before his meeting with Dulles, they must

have been quickly shattered, for at once it became apparent
that Dulles was neither interested in nor prepared to negotiate
about anything beyond the surrender of the Southern German
Army Group. As a result of the conference, Wolff had bound
himself to arrange the capitulation of that Army Group, regardless of any orders which Berlin might issue to the contrary.
In addition he was to prevent any sort of destruction, demoli-
tion, shooting of hostages and operations against the Italian
partisans. This agreement had been given the code-name of
Operation 'Sunrise Crossword'.

Wolff's visit to Switzerland and his negotiations with Dulles
had not passed unobserved. Kaltenbrunner realized at once
that Wolff's independent action would prejudice if not entirely
ruin the enterprise which he himself had decided to support.
If, as was to be assumed, Wolff had offered the surrender of
the Army Group South to the Americans, the whole fabric of
the mythical Alpine defence would be destroyed and the Allies
would be freed of that anxiety. Kaltenbrunner therefore
arranged with Himmler that Wolff was to have no further
dealings with Dulles. Himmler also told Ribbentrop of what
was afoot, and the latter, fearing that the Ambassador's activities
would bring Hitler's wrath upon his own head, decided to recall
Rahn. But Rahn was warned in time and making most skilful
use of his psychological knowledge of Hitler's and Himmler's
characters, he set about showing how indispensable he was in
his present position. He sent a long and sensational report on
events in Mussolini's entourage and in the Foreign Ministry,
some of which was true, some fictitious, but all of such sustained
sensational possibility that his immediate recall was regarded
as out of the question. Wolff too disregarded Himmler's instructions and carried on his negotiations with Dulles, and Kaltenbrunner thus failed all along the line to checkmate the Wolff-
Rahn activities which were threatening such grave danger to his
own scheme.

When Kesselring was transferred to take command of the
Western Army Group, Rahn and Wolff found themselves deprived of their original and chief military protector. But Kesselring's successor General von Vietinghoff and his Chief of Staff
General Roettinger, held precisely the same opinions and they

endorsed all Kesselring's actions. Negotiations then could continue, and Dulles flew to Allied Headquarters at Caserta to expedite them. As a result of this visit the Deputy Chief of Staff of the American Fifth Army, General Lyman-Lemnitzer, and the British Director of Military Intelligence, Allied Forces in Italy, Major-General Airey, were sent under false names to meet the Germans in Switzerland.

The conference took place on 19th March, 1945, and was attended by S.S. General Wolff, his colleagues and the two Allied Generals, as well as Allen Dulles and his expert on German affairs, Dr. Gero von Schulze-Gaevernitz. Complete agreement was reached as to the terms of capitulation, and after the conference Wolff decided to go and see Himmler who was in a state of panic lest Hitler should hear of the negotiations. Wolff was anxious if possible to gain Himmler's firm approval of what had been done but he failed to do so. All Himmler would say was that he must obtain the agreement of Kaltenbrunner who was in a better position to judge than he was.

At this juncture Kaltenbrunner decided that he too would like to take a personal part in the conversations with the Allies, and to this end he arranged to meet Professor Burckhardt, the President of the International Red Cross, at the Austro-Swiss frontier. Far from furthering the negotiations by so doing, he very nearly ruined them. Dulles was informed of this second meeting at once and became suspicious at the appearance of yet a third negotiator, while he was already negotiating with Wolff on the subject of the capitulation of the Army Group, and with the German Secret Service on the question of the Alpine redoubt. On top of all this, Mussolini found out that two of the most prominent partisan leaders had been liberated at Wolff's instigation and made the most bitter protests to the German Ambassador. These events alone sufficed to slow up action on the German side but then an event occurred on the Allied side which threatened to blow all the plans sky-high.

After the talks between General Wolff and the representatives of the Allied Commander-in-Chief in Italy, General Sir Harold Alexander's report on the negotiations was communicated to the American Ambassador in Moscow. The negotiations were

10*

described as purely military. It was added that on orders from Allied Supreme Headquarters General Alexander would await instructions from the British and Soviet Governments before sending negotiators to Switzerland. The American Ambassador, Averell Harriman, passed on this report in the form of a note to the Soviet Foreign Minister, Molotov.

Recognizing the great significance of the opportunity, Molotov made strenuous endeavours to use it to increase Soviet influence in the affairs of the West. He demanded that the Russian Generals who happened to be on liaison duties in France at the time should forthwith be allowed to take part in the negotiations, but as diplomatic relations did not exist between the Soviet Union and Switzerland and a visit of Russian Generals to that country could not be readily arranged, the Americans found a welcome excuse for refusing the request. The Soviet Government protested and demanded the immediate abandonment of the capitulation negotiations.   When the Western Powers rejected this demand, Stalin sent a violent personal telegram to Roosevelt in which he reproached the Americans with a flagrant breach of faith, adding that as a result of this breach of treaty obligations the Soviet Government now regarded itself as justified in acting independently in Poland.

At this crucial moment, when Roosevelt was about to reply to Stalin's telegram he was overcome by a stroke and died on 12th April.

In addition to his duties in the Office of Strategic Services, Dulles was also Roosevelt's personal representative. The death of the President in conjunction with the violent Soviet protest seems to have weakened the position of this principal American negotiator and the United States Government directed him to break off the negotiations. Dulles, however, would not give in without a struggle. He got in touch with General Alexander, who undertook to recommend the acceptance of the German proposals to the British and American Governments on his own responsibility. More clearly than those responsible in Washington and London, Alexander saw through the Russian tactics, the object of which was to delay a cessation of hostilities and thus to give the Soviet forces time both to push further westwards and to turn south and open the gateway to the Po

plain for Tito. General Alexander's intervention was crowned
with success.

It may be assumed that the Church also brought the whole
weight of its advice and influence to bear in persuading the
Allies not to cede to Soviet aspirations. The Archbishop of
Milan, Cardinal Ildefonso Schuster, was kept fully informed of
all stages of the negotiations. There were still some difficulties
to be overcome, but at last on 27th April, 1945, the capitulation
was signed at Caserta. With this act the greater project of the
Alpine redoubt—whether as the scene of a last stand or as a
basis for bargaining—also came to its end. Without the German
Southern Army Group, the nucleus and the mass for manning
the redoubt were both lacking. The Allies had nothing more
to worry about in the South, and in the meanwhile they had
also come to know that their original misgivings had been
exaggerated.

When Field-Marshal Model's Army Group surrendered in
the Ruhr, the Americans, armed with large-scale maps, organized
a meticulous and detailed interrogation of German Staff officers
on the subject of the Alpine redoubt. They were greatly surprised to find that the majority of these Staff officers had either
heard nothing at all of the project or had dismissed what they
had heard as of no practical consequence.

The Swiss General Staff had reached the same conclusion.
Detailed investigation had been undertaken as Swiss interests
were considered to be vitally concerned, and Switzerland could
not remain indifferent to the setting up of a German defensive
zone on her immediate frontiers in the final phase of the war.
Swiss concern had been further accentuated by reports that it
was the intention of the Allies to ask for the co-operation of
Swiss specialist mountain warfare units in the breaking of this
last German resistance. Such Swiss intervention was to be
termed 'Police measures' and would therefore not affect Swiss
neutrality.

My agents were in touch with Dulles between December 1944
and May 1945, superseding the unlucky opposition. Although
we did not achieve the far-reaching results for which we had
striven, the contact of the German Secret Service with Dulles
did at least ensure that the occupation of Austria and the assump-

tion of government in that country were accomplished without vain bloodshed and senseless destruction. In the western zones the seizing of power by the Communists and other political adventurers was prevented, and prominent statesmen were installed in all the key positions. These men had played leading parts in the political life of the country before 1938 and were imbued with the desire to protect the fabric and the substance of their country against fatal loss and damage. Austria was spared from revolutionary destruction. There was neither chaos nor the lawlessness inseparable from an interregnum. The economic life of the country was continued with the minimum of interruption. Only those elements which had relied on total catastrophe and complete disruption of law and order to raise them to power lost by our exploitation of the myth of the Alpine redoubt.

CHAPTER XVII

THE SECRET FRONT NOW

THE Alpine tourist centre of Alt-Aussee, at the foot of the Austrian *Totengebirge* or Dead Mountains was more full of people in May 1945 than even in the best months of the peacetime season. Its visiting population had always been cosmopolitan, but at that moment with the German Reich collapsing, its international character was more marked than ever, and a dozen foreign tongues were heard in its hotels.

I think that I have fairly established that never at any time did Hitler seriously intend to construct in the massif of the Austrian Alps a fortress redoubt, in which the remnants of the Wehrmacht were to make their last stand. But equally, he did nothing to discourage belief in this legend, and to the end many of his supporters, and particularly his allies in S.E. Europe, who had been encouraged to hold on by hints of new secret weapons and truce talks believed also in the myth of the redoubt. When, at the turn of the year 1944–45 Dr. Guenther Altenberg, the responsible Minister at the German Foreign Ministry, sought quarters in Alt-Aussee for the various South-east European Governments-in-exile, their members were more convinced than ever that Hitler was resolved to carry on the fight in his mountain redoubt. They compared the position of Germany to that of Britain in 1940, when the Governments-in-exile sought refuge in the beleaguered island. If further evidence were needed, it was supplied by the presence of innumerable senior German civil servants in Alt-Aussee and the neighbouring districts of the Salzkammergut. There was also a collection of works of art stored in the shafts of the Salzberg mines, the greatest collection that the world had ever seen.

The position of Alt-Aussee as the Command Post for mountain warfare was ideal. Nestling in a narrow valley between the towering ten-thousand foot precipices of the Dachstein and the Dead Mountains, it was all but invisible and inaccessible to aircraft, and two major demolitions would render the only two roads impassable for a very long time. It was to this spot that August Eigruber, the Gauleiter of Upper Austria, wished to see the leaders of Germany come, if the safety of the Berghof were ever in jeopardy. It was here that he wanted to construct the great defensive redoubt. He did not, however, then know that Hitler had no intention of leaving Berlin. But Hitler had meant every word when, as he entered the Reich Chancellery in Berlin on his assumption of power, he had turned to his trusted friend Max Amann and said: 'Only as a corpse will they ever get me out across this threshold again.' When he remained awaiting the end in his bunker below the Chancellery he had not suddenly changed his mind. He was simply being completely consistent. Nevertheless, a whole staff of Party officials, ignorant of his real intentions, were busily at work preparing a new Head-quarters at Alt-Aussee.

Eigruber, a bull of a man, had little interest in the collection of art treasures, which had come from all over Europe. The Commandant of 'Fortress Upper Danube', as he called himself, would not have spared a lorry, a man and certainly not a drop of precious petrol for the transportation of the stuff. But even Eigruber could not ignore a direct order from the Fuehrer, although he was one of the few senior officials who dared occasionally to stand up to him. Once indeed Hitler's whole entourage had been horrified when Eigruber said to him in his broad Austrian dialect:

'You know, mein Fuehrer, we folk down here don't call your Foreign Minister—Ribbentrop; we call him Ribbentropf'.

Hitler, who no longer thought much of Ribbentrop but who could not admit the fact, was displeased. The ridiculed Foreign Minister from that moment nursed a deadly hatred against Eigruber. Even when they met face to face in the Court House at Nuremberg during the trial of the major war criminals, he used to cut him dead.

Art may have bored him, but Eigruber was intensely anxious to transfer the State secret archives to the security of the inaccessible mines in the Salzberg. At the last Gauleiters' Assembly, which Hitler held in Berlin at the end of February 1945, Eigruber asked him privately when he intended coming down to organize the defence of the mountain redoubt. Hitler gave an evasive reply, but he probably told Eigruber that he would shortly be sending him the most important of the documents and the whole of his personal archives, which he must guard with his life.

To-day we know for a fact that Hitler's private papers never got to Alt-Aussee, though the agents of the Allied secret services searched for years to find them there. I am however in a position to give an exact account of what really happened to Hitler's private papers, the undoubted destruction of which is a loss of unique importance for future historians. My principal source of information is Hitler's senior Adjutant, S.S. General Julius Schaub, who from 1933 until a few days before his death never left Hitler's side. In the truest sense of the saying, Schaub was the faithful servant of his lord and master, and faithfully he carried out his last order to destroy all his private papers.

On 22nd April, 1945, in the Fuehrer's bunker under the shattered Chancellery in Berlin, Hitler admitted for the first time that the war was lost, the end approaching and nothing now could save Berlin. He screamed this at Keitel, Jodl, Bormann and Burgdorf at the daily situation conference, and on this note of hysterical rage brought the conference to an end.

Immediately afterwards he sent for his Adjutant, Julius Schaub, who during twenty years had accompanied him from the back parlours of the Munich inns to the Chancellery of the Reich. Schaub told me what happened. Hitler instructed him to destroy the contents of all the safes in which his private documents were kept. These were placed all over the country. Some were in the Fuehrer's bunker in Berlin, others in Hitler's bedroom in the badly damaged Chancellery, in his Munich residence at 16 Prinzregentenplatz and yet others in the Berghof in Berchtesgaden. The keys of these safes had never left Hitler's person, and no one had ever even so much as glanced at their contents.

Schaub started at once on the task entrusted to him. With the help of S.S. officers and under a heavy bombardment which was destroying the last remaining wing of the Chancellery, in which Hitler had his bedroom, he gathered the papers out of the two safes which by some miracle had escaped all damage and, with those from the safe in the bunker, he started to burn them with the utmost care in a bomb crater in the Chancellery garden. For some time Hitler watched him, without saying a word.

It was only on the evening of 25th April that Hitler again sent for Schaub and ordered him to flee. In the east the Russians were already in the Alexander Platz, a bare two thousand yards away, shells were bursting everywhere, and the streets were heaped with fallen and falling debris. But after a difficult and dangerous drive Schaub succeeded in reaching Gatow airport, where one solitary aircraft, a Junkers 52, remained airworthy. Early on the morning of 26th April he left Berlin under a fusillade of rifle fire from advancing Russian infantry. He landed at Munich airport and in spite of an air raid salved the papers from the small safe in Hitler's bedroom in the house on the Prinzregentenplatz, packed them in a suitcase and went on to Berchtesgaden. There too he found the safe in Hitler's study undamaged. On the same day he set fire to the last of Hitler's private papers on a rubbish heap outside.

For years Schaub remained silent about the part he had played. It was only when a German illustrated paper, having found some slight clue, published a distorted account, that he felt compelled to make known the true story, which has been reproduced above. Interrogation of others of Hitler's immediate entourage confirms the accuracy of Schaub's statement in every detail. So we know now what happened to some of the most important documents of the Third Reich.

Until 8th May, 1945, Eigruber himself stayed in the capital of his Gau. Then Linz fell. He kept one of his subordinates stationed in Alt-Aussee with instructions to await a courier bringing Hitler's private papers and to bury them in the local salt mine. No such courier ever started, but Eigruber did not know that to the day of his death, although he was in prison with Schaub in Nuremberg for many months. Schaub maintained absolute silence until he was convinced that Hitler was really dead.

Another man was awaiting the arrival of important documents in Alt-Aussee, and waited in vain. But in this case it is not known whether the papers were destroyed or not. The Chief of the Security Services, Dr. Kaltenbrunner, spent most of the last few weeks before the collapse of Germany in Alt-Aussee. From the time he assumed his duties of Chief of the Security Services in 1943, Kaltenbrunner had always been inclined to favour the idea of shortening the war by means of a separate peace with the Western Powers. But he lacked both the personality and the greatness to impose his will. It must not be forgotten that although Kaltenbrunner had risen to become the second most powerful man in Germany, he had not done so on his own ability, but thanks rather to the immense power with which his predecessor Heydrich had endowed the appointment. Kaltenbrunner rose too, as Hitler realized more and more what a really insignificant person Himmler was. But those who were working for an early peace with the Western allies could largely count on Kaltenbrunner's support. Of this mention has already been made.

The phlegmatic Kaltenbrunner returned to Alt-Aussee from his visit to Berlin at the end of March 1945 in an astonishingly optimistic frame of mind, for Hitler had succeeded in inspiring the waverers with new confidence. But as one nightmare report came in after another, even he began to get nervous. He was anxious to obtain some papers which he had put in his personal safe in Berlin. These, he had felt compelled to leave behind on the occasion of his last visit, because he did not wish to be suspected of thinking that Berlin must fall and that he would never be able to return there. And so he had left them for safe custody with Mueller, the Gestapo Chief, who had remained in Berlin as his liaison officer with Hitler. Kaltenbrunner had telegraphed, telephoned and even sent a special messenger, but Mueller neither replied nor sent the papers.

We can only guess what these papers were that were causing Kaltenbrunner so much concern. Among them were certainly the personal files of the leading personalities of the Third Reich, which had been maintained for many years, and the most important of which were kept, so Kaltenbrunner told me, in his own private safe. Among them were a number of important 'Plans for the Fuehrer's consideration'—suggestions of various kinds which Kaltenbrunner had submitted to Hitler. Kaltenbrunner was particularly interested in some of these because he hoped they would furnish proof to the Allies of the soundness of foreign policy proposals which he had submitted to the Fuehrer. He used this line of argument at the Nuremberg trial, and he seemed unable to grasp the fact that he was not being tried on account of his activities as Chief of the German Secret Service, but solely in his capacity as the Head of Section V, the Secret State Police (Gestapo).

It also availed him nothing when in his defence he quoted with a wealth of detail the activities of those of his subordinates in the overseas section of the German Secret Service whom he had entrusted with the passing on of his proposals for a separate peace with the Western Allies. But then, Kaltenbrunner always had a fairly elastic conscience. At the Nuremberg trial he even invited me, whom he had arrested on 23rd April on account of my contacts with the Dulles group, as the chief witness in his defence. I wrote an affidavit on the points that he raised.

According to Kaltenbrunner, among the papers he had sent for while in Austria in April 1945 was the famous diary of Admiral Canaris, which later caused such a sensation. It cannot have been the original, which was produced by the prosecution at the Admiral's trial. It was probably among those important documents of which photo copies or micro-films had been made and kept at Headquarters of the Security Services.

What became of the Gestapo Chief, S.S. General Heinrich Mueller? There is little doubt that Mueller succeeded in making good his escape from Berlin and that he is still alive. The story of the carefully prepared escape of this redoubtable man reads like a thriller, but it seems nevertheless to be true.

After the death of Hitler and the execution of the principal war criminals condemned at Nuremberg, the entire resources of the Allied Criminal Investigation Branches were concentrated on the finding of three men, who were most intimately connected with the major war criminals. In the opinion of many experienced members of the Allied secret services, these three were more important than any of the men who had been executed. These were the Head of the Chancellery, Reichsleiter Bormann, the Head of Section IV of the Security Services, Heinrich Mueller, and Mueller's subordinate in charge of his Jewish section, Adolf Eichmann.

So much has already been written about Bormann's fate that unless new facts could be quoted, comment is superfluous here. Except for the activities of a small group of Secret Service experts, the hunt for the other two has died down. For some reason neither the public nor the illustrated press, which seldom if ever misses the chance of so sensational a story, has shown the slightest interest in them. Yet one was the Chief of the Gestapo, the man who during the period of Germany's greatest expansion exercised powers of life and death over practically the whole of the continent of Europe. The other was the man who with gruesome efficiency put into practice the terrible plan for the extermination of the Jewish people.

Adolf Eichmann, now a man of forty-three years of age, is of Austrian origin. Short of stature, Jewish in appearance ,energetic, talkative, a great organizer, he was born in Germany, but he spent his youth with his father in Linz. At first he seems to have led a normal existence. He was an employee in some small business, became a Nazi member and S.S.-man and fled to Germany when the Party was declared illegal in Austria in 1933. He joined the Austrian Legion and finally transferred to the Secret Service. Although he was anything but a distinguished member of the Service, his tremendous zeal attracted attention, and in 1937 he was sent by Heydrich to Palestine to study conditions there. Then he laid no claim to being an expert on Jewish affairs. He regarded the journey much more as a pleasure trip, telling his friends later that there were pretty girls there and that the Party racial laws could not be taken seriously in Palestine. At that time he took no offence when his own pronounced Jewish appearance was mentioned. He got on well with Jews, and had a certain knowledge of Hebrew and Yiddish. His great chance came when Austria was incorporated into the Reich. He was then promoted to S.S.-Fuehrer and adviser on Jewish affairs to the newly set-up S.D. branch in Vienna. The wave of Jewish emigration which immediately set in gave him an idea which Heydrich permitted him to put into practice. He founded the 'Central Bureau for Jewish Emigration'.

This organization, which swept aside bureaucratic procedure, took under its control every activity connected with emigration, from the issue of passports and the obtaining of visas to the procurement of passages. Whoever wished to emigrate and was willing to pay the rather high State emigration tax must apply there. Eichmann's bureau did the rest. In a few days the emigrant could depart. The success of the Bureau was so great that branches were set up in Berlin and Prague—all subordinated to Eichmann. Then he had a really large idea—nothing less than to organize the mass emigration of Jews from Europe based on international agreement.

This idea took hold of him after France had been defeated. Eichmann revived a proposal for making Madagascar the home of the European Jews. Negotiations were already in progress with the Vichy Government, and a liaison office had been organized in Paris, when suddenly the Russian campaign started. Eichmann continued his planning but Heydrich vetoed it. In the latter's brain the seed of his own atrocious plan for the 'final solution of the Jewish problem' had already taken root. Having obtained Hitler's concurrence, Heydrich placed Eichmann in charge of the first stage of the project—the mass collection of the victims. Eichmann brought his talent for organization to the task, and in the course of the next few years he delivered millions of Jews from every country in Europe to the extermination camps in the East.

Eichmann's anxiety became acute in 1944 when he heard through the German monitoring service that the allied radio programmes constantly mentioned his name as one of the principal war criminals. He realized that he would have no chance of survival, and from that moment he started to make preparations for escape. He could have fled straightway to some neutral country, but he had no intention of doing that. He was determined to stick to his post to the last possible moment and then to dive into oblivion.

After the Gestapo Headquarters in the Prinz Albrecht Strasse had been destroyed by bombs, he set up his Berlin office in the Kurfuersten Strasse. When air-raid shelters were being constructed beneath his new offices, he took the opportunity of organizing what he called his 'fox-lair'. Underground rooms were built and stocked with food, water, medicine and first aid appliances. Lighting and plumbing were installed for a prolonged stay. These shelters were not built under the offices but some way off and were connected to them by a labyrinth of passages which could be sealed by a variety of devices. The exits and air shafts debouching into various bomb-damaged sites, were camouflaged to harmonize with their surroundings. The longest of the passages was said to be more than a mile long.

This fox-lair was no mere phantasy. Eichmann showed it to Kaltenbrunner, who was greatly impressed. He had no intention of using it for the purpose for which it had been constructed. Kaltenbrunner's idea was to go south to some Alpine stronghold which had yet to be built. When the time came, Eichmann too was unable to use the place. He was kept for some weeks on official business in Prague and Vienna during March 1945 and when he was ready to return to Berlin in April, he could no longer get through. The end of the war found him at Alt-Aussee among the Austrian lakes at the foot of the Dead Mountains. Someone else however, moved most gratefully into the underground hide-out—Heinrich Mueller, Chief of the Gestapo and his henchman, Scholz.

Mueller had been left in Berlin by Kaltenbrunner as his Liaison Officer with Hitler. As Chief of the Gestapo he could easily have found a reason for leaving the beleaguered city to which even Hitler could have taken no exception. Apparently he made no attempt to do so. He reported daily to the bunker in the Chancellery and then disappeared, presumably to his office on the Kurfuersten Strasse. Nobody visited him there. With the country tottering to its final collapse no one had any particular reason to contact the Chief of the Gestapo. On the contrary most people preferred to keep well out of the way of this detestable official. As far as can be ascertained he visited the Chancellery for the last time on 29th April. All survivors are unanimous in saying that he certainly was not there when Hitler died and the last attempt was made to break out of Berlin. From that moment Mueller disappeared, and what happened to him is pure conjecture. The most interesting theory is that of Schellenberg.

Since 1944 Schellenberg had suspected that Mueller had exploited certain wireless intelligence links used for deception of the enemy to establish genuine contact with the Russians. He claimed to have obtained proof of the fact, when he set a watch on a number of these wireless sections. At any rate he told Kaltenbrunner that he was prepared to bring proofs of his accusation. Kaltenbrunner did not take the matter seriously and attributed Schellenberg's accusations to professional jealousy. Schellenberg nevertheless insisted, and declared that if Kaltenbrunner would do nothing, he himself would keep his evidence and in years to come would show that the Chief of the German Gestapo had worked for the Russians. He asserted that after Mueller had taken up his residence in the Kurfuersten Strasse fox-lair, he had continued his wireless communications with the Russians.

If Mueller indeed continued his wireless operations from the fox-hole, that fact itself would go a long way towards substantiating Schellenberg's statement. For what man in his senses— and Mueller was a cold enough realist—would continue in the last days before a final collapse to operate a complicated system designed to mislead the enemy, when that same advancing enemy was already only a mile or so away? So if Mueller were really using his wireless, he was most probably doing so, as Schellenberg claims, in genuine contact with the Russian Secret Service. Nobody knows how Mueller and Scholz eventually got out of Berlin. Statements from senior German officers who took part in the final battle for the city prove that on 29th April the locality in which Mueller had his office was still free of the enemy. He would therefore have had no difficulty in getting back there from the Chancellery, and he could then have made his escape through one of the numerous passages which debouched behind the advancing Russians. Civilian clothes, false papers of every kind were always available for the Gestapo Chief and his henchman. Once in rear of the Russians, he might bide his time. If the suspicions of Schellenberg were founded and he was working for the Russians Mueller probably awaited their arrival quietly in his fox-hole.

Since 1945 there have been certain indications that Mueller is still working for the Russians. That the Russians should not scruple to make use even of a man who had done them so much harm is nothing new. There are any number of examples of ex-Gestapo officials and senior officers of the Military Security Services—General Bamler for one—working for the State

Security Service of the east zone, in spite of previous service against the Russians.

At Gestapo Headquarters in Vienna a man named Sanitzer was working in the close wartime co-operation with Mueller and Scholz. He had quite outstanding success in wireless deception of the Russians. Sanitzer was one of the ablest criminologists in the Austrian State Police. After the war, he was sentenced by an Austrian Peoples' Court to penal servitude for life. He had without demur accepted full responsibility for all the activities in which his section had been engaged. From his prison in Vienna he had tried to get into touch with the American Secret Service and had begged to be transferred to a prison in the western zone of Austria. In return he would be willing to give valuable information about the wireless deceptions practised on the Russians. The Americans refused to have anything to do with a condemned war criminal. But the moment he was transferred to the penal settlement in the Russian zone, where he was to serve his sentence, a car of the M.V.D. called for him and took him away. Since then there has been no further trace of him. But there is one man who apparently knows what subsequently befell him—Dr. Adolf Slawik.

Slawik, the leader of the so-called National League, was formerly an insignificant Hitler Youth and S.S. leader in Vienna. Some thirty-five years of age, he was selected by the Russians to try and win over the National-Socialists in Austria to the Russian cause. His National League is organized on the lines of the Nazi Party, although it has not the mass following which that Party once had in Austria. Slawik's followers have never exceeded a few thousands. Although the Russians fully realize these limitations, they still support him and have told him that instead of trying to organize a political party of the masses, he is to form special cadres for a Communist Austria of the future.

It is his task to gather together from among the former National Socialists experts of all kinds—technicians, propagandists, specialists in Secret Service and military experts. These men are not to be used at once, but are to be kept available as a Fifth Column. Slawik travels up and down the country interviewing men whose names have been given to him by the

Russian Secret Service or whom he himself has suggested from among his former colleagues. He seeks to persuade them that their real chance lies in collaboration with the Russians, and he organizes meetings for them with Russian officers, to whom subsequent negotiations are then left.

The Austrian penalizing laws against former Nazi Party members afforded him wide scope among disinherited men ready to be his recruits. In spite of this, Slawik's success has been meagre, as he himself admits.

In the early 'fifties he was seeking young men to take part in a course of instruction in wireless, which was to be held in Bautzen in the Russian zone of Germany. The prospective students, who had apparently been most carefully selected, were required to bind themselves to do a year's study, after which they would be free to leave. Slawik's proposals seem to have met with little enthusiasm. In order to persuade one young man, on whose services great store had been set, he had to give away a secret. He assured the young man that the proposal really came from the C.I.D. official, Sanitzer, who knew of his ability in electronics, and wished to employ him after a brief training as an instructor. This was not ordinary military wireless, Slawik explained, but the training of agents for a secret wireless organization. The man in charge of the course was Sanitzer himself. After training some of the agents would be employed in western Europe, while others would be sent to wireless stations which were at present still silent, but which would come into action in certain circumstances.

The young man in question still refused to join, even after hearing this exciting explanation. He was foolish enough to talk about the proposal, and one day he disappeared for ever. Some witnesses state that they saw him hustled into a black car by three men in the vicinity of Vienna. That is all that has since been heard of him. Slawik is still trying to recruit men for this course, but as a result of this episode, the school itself is said to have been transplanted to Poland.

The truth or otherwise of Slawik's assertions and indeed of the whole conspiracy might be proved if some student accepted the offer and enlisted for the course. Then—if he ever returned —he would know a great deal; among other things, whether, as

Schellenberg asserts, Mueller is the Chief of the whole organization over Sanitzer.

When the Soviet Army occupied Iran in 1941, it did so according to Molotov on account of the activities of 'two Gestapo agents', Gamottha and Mayer. These two men had indeed been sent to Iran by Section VI of the German Secret Service in 1939. They were not very effective, and in 1941 they both fled to the mountains, taking refuge with the Persian hill clans. Eventually Mayer was captured by the British, while Gamottha, who had parted company with him some time previously, remained in hiding. A report came from another source of the German Secret Service to the effect that he had fallen into the hands of the Russians. This could not be verified. Then, at the end of 1943, Gamottha suddenly appeared in Turkey, arriving after what he described as a most adventurous 70-day journey on foot through the Persian mountains. He was welcomed by the German colony and shortly afterwards went to Berlin, where he became Adviser to Section VI on Iran. He failed, however, to get on with his chief, who somewhat distrusted him from the beginning. After some minor episode, which has nothing to do with this story, he was dismissed and sent to Vienna, and resumed his University studies there.

When in the face of the advancing Russians, the various groups of the German Secret Service prepared to evacuate Vienna at the end of March 1945, Gamottha appeared to be in more danger than most. He was not forgotten. A car was sent to fetch him and bring him to safety in the west; but he refused the offer and remained in Vienna! This man whom Molotov had described as a war criminal in Persia, whose activities had been the pretext for the Russian occupation of that country, elected to remain in Vienna and await the arrival of the Red Army!

He was not molested until the summer of 1945. Then he suddenly disappeared. His wife received a smuggled note in his handwriting, which he is said to have dropped as he was being taken away. Gamottha wrote that he had been sentenced to 25 years' forced labour and was on his way to Siberia. Those acquainted with the methods of the Russian police consider that a man as interesting and important as Gamottha would hardly be convicted within a few days of his arrest. A case of this kind would go on for months—and would probably be handled by Headquarters in Russia itself. The conviction and the journey to Siberia seem to me to be suspect, though the handwriting was Gamottha's without any doubt. It did not seem improbable that he had been working for the Russians since his days in Persia.

Gamottha is moreover an old friend of Slawik. They were together in the Hitler Youth and the S.S. and, from the moment he appeared on the scene, Slawik has always made use of Gamottha's name, particularly among former members of the Hitler Youth and such people as knew Gamottha in the days of the German Secret Service. According to Slawik, he is now in charge of a bureau in Prague, which operates a Secret Service against Austria and Western Germany. In the opinion of many who have a good insight into the affairs of the National League, it is this bureau in Prague which issues orders to the League, and Slawik himself certainly goes to Prague very frequently, being escorted secretly across the frontier by the Russians. It would appear then that the primary task of this mysterious bureau in Prague is not Secret Intelligence work, but rather to penetrate former National-Socialist and Fascist circles. Its network is spread not only all over Italy and Spain, but also over the countries of the Middle East.

Before leaving the subject of Mueller and his flight, another version, which certainly merits consideration, must be quoted to complete the picture. A former chauffeur of the Gestapo Chief, who claims also to have known Scholz well, was condemned to death by a Military Court at Dachau for his part in the murder of an allied airman. In 1947 he told me as a fellow prisoner in internment that he knew the exact whereabouts of Mueller and Scholz, who were running an ironmongery business in a small German provincial town, and that he had even been in touch with them after their flight. He said that Mueller was one who deserved no mercy, and about him he would gladly give all details to the Americans; but Scholz was a thoroughly decent fellow, and he would be sorry to get him into serious trouble.

I persuaded the man to tell his story to the American authorities. The latter refused to believe it, declaring that the man had invented it in order to save himself from hanging. Their view may well have been correct, but the story would have been well worth verifying.

Schellenberg was sentenced to six years' penal servitude at the trial of German Foreign Service officials by the Allies. But the former Chief of German intelligence services was a sick man, and the sentence was regarded only as a token. He was admitted to hospital, and was then discharged long before the expiration of his sentence. On the invitation of the Swiss General Guisan, or of his war-time Chief of Intelligence, Colonel Masson, Schellenberg went first to Switzerland, and then on to Spain. There he tried to get in touch with some of his former colleagues, whom he knew to be in good financial circumstances. He failed to find a foothold there and made his way to Italy, where he started to write his memoirs for a Swiss publishing firm. With the advance paid to him by the firm he managed to exist, but he could not afford the medical treatment which was essential in his poor state of health. In the summer of 1952 he had a relapse, and died after an operation which was either unsuccessful or performed too late. His death passed unnoticed by the rest of the world.

To return now to Alt-Aussee and the last days of the Third Reich. Eichmann, accompanied by his closest colleagues, arrived there to obtain instructions from Kaltenbrunner. His Deputy in Prague, Guenther, had committed suicide, and he realized that he and his sort could expect no mercy. He was furious at being prevented from returning to Berlin and his hideout, in which he had complete confidence. Kaltenbrunner's instructions were far from helpful.

'You'd better have a crack at getting away,' he had said, 'with any luck you might get through to Spain.'

All he did for him was to give him a large sum of money in gold and negotiable foreign currency—assistance of which he stood in no need, for he had brought the famous 'Jewish Treasure' with him from Prague. Eichmann was strict in money matters. He had been offered literally millions in bribes and could have salted away a fortune abroad, had he accepted them. But he always refused, and he punished most severely any subordinate whom he caught taking bribes.

Eichmann next turned to Skorzeny. Skorzeny was in Alt-Aussee, busily making preparations for guerrilla warfare, setting up food and ammunition dumps in the mountains, erecting wireless stations and threatening death to any traitors who refused to join him in the fight. But Skorzeny had no use for Eichmann, although the latter in his desperate situation would undoubtedly have fought to the bitter end.

Finally he joined forces with a foreigner, Horia Sima, the Prime Minister of the Rumanian Government in exile. It was probably due to the latter's great experience in guerrilla methods that Eichmann survived the first few critical weeks. While one of the advanced guards of the Third American Army under Major Ralph E. Pearson (he later styled himself 'the conqueror of Alt-Aussee' and has written a book about his experiences) marched peacefully into one end of a village, Eichmann and his column slipped out of the other. Then he ran into trouble. The narrow forest track to Bad Ischl was still snow-bound and quite impassable for Eichmann's heavy wireless lorry. What could not be carried had to be destroyed or buried—and there is no doubt that a whole heap of gold and other valuables was buried somewhere in the forest. Later Alt-Aussee became a veritable second Klondyke. Treasure hunters came from far and near. In 1951 a car bearing a French number-plate arrived with a team of divers to search the lake itself and are said to have found treasure. The American field police discovered afterwards that the party was not French, and it may well have been friends or colleagues of Eichmann himself. Even to this day parties appear on the scene, searching for gold with radar and geiger apparatus.

All the Balkan political leaders who spent the last few months before the collapse of Germany in Alt-Aussee were also well found with gold and foreign currency. They too buried their treasure and returned later to retrieve it. There were then numerous and valuable caches of treasure dotted about in the forests around Alt-Aussee, Eichmann and Sima were both skilful and successful. All Eichmann's people escaped and are now presumably living abroad on the proceeds of the treasure which they must have hidden very cleverly and later retrieved.

When Eichmann parted from Sima a few weeks later, his luck deserted him. He fell into the hands of an American patrol and gave himself up for lost. Without hesitation he gave his right name. Then in a flash he realized that he still had just a chance. He had not been recognized, and his name had conveyed nothing to the Sergeant, who wrote him down as ECKmann. Otto Eckmann, Lieutenant of the S.S. he immediately became!

As such he was of no particular interest and soon found himself in an ordinary prisoner-of-war camp near Nuremberg, where he was put in charge of a working party cutting wood. So the criminal more sought after than any other by the allies, was sitting as an ordinary prisoner of war in an American camp. He could, of course, have escaped while on duty in the forest at any time he liked. But for some queer reason he felt absolutely secure as he was, and he gave no thought to flight.

Then the trial of the major war criminals began in Nuremberg. In their camps prisoners of war rigged up receiving sets and followed the proceedings with intense interest. One of Eichmann's subordinates took his stand in the witness box in November 1945, and for the first time the whole dreadful story was told. For the first time, too, the name of Eichmann became hideously familiar to the German people. For Eichmann himself the time had obviously come to disappear. He remained two days more in the camp, and then he fled through the forest. His flight caused no great excitement. Such things were a daily occurrence in every camp. It seems correct that to this very day the American authorities have not realized that the man they had sought so intently had all the time been in their hands for months on end. A search for him in Cairo petered out, and the hunt died down.

Interest in Eichmann waned, but Skorzeny was never absent from the headlines of the international Press for very long. He made certain of that.

In May 1945 Skorzeny undoubtedly flattered himself that he was the Commander-in-Chief of the coming German guerrilla war, though later he was unwilling to admit the fact. He reported fully to Kaltenbrunner on the progress of preparations, much to Kaltenbrunner's amusement, who nicknamed him 'the Partisan Napoleon'.

Skorzeny developed into an unpleasant type in the last stages of the war and immediately afterwards. His pretentions to greatness had increased enormously as a result of his apparent triumphs. He became obsessed with a boundless ambition and he felt himself destined to scale the heights of fame to their very peak. At first he intrigued against his own Chief, Schellenberg. Early in April 1945 he managed to persuade Kaltenbrunner to relieve Schellenberg from his duties as Chief of Section VI and of Military Security and to entrust the latter to him instead.

Such of Skorzeny's military plans as were practicable were worked out in practice by his 'Chief of Staff'—Captain Folcker-sam and later Lieut.-Colonel Walter. Both were highly trained and efficient General Staff Officers, and the untrained Skorzeny set them many a problem. It is not generally known that Skorzeny failed to pass the examination for Company Commander in 1942. He was serving with the Division 'Das Reich' at the time, and was sent back from the front to Berlin as a driving instructor in an M.T. School. Then Kaltenbrunner singled him out, and within a couple of years he was commanding Divisions. Such meteoric rise could only have occurred in the Third Reich, and is perhaps still possible only in the Red Army. His Director of Secret Political Services was an S.S. Major Karl Radl. In Section VI he was known as 'Skorzeny's Nanny', as his principal activity was to hold his chief on leading strings. Radl was only one rank junior to Skorzeny, who nevertheless referred to him grandiloquently as 'my Adjutant'. Radl accompanied his friend and chief everywhere—even in captivity, and always with the assertion that if he were not there, something unpleasant was bound to happen. It was also undoubtedly thanks to Radl that the case against Skorzeny ended as favourably for him as it did. In a stream of smuggled messages he advised him how to conduct his defence. When released, the two remained together until Skorzeny went to Spain.

Radl's nursing years were shabbily repaid by Skorzeny. In Frankfurt he again met in 1951 the man who had shared all his secrets from 1943 to 1948, and cut him in the street. Radl had offended him by venturing to correct some of Skorzeny's taller stories of his exploits. Skorzeny did not forgive him.

Thanks to the respect in which his name is still held by the Spaniards and the Arabs, Skorzeny to-day succeeds in hob-nobbing with the most important people in these countries.

Apart from that, he is related, through his third wife, to Dr. Schacht, and that is a connection which he exploits.

It is above all in Britain and America that this man enjoys a glowing reputation. From the professional view, Skorzeny accomplished very little, either as a soldier or as a secret agent. The liberation of Mussolini was mainly a feat of flying, after the skilful planning and reconnaissance work. Skorzeny made no contribution to planning or reconnaissance. His orders to the pilots to crash-land prematurely on the Gran Sasso was in conflict with the plan of operation. But for the success of the enterprise, he would have been court-martialled. The German paratroopers who took part are indignant over Skorzeny's version of the adventure.

And what of Kaltenbrunner? His flight and subsequent capture were not in the least dramatic for a Chief of the German Secret Service. He had no faith in Skorzeny as a conspirator, and he refused to take refuge in a hut which Skorzeny had prepared for him in the Dachstein area, preferring to rely on an Austrian guide, little knowing that the guide had already made plans to betray him. Kaltenbrunner was confident that the inhabitants of Alt-Aussee would help him, for he it was who had prevented the blowing-up of the galleries of the Salzberg mines, in which art collections from all over Europe were hidden. This had brought some credit to the Ausseelanders as the saviours of Europe's priceless works of art. Books have been written on the subject, and perhaps it would not be out of place to recapitulate briefly here what really happened.

Eigruber, who was still expecting to receive Hitler's secret archives for safe custody, had the idea of blowing in the entrances to the galleries, in order to preserve these invaluable documents in absolute security until with the aid of the new and secret wonder-weapons the war had been finally won. In preparation he got hold of a number of heavy bombs from the Air Force, marked the cases containing them as 'marble', and stacked them in the entrances to the glistening salt galleries. He did not dismantle his demolitions even when convinced that Hitler was dead. He anticipated that the Salzberg district would be occupied by the Russians, and he became more determined than ever to prevent these treasures from falling easily into the hands of the enemy. It seems not to have occurred to him that his demolitions might well wreck the whole place and destroy the art treasures too.

Meanwhile the salt miners themselves had secretly found out what the cases really contained. They reported their discovery to the foreman; the latter passed on the information to the managing director and those who were responsible for the art treasures. These all did their utmost to thwart Eigruber's intentions. But he remained obstinate. It was then that an ordinary miner named Alois Raudaschl took his courage in both hands and went to Kaltenbrunner, who wasted no time in putting a stop to the project. Exercising the powers which Himmler had given him, he compelled Eigruber to remove his bombs at once.

So the rows of Venetian and Dutch masterpieces were saved. To Kaltenbrunner, later hanged as a major war criminal, and Raudaschl, the simple miner, must go some of the credit. All the rest—the American Major Pearson, the Managing Director of the mines, Poechmueller, who demanded an enormous reward, and the Austrian resistance movement can at the most claim to have had the same aim.

On 7th May, accompanied by his Adjutant, an orderly and his chauffeur, Kaltenbrunner fled to a hut in the Dead Mountains. He had made no preparations for the flight, and the false papers he carried were, for a Chief of the German Secret Service, quite ridiculous—an Army pay-book in the name of a medical officer, with a forged seal accrediting him to the International Red Cross. In any case his outward appearance was unmistakable. He was some six foot four in height, with a face scarred with the duelling marks of his student days. He would have been picked out at once from among thousands. The direction he took was equally stupid, for at that time of the year the Dead Mountains were still under heavy snow, through which there could be no progress without skis. He was in truth only half-heartedly bent on escape. All he really desired was a chance to rest, to sleep and to think. When the American troops sent to hunt for him came upon Kaltenbrunner, he was fast asleep. Over a hundred men, led by the guide who had betrayed him, rushed the hut. Out staggered a man half asleep, who after the briefest interrogation admitted that he was indeed Kaltenbrunner.

His attempts to defend himself, both then and later at his trial, were so primitive that it was hard to believe that he had once been a lawyer. He based his attitude on the assumption that all the papers in his office had been destroyed according to instructions, and that therefore nothing could be proved against him. It is a reproach to the prosecution at Nuremberg that this rough-and-ready method stood him in good stead. The prosecution accused him of actions which he had no difficulty in denying, and when they proceeded to crimes which were known beyond doubt, they failed to produce proof. It was grotesque to hear the Chief of the German Secret Police declare that he had never issued a single warrant for arrest. In the Langwasser Internment Camp in Nuremberg was the official who had been in charge of the Protective Custody Section and who had issued over a rubber stamp of Kaltenbrunner's signature the warrants for the arrest of thousands of people. The Americans had already interrogated the man, everybody knew about him; but the Prosecution at Nuremberg could not produce him! Eventually, as is not surprising, a few original signatures of Kaltenbrunner were brought into Court. But Kaltenbrunner blandly denied that they were genuine, saying he was on terms of intimate friendship with Blaschke, the Mayor of Vienna, to whom the letters were addressed, and that he would certainly have signed himself 'Ernst' and not 'Kaltenbrunner'!

While Kaltenbrunner and the other senior German officials who had taken refuge in Alt-Aussee were mostly captured, the Balkan chieftains all succeeded in getting away without exception. Vancho Mihailoff, the leader of I.M.R.O., the Macedonian Independence Movement, 'the most mysterious man in the Balkans,' as he is still often called, was in Alt-Aussee in May 1945 as the representative of Macedonia. He asked the Germans neither for aid nor for false papers—little things like that Mihailoff could manage for himself. The Russians were so interested in him that they sent a special agent to find out whether or not he was in Alt-Aussee. The agent, having no special knowledge, thought that the search was for the Serbian rebel leader, Mihailovic, and reported that the man sought was

not and never had been in Alt-Aussee. Meanwhile Mihailoff
and his wife, an old fellow-conspirator, disappeared.

This wife of his had had an interesting past. She had originally been Mihailoff's secretary, and had been entrusted with
several particularly difficult missions. Some years before the
Nazis seized Austria she had been detailed to kill a Bulgarian
politician, who had been condemned to death by I.M.R.O. in a
mock trial. She shot him as he sat in a box at the Vienna State
Opera, and then allowed herself to be arrested by the Austrian
police without any attempt at escape or resistance. Forty-eight
hours later she was free again. I.M.R.O. had informed the
Police President that arrangements had been made to blow up
the Soviet Legation if the woman were not released within
forty-eight hours! The Vienna police knew I.M.R.O. well
enough to realize that this was no idle threat, and very quietly
they let the woman go.

To-day Mihailoff is playing a comparatively important part
as leader of an underground movement. In 1951 he published
a book on the future of Macedonia, in which he gives as the
solution of this apparently insoluble problem the foundation of
a State on much the same lines as Switzerland, in which all
three nationalities, the Greeks, the Bulgars and the Albanians,
could all live amicably together.

The Heads of the Axis nations—Hitler, Mussolini, Antonescu,
Szalasi, Filoff, Tiso, and with them Quisling, Mussert and Nedic
—are all dead. Only one survives, one who deserves to die
many times—the 'Poglavnik' of Croatia, Dr. Ante Pavelic.
As early as 1942 the German plenipotentiary in Croatia, General
Glaise von Horstenau, had already given him the honorary title
of War Criminal. Glaise showed me a photo of Pavelic, in
which a painted convict garb had been so realistically super-
imposed on the uniform that it really looked like a genuine
exhibit from a criminal album. Things like this did not help to
make the General a popular man at Fuehrer Headquarters.
Pavelic, 'the strong man'—in reality the ruthless and merciless
thug—stood high in Hitler's estimation at the time. General
von Horstenau, against whom Tito had no grudge and never
demanded his extradition, in spite of the high command that he
had held in Croatia, committed suicide in 1946 in old Lang-

wasser prison camp. He had no sense of guilt, but he had seen the Austria that he had known crumble away. He used to call himself 'the last of the Austrians' and had no desire to live any longer in an abhorrent world.

Pavelic delayed his departure from his capital Zagreb until the beginning of May 1945. Then he and Kasche, the German Minister, and their staffs left together. On their way they heard the news that Germany had capitulated, and the two parties thereupon split up. Pavelic took the road via Carinthia to Styria. In the vicinity of Judenburg he had an unexpected and dramatic meeting with Russian advanced guards. This caused him to decide to proceed in secret. His destination was Alt-Aussee, where he knew his wife and family to be. In Alt-Aussee he saw no one and appears to have stayed only a few hours, long enough to realize that this was no haven of refuge but a deadly trap. He found his family installed at Hintersee near Fuschl and not far from Alt-Aussee. The German Foreign Ministry had assumed responsibility for these various families. During their time in Alt-Aussee they had been well looked after. Some members of the Government, however, had been left behind in Alt-Aussee itself, presumably to bury such of the State treasure as could not readily be removed. In the hotel in Aussee where the Pavelic family had lived, only one sort of currency was accepted—gold coinage. Even in the autumn of 1945 a few old *napoléons d'or* were still to be found buried in the cellars. But the treasure itself was all removed in good time, and this part of the Pavelic organization functioned perfectly.

Pavelic made no secret of his presence in Hintersee. He sent his Adjutant, Rear-Admiral Crisomali, to call officially on the American Divisional Commander at Salzburg, who gave him permission to stay where he was in Hintersee. Surprisingly no one bothered about the people who were really wanted, though in Croatia itself all sorts of junior officials of the Ustase régime were being killed by Tito's partisans. The British and Americans handed over to Yugoslavia not only Ustase adherents but men of the Croatian armed forces. All the time their leader Pavelic sat a few miles away in the vicinity of Salzburg itself!

It was not until 13th June that he disappeared from the district. He still remained in Austria, living with friends in a castle until the end of 1947. For two and a half years he lived peacefully in Austria, while all the Secret Services of the Allies combed the world for him. Tito sent a special agent to Spain to investigate a rumour that Pavelic had settled there. Pavelic was skilled at secrecy, there certainly seems to have been some power protecting him.

From Austria he went over the mountains to Italy and remained there for a further two years. He had the papers of a Hungarian General. Although the efficient Italian Police found out all about him, he was not molested. It was obvious that whoever they were, his protectors were influential. At the end of 1949 Pavelic flew to Buenos Aires. There he found affluence waiting for him—his Balkan treasure hoard?

For this he was indebted to the former Croatian Minister to Berlin, Dr. Benzon. One of the original Ustase leaders, Benzon quickly broke away from a régime which had no attractions for him. In Berlin as in Budapest, where he was stationed as Minister in 1944, this handsome and witty man was popular among the neutral diplomats—and particularly among the ladies. He realized that the war was lost, and he was determined to get away in good time. That was by no means easy for a senior representative of a totalitarian State. The wily Benzon found a way. He persuaded Kaltenbrunner, with whom he was on friendly terms, to send him to Spain as the representative of the German Secret Service. Kaltenbrunner, like his masters Hitler and Himmler, had a great weakness for this section of the Service. He was fond of setting up little organizations of his own. When Benzon hinted with the utmost caution that perhaps he might be able to arrange some little place of refuge in Spain for Kaltenbrunner himself, the latter refused the offer most abruptly. This amiable offer nearly wrecked Benzon's plans for himself.

Kaltenbrunner did not take this opportunity of salting away a large sum of gold and foreign currency in Spain. He was far too short sighted to think of such a thing. The story appears to have arisen as the result of a mistake in identities. The Police Attaché in Lisbon had at that same time been in Berlin for a conference. As the south of France was already in the hands of the Allies, and to maintain his organization in the event of communications with Germany being cut off, he took a very large sum in gold and foreign currency with him when he returned to his post. German planes at that time had to fly either by night or make a detour out to sea. The aircraft in which the Police Attaché was flying crashed, and the wreckage is said to have been found in the Pyrenees by French maquisards. This story has never been substantiated, but it seems to fit in with the suggested mistake in identities.

Thanks to Kaltenbrunner, Benzon got a seat on one of the last German aircraft to reach Spain. Fortunes were being offered at the time for a seat. As far as is known, not a single important personage of the Third Reich escaped by this means. When the war was over, Benzon went on from Spain to the Argentine, where he quickly became intimate with Peron. He had apparently to thank Eva Peron, whom he treated as a doctor. Before entering the diplomatic service, Benzon had been an eminent heart specialist. He was therefore able to prepare the way for Pavelic. There is no doubt that Peron at the time valued Pavelic and thought he would be useful.

To Pavelic clearly both the Russian and the Anglo-Saxon side seemed closed. He aimed at becoming the protagonist of a 'third force', and in Peron and Franco he saw his partners and protectors. He wished to organize in Europe a species of Fascist International. Italy seemed to offer an ideal base, for since 1945 thousands of political refugees from every country in Europe had found refuge there. At the same time he wished to include the Arab States, in which he counted on finding many friends. Pavelic had always treated the Mohammedan minority in his country well. He knew that, in the Arab States in particular, Bosnian officers were highly esteemed on account of their soldierly virtues and had for generations served in the Middle East.

Initially his plans met with some success. On 10th April, 1951, on the tenth anniversary of the foundation of the independent Croat State, Pavelic announced over the Montevideo radio a 'reconstruction' of the Croat Government. He still regarded his Government-in-exile as the only legal Government of the country. Montevideo radio was used because Peron was unwilling to make known his association with Pavelic, and refused to put any Argentine station at his disposal.

Pavelic himself, of course, retained the post of 'Poglavnik'. Dr. Kulenovic was appointed Prime Minister. Dr. Pejacevic and General Boban were given the Ministries for Foreign Affairs and War. Kulenovic was one of the best known men of the Yugoslav Mohammedan community. He had been their leader in the Belgrade parliament, and when the independent State of Croatia was founded, Pavelic used him skilfully as a figurehead in the post of Deputy Prime Minister, although Kulenovic had little in common with the very radical Ustase régime.

Other exiles are forming their Secret Fronts under the protection of Peron in the Argentine. There is Dr. Durcansky, Croat Foreign Minister under Tiso. He has held himself rigidly and completely aloof from Pavelic. Durcansky's flight was also through Alt-Aussee. His mission there had nothing whatever to do with politics. After he had been thrown out of the Croat Government at the instigation of Ribbentrop, Durcansky turned his attention to business and took over a small chemical factory. When fleeing from the advancing Russians, he thought he could best ensure his future by taking with him the more valuable of his chemical products, which would find a ready market all over the world. Among these were twenty cases of crude morphia, which were promptly confiscated at the Austrian frontier, where Eigruber had set up a Customs Department of his own. Durcansky then appealed successfully to Kaltenbrunner for the return of his luggage, but Eigruber had in the meantime divided up the contents of the twenty cases among the various Wehrmacht hospitals, without realizing that in its crude state the morphia was of no use to them. By so doing he let loose a flood of misery, for there were plenty of people who knew that crude morphia was a profitable commodity in the black market. There were over five hundred pounds of the stuff, and a stream of morphia flowed in every direction. The Drug and Narcotic Section of the Austrian Police had their hands full for years. Yet Durcansky won through to South America.

It seems strange as I look out over this peaceful lake and mountains, that this placid Alpine resort was eight years ago the refuge of half the 'wanted' men of Europe and the hiding-place of Hitler's loot and stolen property of Europe's oppressed peoples. The German Secret Service is broken and scattered both to East and West. Some serve the Americans and some the Russians. Others lie low and watch which way the wind blows. Some play with fire on both sides of the Iron Curtain, and some in South America and the Middle East have taken with them the unrest that surrounded them here. So too with the political adventurers of the Balkans who throve under Hitler.

I knew some of these men well, and met most of them in my busy seven years with the Secret Service. I have not, contrary to some sensational reports in the German weekly press, managed to discover and squander the buried treasure that they are said to have left here in Aussee. I have taken to publishing and printing. All I have found here has been the solitude and peace to write my own story of what was the Secret Front in Europe.

Alt-Aussee, May 1953.

FINIS

INDEX